John Wesley

THE LIFE

OF

REV. JOHN WESLEY, A. M.,

SOMETIME FELLOW OF LINCOLN COLLEGE, OXFORD,

FOUNDER OF THE METHODIST SOCIETIES.

BY RICHARD WATSON.

Ἐν κόποις περισσοτέρως.

[In labors more abundantly.]

FIRST AMERICAN OFFICIAL EDITION,

WITH TRANSLATIONS AND NOTES,

BY JOHN EMORY.

Cincinnati:

PUBLISHED BY L. SWORMSTEDT & A. POE,

FOR THE METHODIST EPISCOPAL CHURCH, AT THE WESTERN BOOK CONCERN

CORNER OF MAIN AND EIGHTH STREETS.

R. P. THOMPSON, PRINTER.

1857.

Entered, according to Act of Congress, in the year 1831,

BY J. EMORY & B. WAUGH,

In the Clerk's Office of the District Court of the Southern District of New York.

CONTENTS.

CHAPTER VII.

CHAPTER VIII.

CHAPTER IX.

CHAPTER X.

CHAPTER XI.

CHAPTER XII.

CHAPTER XIII.

CHAPTER XIV.

CHAPTER XV.

ADVERTISEMENT.

VARIOUS Lives or Memoirs of the Founder of Methodism have already been laid before the public. But it has been frequently remarked that such of these as contain the most approved accounts of Mr. Wesley, have been carried out to a length which obstructs their circulation, by the intermixture of details comparatively uninteresting beyond the immediate circle of Wesleyan Methodism. The present Life, therefore, without any design to supersede larger publications, has been prepared with more special reference to general readers. But, as it is contracted within moderate limits chiefly by the exclusion of extraneous matter, it will, it is hoped, be found sufficiently comprehensive to give the reader an adequate view of the life, labors, and opinions of the eminent individual who is its subject; and to afford the means of correcting the most material errors and misrepresentations which have had currency respecting him. On several points the author has had the advantage of consulting unpublished papers, not known to preceding biographers, and which have enabled him to place some particulars in a more satisfactory light.

London, May 10, 1831.

ADVERTISEMENT TO THIS EDITION.

IN this edition, *translations* are given of such passages in the dead languages as are left untranslated in the London edition. It is enlarged, too, and we hope enriched, by a variety of *notes*, on points of peculiar importance in an American edition. The price, nevertheless, is so extremely low as to be justified solely by the confident anticipation of very extensive sales. The profits, if any—as of all other publications from the Methodist Episcopal Press—will be scrupulously applied to the spread of the Gospel, and to strictly-charitable objects.

THE LIFE

OF

REV. JOHN WESLEY, A. M.

CHAPTER I.

John and Charles Wesley, the chief founders of that religious body now commonly known by the name of the Wesleyan Methodists, were the sons of Rev. Samuel Wesley, rector of Epworth, in Lincolnshire.

Of this clergyman, and his wife, Mrs. Susannah Wesley, who was the daughter of Rev. Dr. Annesley, as well as of the ancestors of both, an interesting account will be found in Dr. Adam Clarke's "Memoirs of the Wesley Family," and in the "Life of Mr. John Wesley" by Dr. Whitehead, and the more recent one by Mr. Moore. They will be noticed here only so far as a general knowledge of their character may be necessary to assist our judgment as to the opinions and conduct of their more celebrated sons.

The rector of Epworth, like his excellent wife, had descended from parents distinguished for learning, piety, and non-conformity. His father dying while he was young, he forsook the Dissenters at an early period of life; and his conversion carried him into High Church principles, and political toryism. He was not, however, so rigid in the former as to prevent him from encouraging the early zeal of his sons, John and Charles, at Oxford, although it was even then somewhat irregular, when tried by the strictest rules of Church order and custom; and his toryism, sufficiently high in theory, was yet of that class which regarded the rights of the subject tenderly in practice. He refused flattering overtures made by the adherents of James II, to induce him to support the measures of the court, and wrote in favor of the revolution of 1688; admiring it, probably, less in a political view than as rescuing a Protestant Church from the dangerous influence of a Popish head. For this service he was presented with the living of Epworth, in Lincolnshire, to which, a few years afterward, was added that of Wroote, in the same county.

He held the living of Epworth upward of forty years, and was distinguished for the zeal and fidelity with which he discharged his parish duties. Of his talents and learning, his remaining works afford honorable evidence.

Mrs. Susannah Wesley, the mother of Mr. John Wesley, was, as might be expected from the eminent character of Dr. Samuel Annesley, her father, educated with great care. Like her husband, she also, at an early period of life, renounced non-conformity, and became a member of the Established Church, after, as her biographers tell us, she had read and mastered the whole controversy on the subject of separation; of which, however, great as were her natural and acquired talents, she must, at the age of thirteen years, have been a very imperfect judge. The serious habits impressed upon both by their education, did not forsake them; "they feared God, and wrought righteousness;" but we may perhaps account for that obscurity in the views of each on several great points of evangelical religion, and especially on justification by faith, and the offices of the Holy Spirit, which hung over their minds for many years, and indeed till toward the close of life, from this early change of their religious connections. Their theological reading, according to the fashion of the Church people of that day, was now directed rather to the writings of those divines of the English Church who were tinctured more or less with a Pelagianized Arminianism, than to the works of its founders; their successors, the Puritans; or of those eminent men among the Non-Conformists, whose views of discipline they had renounced. They had parted with Calvinism; but, like many others, they renounced with it, for want of spiritual discrimination, those truths which were as fully maintained in the theology of Arminius, and in that of their eminent son, who revived, and more fully illustrated it, as in the writings of the most judicious and spiritual Calvinistic divines themselves. Taylor, Tillotson, and Bull, who became their oracles, were Arminians of a different class.

The advantage of such a parentage to the Wesleys was great. From their earliest years they had an example in the father of all that could render a clergyman respectable and influential; and in the mother there was a sanctified wisdom, a masculine understanding, and an acquired knowledge, which they regarded with just deference after they became men and scholars. The influence of a piety so steadfast and uniform, joined to such qualities, and softened by maternal tenderness, could scarcely fail to produce effect. The firm and manly character, the practical sense, the active and unwearied habits of the father, with the calm, reflecting, and stable qualities of the mother, were in particular inherited by Mr. John Wesley, and in him were most happily blended. A large portion of the ecclesiastical principles and prejudices of the rector of Epworth was also transmitted to his three sons; but while Samuel and Charles retained them least impaired, in John, as we shall see, they sustained in future life considerable modifications.

Samuel, the eldest son, was born in 1692; John, in 1703; and Charles, in 1708.

Samuel Wesley, junior, was educated at Westminster school, and in 1711 was elected to Christ Church, Oxford. He was eminent for his learning, and was an excellent poet, with great power of satire, and an elegant wit. He held a considerable rank among the literary men of the day, and finally settled as head master of the free school of Tiverton, in Devonshire, where he died in 1739, in his forty-ninth year.

Mrs. Wesley was the instructress of her children in their early years. "I can find," says Dr. Whitehead, "no evidence that the boys were ever put to any school in the country, their mother having a very bad opinion of the common methods of instructing and governing children." She was particularly led, it would seem, to interest herself in John, who, when he was about six years old, had a providential and singular escape from being burned to death, upon the parsonage house being consumed.* There is a striking passage in one of her private meditations, which contains a reference to this event, and indicates that she considered it as laying her under a special obligation "to be more particularly careful of the soul of a child whom God had so mercifully provided for." The effect of this special care on the part of the mother was, that, under the Divine blessing, he became early serious; for at the age of eight years he was admitted by his father to partake of the sacrament. In 1714 he was placed at the Charter House, "where he was noticed for his diligence, and progress in learning." (Whitehead's Life.) "Here, for his quietness, regularity, and application, he became a favorite with the master, Dr. Walker; and through life he retained so great a predilection for the place, that on his annual visit to London, he made it a custom to walk through the scene of his boyhood. To most men, every year would render a pilgrimage of this kind more painful than the last,

* The memory of his deliverance, on this occasion, is preserved in one of his early portraits, which has, below the head, the representation of a house in flames, with the motto, "Is not this a brand plucked from the burning?"

but Wesley seems never to have looked back with melancholy upon the days that were gone; earthly regrets of this kind could find no room in one who was continually pressing onward to the goal." (Southey's Life.) When he had attained his seventeenth year, he was elected to Christ Church, Oxford, "where he pursued his studies with great advantage, I believe under the direction of Dr. Wigan, a gentleman eminent for his classical knowledge. Mr. Wesley's natural temper in his youth was gay and sprightly, with a turn for wit and humor. When he was about twenty-one years of age, 'he appeared,' as Mr. Babcock has observed, 'the very sensible and acute collegian; a young fellow of the finest classical taste, of the most liberal and manly sentiments.' (Westminster Magazine.) His perfect knowledge of the classics gave a smooth polish to his wit, and an air of superior elegance to all his compositions. He had already begun to amuse himself occasionally with writing verses, though most of his poetical pieces, at this period, were, I believe, either imitations or translations of the Latin. Some time in this year, however, he wrote an imitation of the sixty-fifth Psalm, which he sent to his father, who says, 'I like your verses on the sixty-fifth Psalm, and would not have you bury your talent.'" (Whitehead's Life.)

Some time after this, when purposing to take deacon's orders, he was roused from the religious carelessness into which he had fallen at college, and applied himself diligently to the reading of divinity. This more thoughtful frame appears to have been indicated in his letters to his mother, with whom he kept up a regular correspondence; for she replies, "The alteration of your temper has occasioned me much speculation. I, who am apt to be sanguine, hope it may proceed from the operations of God's Holy Spirit, that, by taking off your relish for earthly enjoyments, he may prepare and dispose your mind for a more serious and close application to things of a more sublime and spiritual nature. If it be so, happy are you if you cherish those dispositions; and now, in good earnest, resolve to make religion the business of your life; for, after all, that is the one thing which, strictly speaking, is necessary: all things beside are comparatively little to the purposes of life. I heartily wish you would now enter upon a strict examination of yourself, that you may know whether you have a reasonable hope of salvation by Jesus Christ. If you have, the satisfaction of knowing it will abundantly reward your pains; if you have not, you will find a more reasonable occasion for tears than can be met with in a tragedy. This matter deserves great consideration by all, but especially by those designed for the ministry, who ought, above all things, to make their own calling and election sure, lest, after they have preached to others, they themselves should be cast away."

This excellent advice was not lost upon him; and indeed his mother's admirable letters were among the principal means, under God, of producing that still more decided change in his views which soon afterward began to display itself. He was now about twenty-two years of age.

The practical books most read by him at this period, which was probably employed as a course of preparation for holy orders, were, "The Christian's Pattern," by Thomas a Kempis; and Bishop Taylor's "Rules of Holy Living and Dying;" and his correspondence with his parents respecting these authors shows how carefully he was weighing their merits, and investigating their meaning, as regarding them in the light of spiritual instructors. The letters of his mother on the points offered to her consideration by her son, show, in many respects, a deeply-thinking and discriminating mind; but they are also in proof that both she and her husband had given up their acquaintance, if they ever had any, with works which might have been recommended as much more suitable to the state of their son's mind, and far superior as a directory to true Christianity. This to him would have been infinitely more important than discussing the peculiar views, and adjusting the proportion of excellency and defect, which may be found in such a writer as Kempis, whose "Christian's Pattern" is, where in reality excellent, a manual rather for him who is a Christian already, than for him who is seeking to become one.

A few things are, however, to be remarked in this correspondence which are of considerable interest, as showing the bearings of Mr. Wesley's views as to those truths of which he afterward obtained a satisfactory conviction, and then so clearly stated and defended.

The son, in writing to his mother on Bishop Taylor's book, states several particulars which Bishop Taylor makes necessary parts of humility and repentance; one of which, in reference to humility, is, that "we must be sure, in some sense or other, to think ourselves the worst in every company where we come." And in treating of repentance, he says, "Whether God has forgiven us or no, we know not; therefore, be sorrowful for ever having sinned." "I take the more notice of this last sentence," says Mr. Wesley, "because it seems to contradict his own words in the next section, where he says, that by the Lord's supper all the members are united to one another, and to Christ, the head. The Holy Ghost confers on us the graces necessary for, and our souls receive the seeds of, an immortal nature. Now, surely, these graces are not of so little force as that we can not perceive whether we have them or not: if we dwell in Christ, and Christ in us, which he will not do unless we are regenerate, certainly we must be sensible of it. If we can never have any certainty of our being in a state of salvation, good reason it is that every moment should be spent, not in joy, but in fear and trembling; and then undoubtedly, in this life, we are of all men most miserable. God deliver us from such a fearful expectation as this! Humility is, undoubtedly, necessary to salvation; and if all these things are essential to humility, who can be humble? who can be saved?"

The mother, in reply, suggests to him some good thoughts and useful distinctions on the subject of humility; but omits to afford him any assistance on the point of the possibility of obtaining a comfortable persuasion of being in a state of salvation, through the influence of the Holy Spirit, which he already discerned to be the privilege of a real believer, though as yet he was greatly perplexed as to the means of attaining it. At this period, too, he makes the important distinction between assurance of *present*, and assurance of *future*, salvation; by confounding which, so many, from their objection to the Calvinistic notion of the infallible perseverance of the saints, have given up the doctrine of assurance altogether. "That we can never be so certain of the pardon of our sins as to be assured they will never rise up against us, I firmly believe. We know that they will infallibly do so if ever we apostatize; and I am not satisfied what evidence there can be of our final perseverance, till we have finished our course. But I am persuaded we may know if we are now in a state of salvation, since that is expressly promised in the holy Scriptures to our sincere endeavors; and we are surely able to judge of our own sincerity."

The latter part of this extract will, however, show how much he had yet to learn as to "the way to the Father." Mrs. Wesley also corrects a defective definition of faith, which her son's letter had contained, in the following sensible remarks, which are just, as far as they go, but below the true Scriptural standard, and the proper conception of that saving faith after which her son was inquiring: "You are somewhat mistaken in your notions of faith. All faith is an assent, but all assent is not faith. Some truths are self-evident, and we assent to them because they are so. Others, after a regular and formal process of reason, by way of deduction from some self-evident principle, gain our assent. This is not properly faith, but science. Some again we assent to, not because they are self-evident, or because we have attained the knowledge of them in a regular method by a train of arguments, but because they have been revealed to us, either by God or man; and these are the proper objects of faith. The true measure of faith is the authority of the revealer, the weight of which always holds proportion to our conviction of his ability and integrity. Divine faith is an assent to whatever God has revealed to us, because he has revealed it."

Predestination was another subject touched upon in this interesting correspondence. Mr. Wesley was probably led to it by his review of the Articles of the Church previous to his ordination, and he thus expresses himself on this controverted subject: "What, then, shall I say of predestination? An everlasting purpose of God to deliver some from damnation, does, I suppose, exclude all from that deliverance who are not chosen. And if it was inevitably decreed from eternity that such a determinate part of mankind should be saved, and none beside them, a vast majority of the world were only born to eternal death, without so much as a possibility of avoiding it. How is this consistent with either the Divine justice or mercy? Is it merciful to ordain a creature to everlasting misery? Is it just to punish a man for crimes which he could not but commit? That God should be the author of sin and injustice, which must, I think, be the consequence of maintaining this opinion, is a contradiction to the clearest ideas we have of the Divine nature and perfections." (Whitehead's Life.)

From these views he never departed; and the terms he

uses contain indeed the only rational statement of the whole question.

He was ordained deacon in September, 1725, and the year following was elected fellow of Lincoln College. His previous seriousness had been the subject of much banter and ridicule, and appears to have been urged against him, in the election, by his opponents; but his reputation for learning and diligence, and the excellence of his character triumphed; and, what was probably to him the greates pleasure, he had the gratification of seeing the joy this event gave to his venerable parents, and which was emphatically expressed in their letters. Several specimens of his poetry, composed about this time, are given by his biographers, which show that, had he cultivated that department of literature, he would not have occupied an inferior place among the tasteful and elegant votaries of verse; but he soon found more serious and more useful employment.

He spent the summer after his election to the fellowship with his parents, in Lincolnshire, and took that opportunity of conversing with them at large upon those serious topics which then fully occupied his mind. In September he returned to Oxford, and resumed his usual studies. "His literary character was now established in the university; he was acknowledged by all parties to be a man of talents, and an excellent critic in the learned languages. His compositions were distinguished by an elegant simplicity of style, and justness of thought, that strongly marked the excellence of his classical taste. His skill in logic, or the art of reasoning, was universally known and admired. The high opinion that was entertained of him in these respects was soon publicly expressed, by choosing him Greek lecturer, and moderator of the classes, on the 7th of November; though he had only been elected fellow of the college in March, was little more than twenty-three years of age, and had not proceeded master of arts." (Whitehead's Life.) He took this degree in February, 1727; became his father's curate in August the same year; returned to Oxford in 1728, to obtain priest's orders, and paid another visit to Oxford in 1729; where, during his stay, he attended the meetings of a small society formed by his brother Charles, Mr. Morgan, and a few others, to assist each other in their studies, and to consult how to employ their time to the best advantage.

After about a month, he returned to Epworth; but upon Dr. Morley, the rector of his college, requiring his residence, he quitted his father's curacy, and in November again settled in Oxford. He now obtained pupils, and became tutor in the college; presided as moderator in the disputations six times a week; and had the chief direction of a religious society. From this time he stood more prominently forward in his religious character, and in efforts to do good to others; and began more fully to prove that "they that will live godly in Christ Jesus must suffer persecution." It is, however, necessary to turn to the history of Mr. Charles Wesley, whose labors in the early periods of Methodism were inferior only to those of his brother.

Charles Wesley was, as above stated, five years younger than his brother John; and was educated at Westminster school, under his eldest brother, Samuel, from whom he is said to have derived a still stronger tincture of High Church principles than was imbibed under the paternal roof. "When he had been some years at school, Mr. R. Wesley, a gentleman of large fortune in Ireland, wrote to his father, and asked if he had any son named Charles; if so, he would make him his heir. Accordingly, a gentleman in London brought money for his education several years. But one year another gentleman called, probably Mr. Wesley himself, talked largely with him, and asked if he was willing to go with him to Ireland. Mr. Charles desired to write to his father, who answered immediately, and referred it to his own choice. He chose to stay in England." (Whitehead's Life, vol. i, p. 98.) "Mr. John Wesley, in his account of his brother, calls this a fair escape. The fact is more remarkable than he was aware of; for the person who inherited the property intended for Charles Wesley, and who took the name of Wesley, or Wellesley, in consequence, was the first Earl of Mornington, grandfather of Marquis Wellesley and the Duke of Wellington." (Southey's Life.)

The lively disposition of Charles, although he pursued his studies diligently, and was unblamable in his conduct, repelled all those exhortations to a more strictly-religious course which John seriously urged upon him, after he was elected to Christ Church. During his brother's absence, as his father's curate, his letters, however, became more grave; and when Mr. John Wesley returned to Oxford, in November, 1729, "I found him," he observes, "in great earnestness to save his soul." His own account of himself is, that he lost his first year at college in diversions; that the next, he set himself to study; that diligence led him into serious thinking; that he went to the weekly sacrament, persuading two or three students to accompany him; and that he observed the method of study prescribed by the statutes of the university. "This," says he, "gained me the harmless name of *Methodist*."* Thus

* From the name of an ancient sect of physicians, say some of Mr. Wesley's biographers; but probably the wits of Oxford, who imposed the name, knew nothing of that sect of the middle ages. The Non-Conformists were often called, in derision, Methodists; and the name was probably transmitted from them; or it might be given merely from the rigid adherence to method in study by Mr. Charles Wesley. It is, however, somewhat worthy of notice, that before the times of non-conformity, properly so called, we find Methodists mentioned as one of the minor sects in conjunction with the Anabaptists; for, as early as 1639, in a sermon preached at Lambeth, they are rated in good set style for

it appears that Charles was the first modern Methodist, and that he in fact laid the foundations of the religious society which continues to be distinguished by that appellation. To this society Mr. John Wesley joined himself on his return to reside at Oxford; and by his influence and energy gave additional vigor to their exertions to promote their own spiritual improvement and the good of others. The union of system and efficiency which this association presented well accorded with his practical and governing mind; and, no doubt, under the leadings of a superior agency, of which he was unconscious, he was thus training himself to those habits of regular and influential exertion and enterprise which subsequently rendered him the instrument of a revival of religion throughout the land. Of the little society of which, by the mere force of his character, he thus became the head, Mr. Hervey, the author of the "Meditations," and the celebrated Whitefield, were members.

CHAPTER II.

The strictly-religious profession which Mr. Wesley must now be considered as making at Oxford—a profession so strongly marked as to become matter of public notice, and accompanied with so much zeal as to excite both ridicule and opposition—requires to be carefully examined. After

their aversion to rhetorical sermons: "Where are now our Anabaptists and *plain pack-staff Methodists*, who esteem of all flowers of rhetoric in sermons no better than stinking weeds, and of all elegancies of speech no better than profane spells?" etc. Their fault in those days, it appears, was to prefer plain preaching; no bad compliment, though an undesigned one. The epithet used to describe them may also intimate that they were *plain* in dress and manners. At a later period, in 1693, some of the Non-Conformists who had renounced the imputation of Christ's righteousness in justification, except in the merit of

all, he thought himself to be but "almost," and not "alto gether," a Christian—a conclusion of a very perplexing kind to many who have set up themselves for better judges in his case than he himself. From a similar cause, we have seen St. Paul all but reproved by some divines for representing himself "as the chief of sinners," at the time when he was "blameless" as to "the righteousness of the law;" and, but for the courtesy due to an inspired man, he would, probably, in direct contradiction to his own words, have been pronounced the chief of saints; although his heart remained a total stranger to humility and charity.

The Wesleys at Oxford were indeed not only in a *higher* but in an *essentially-different* state of religious experience from that of Saul of Tarsus, notwithstanding his array of legal zeal and external virtue; but if our views of personal religion must be taken from the New Testament, although as to men they were blameless and exemplary, yet, in respect to God, those internal changes had not taken place in them which it is the office of real Christianity to effect. They were, however, most sincere; they were "faithful in that which is little," and God gave them "the true riches." They "sought God with all their heart;" and they ultimately found him, but in a way which at that time "they knew not." The very writers, Bishop Taylor and Mr. Law, who so powerfully wrought upon their consciences, were among the most erring guides to that "peace of God which passeth all understanding," for which they sighed; and those celebrated divines, excelled by none for genius and eloquence, who could draw the

it, and whose views were somewhat similar to those of the Wesleyan Methodists on the imputation of faith for righteousness, were called by their brethren, the New Methodists. They were not, however, a sect but were so denominated from the new method which they took in stating the doctrine of justification. Thus we have a Calvinistic pamphlet, under this date, written against "the principles of the *New Methodists* in the great point of justification."

picture of a practical piety so copious and exact in its external manifestations, were unable to teach that mystic connection of the branches with the vine, from which the only fruits which are of healthy growth and genuine flavor can proceed. Both are too defective in their views of faith, and of its object, the atonement of Christ, to be able to direct a penitent and troubled spirit into the way of salvation, and to show how all the principles and acts of truly Christian piety are sustained by a life of "faith in the Son of God." To this subject, however, Mr. Wesley's own account of himself will, subsequently, again call our attention.

Bishop Taylor's chapter on purity of intention first convinced Mr. Wesley of the necessity of being holy in heart, as well as regular in his outward conduct; and having, for the first time, formed an acquaintance with a religious friend, "he began to alter the whole form of his conversation, and to set in earnest upon a new life." "He communicated every week. He watched against all sin, whether in word or deed, and began to aim at, and pray for, inward holiness," (Journal;) but still with a painful consciousness that he found not that which he so earnestly sought. His error, at this period, was drawn from his theological guides just mentioned; he either confounded sanctification with justification, that is, a real with a relative change, or he regarded sanctification as a preparation for, and a condition of, justification. He had not yet learned the apostle's doctrine, the gratuitous justification of "the ungodly," when penitent, and upon the sole condition of believing in Christ; nor that upon this there *follows* a "death" to all inward and outward sin; so that he who is so justified can "no longer continue therein." It is, however, deeply interesting to trace the progress of his mind through its agitations, inquiries, hopes, and fears, till the moment when he found that steadfast peace which never afterward forsook him, but gave serenity to his countenance, and cheerfulness to his heart, to the last hour of a prolonged life.

The effects of the strong impression which had been made upon him by the practical writings of Taylor and Law promptly manifested themselves. The discipline he maintained as a tutor over his pupils was more strict than the university had been accustomed to witness; and for this reason, that it was more deeply and comprehensively conscientious. He regarded himself as responsible to God for exerting himself to his utmost, not only to promote their learning, but to regulate their moral habits, and to form their religious principles. Here his disciplinary habits had their first manifestation. He required them to rise very early; he directed their reading, and controlled their general conduct, by rules to which he exacted entire obedience. This was not well taken by the friends of some; but from others he received very grateful letters; and several of his pupils themselves were not insensible of the obligations they owed to him, not only on a religious account, but for thus enabling them to reap the full advantages of that seat of learning, by restraining them from its dissipations.

The little society of Methodists, as they were called, began now to extend its operations. When Mr. Wesley joined them, they committed its management to him, and he has himself stated its original members:

"In November, 1729, four young gentlemen of Oxford, Mr. John Wesley, fellow of Lincoln College; Mr. Charles Wesley, student of Christ Church; Mr. Morgan, commoner of Christ Church; and Mr. Kirkman, of Merton College, began to spend some evenings in a week together, in reading chiefly the Greek Testament. The next year, two or three of Mr. John Wesley's pupils desired the liberty of meeting with them; and afterward one of Mr.

Charles Wesley's pupils. It was in 1732 that Mr. Ingham, of Queen's College, and Mr. Broughton, of Exeter, were added to their number. To these, in April, was joined Mr. Clayton, of Brazen-nose, with two or three of his pupils. About the same time Mr. James Hervey was permitted to meet with them, and afterward Mr. Whitefield." (Journal.)

Mr. Morgan led the way to their visiting the prisoners in the Oxford gaol, for the purpose of affording them religious instruction. They afterward resolved to spend two or three hours a week in visiting and relieving the poor and the sick, generally, where the parish ministers did not object to it. This was, however, so novel a practice, and might be deemed by some so contrary to Church order, that Mr. Wesley consulted his father upon the point. Mr. Wesley, senior, answered the inquiry in a noble letter, equally honorable to his feelings as a father and a minister of Christ. They had his full sanction for prosecuting their pious labors; he blessed God who had given him two sons together at Oxford, who had received grace and courage to turn the war against the world and the devil; he bids them defy reproach, and animates them in God's name to go on in the path to which their Savior had directed them. At the same time, he advises them to consult with the chaplain of the prison, and to obtain the approbation of the bishop. This high sanction was obtained; but it was not sufficient to screen them from the rebukes of the gravely lukewarm, or the malignantly vicious. Sarcasm and serious opposition robbed them of one of their number, who had not fortitude to bear the shafts of ridicule, or to resist the persuasion of friends; and the opposition being now headed by some persons of influence, Mr. Wesley had again recourse, by letter, to his father's counsel. The answer deserves to be transcribed at length:

"This day I received both yours, and this evening, in the course of our reading, I thought I found an answer that would be more proper than any I myself could dictate; though since it will not be easily translated, I send it in the original. Πολλή μοι καύχησις ὑπὲρ ὑμῶν· πεπλήρωμαι τῇ παρακλήσει· ὑπερπερισσεύομαι τῇ χαρᾷ.* What would you be? Would you be angels? I question whether a mortal can arrive to a greater degree of perfection than steadily to do good, and for that very reason patiently and meekly to suffer evil. For my part, on the present view of your actions and designs, my daily prayers are, that God would keep you humble; and then I am sure that if you continue 'to suffer for righteousness' sake,' though it be but in a lower degree, the Spirit of God and of glory shall in some good measure rest upon you. And you can not but feel such a satisfaction in your own minds as you would not part with for all the world. Be never weary of well doing; never look back, for you know the prize and the crown are before you; though I can scarce think so meanly of you, as that you should be discouraged with the 'crackling of thorns under a pot.' Be not high-minded, but fear. Preserve an equal temper of mind under whatever treatment you meet with, from a not very just or well-natured world. Bear no more sail than is necessary, but steer steady. The less you value yourselves for these unfashionable duties—as there is no such thing as works of supererogation—the more all good and wise men will value you, if they see your works are all of a piece; or which is infinitely more, He by whom actions and intentions are weighed will both accept, esteem, and reward you.

"I hear my son John has the honor of being styled the 'Father of the Holy Club;' if it be so, I am sure I must be the grandfather of it; and I need not say, that I

* 2 Cor. vii, 4. Great is my glorying of you. I am filled with comfort. I am exceeding joyful.—*Authorized Version.*

had rather any of my sons should be so dignified and distinguished than to have the title of HIS HOLINESS." (Whitehead's Life.)

Thus encouraged they proceeded in their course with meekness and constancy; to relieve the poor they sacrificed all the superfluities, and sometimes the conveniences of life; and they redoubled their efforts to produce religious impressions upon their college acquaintances, as well as upon the ignorant, the poor, and the sick. The apology for these pious and praiseworthy efforts, which, on the increase of the outcry made against them, Mr. Wesley published in the modest form of queries, amply indicates the low state of religious feeling in the university; and we may well conclude with one of Mr. Wesley's biographers, that "a voluntary scheme of so much private and public good, such piety, with such beneficence, certainly merited a different return; and, if the university in general, instead of ridiculing or persecuting them, had had the grace to imitate their example, it would have been much better both for the public and themselves."

Even their eldest brother Samuel added his seasonable exhortations to perseverance, in a short but vigorous letter: "I can not say, I thought you always in every thing right; but I must now say, rather than you and Charles should give over your whole course, especially what relates to the castle, I would choose to follow either of you, nay, both of you, to your graves. I can not advise you better, than in the words I proposed for a motto to a pamphlet, Στηθ' ἱδραῖος ὡς ἀκμων τυπτόμενος· καλȣ γὰρ ἀθλητȣ δέρεσθαι καὶ νικᾳν. 'Stand thou steadfast as a beaten anvil; for it is the part of a good champion to be flayed alive and to conquer.'" (Whitehead's Life.)

Sickness, and cowardly desertion arising from weariness of the cross, some time after this, reduced the number of this little society of zealous young men, and the brothers were left to stand almost alone; but they still persevered with unabated zeal and diligence in their attempts to do good, exhibiting a rare example of decision, only to be accounted for by a preparing influence of God upon their hearts, thus training them up for still more arduous service. This it was which had implanted in them those admirable principles, which are unreservedly laid open in a letter of Mr. John Wesley to his brother Samuel, who had begun to think that they were pushing the strictness of their personal piety too far:

"1. As to the end of my being, I lay it down for a rule, that I can not be too happy, or, therefore, too holy; and thence infer that the more steadily I keep my eye upon the prize of our high calling, and the more of my thoughts, and words, and actions are directly pointed at the attainment of it, the better. 2. As to the instituted means of attaining it, I likewise lay it down for a rule, that I am to use them every time I may. 3. As to prudential means, I believe this rule holds of things indifferent in themselves; whatever I know to do me hurt, that to me is not indifferent, but resolutely to be abstained from: whatever I know to do me good, that to me is not indifferent, but resolutely to be embraced." (Whitehead's Life.)

Adverting to this charge of over-strictness, and being "righteous overmuch," he also earnestly requests his mother to point out any instance in which she might judge, from their unreserved communications to her of every part of their conduct, that they were too superstitious or enthusiastic on the one hand, or too remiss on the other. Some anxiety had, indeed, been created at home by the singularity of their proceedings, and the opposition they had roused at Oxford, which was, probably, the chief reason why the father extended his journey from London to Oxford at the close of the year 1731. He was, however, evidently satisfied with his personal observations and inquiries; for on his return to London he writes to Mrs. Wesley, that he had been well repaid for the expense and labor of his journey to Oxford, "by the shining piety of our two sons."

In the midst of all this zeal, devotedness, and patience of reproach, when the eye of man could see nothing but a mature and vital Christianity, we are enabled to ascertain the state of Mr. Wesley's own heart as laid open by himself. Speaking of a time a little subsequent to the decided impressions he had received from the reading of Bishop Taylor's "Holy Living and Dying," and Mr. Law's "Serious Call," he says, "I was convinced, more than ever, of the exceeding hight and breadth and depth of the law of God. The light flowed in so mightily upon my soul, that every thing appeared in a new view. I cried to God for help, and resolved not to prolong the time of obeying him as I had never done before. And by my continued endeavor to keep his whole law, inward and outward, to the best of my power, I was persuaded that I should be accepted of him; and that I was even then in a state of salvation."

He was now manifestly seeking justification before God by efforts at a perfect obedience to his law; nor was he then quite hopeless as to success. Some time afterward, still clearly convinced, as he had been from the first, that he was not in that state of mind, that settled enjoyment of conscious peace with God—that love to him, delight in him, and filial access to him, which the New Testament describes as the privilege of a true believer—but still diligently persevering in the rigid practice of every discovered duty, in the hope of seizing the great prize by this means, he became greatly surprised that he was so far from obtaining it. He was often dull and formal in the use of the ordinances, and was on that account thrown "into distress and perplexity; so that he seemed at a loss which way to proceed, to obtain the happiness and security he wanted." (Whitehead.) The deep tone of feeling, and the earnestness of his inquiries, in the following passages from a letter to his mother, written in 1732, present this state of his mind in a very affecting light. He then needed some one more fully instructed in the true doctrine of salvation, than even this excellent and intelligent "guide of his youth," to teach him to lay down the burden of his wounded and anxious spirit, in self-despair as to his own efforts, at the foot of the cross of Christ.

After mentioning Mr. Morgan, he observes: "One consideration is enough to make me assent to his and your judgment concerning the holy sacrament; which is, that we can not allow Christ's human nature to be present in it, without allowing either con-substantiation or tran-substantiation. But that his divinity is so united to us then, as he never is but to worthy receivers, I firmly believe; though the manner of that union is utterly a mystery to me.

"That none but worthy receivers should find this effect is not strange to me, when I observe how small effect many means of improvement have upon an unprepared mind. Mr. Morgan and my brother were affected, as they ought, by the observations you made on that glorious subject; but, though my understanding approved what was excellent, yet my heart did not feel it. Why was this, but because it was pre-engaged by those affections with which wisdom will not dwell? Because the animal mind can not relish those truths which are spiritually discerned. Yet I have those writings which the good Spirit gave to that end! I have many of those which he hath since assisted his servants to give us; I have retirement to apply these to my own soul daily; I have means both of public and private prayer; and, above all, of partaking in that sacrament once a week. What shall I do to make all these blessings effectual? to gain from them that mind which was also in Christ Jesus?

"To all who give signs of their not being strangers to it, I propose this question—and why not to you rather than any?—Shall I quite break off my pursuit of all learning, but what immediately tends to practice? I once desired to make a fair show in languages and philosophy; but it is past; there is a more excellent way; and if I can not attain to any progress in the one, without throwing up all thoughts of the other, why, fare it well! yet a little while, and we shall all be equal in knowledge, if we are in virtue.

"You say you have renounced the world. And what have I been doing all this time? What have I done ever since I was born? Why, I have been plunging myself into it more and more. It is enough: awake, thou that sleepest. Is there not one Lord, one Spirit, one hope of our calling? one way of attaining that hope? Then I am to renounce the world as well as you. That is the very thing I want to do: to draw off my affections from this world, and fix them on a better. But how? What is the surest and the shortest way? Is it not to be humble? Surely this is a large step in the way. But the question recurs, How am I to do this? To own the necessity of it, is not to be humble. In many things you have interceded for me and prevailed. Who knows but in this, too, you may be successful. If you can spare me only that little part of Thursday evening which you formerly bestowed upon me in another manner, I doubt not but it would be as useful now, for correcting my heart, as it was then for forming my judgment.

"When I observe how fast life flies away, and how slow improvement comes, I think one can never be too much afraid of dying before one has learned to live. I mean, even in the course of nature. For were I sure that 'the silver cord should not be violently loosed,' that 'the wheel' should not be 'broken at the cistern,' till it was quite worn away by its own motion, yet what a time would this give me for such a work! a moment, to transact the business of eternity! What are forty years in comparison of this? So that, were I sure, what never man yet was sure of, how little would it alter the case! How justly still might I cry out,

> 'Downward I hasten to my destined place;
> There none obtain thy aid, none sing thy praise!
> Soon shall I lie in death's deep ocean drown'd;
> Is mercy there, is sweet forgiveness found?
> O save me yet, while on the brink I stand,
> Rebuke these storms, and set me safe on land.
> O make my longings and thy mercy sure!
> Thou art the God of power.' " (Whitehead's Life.)

It was not, therefore, as it has been hastily stated, that he first learned from the Moravians that he was not a true Christian. He had, at Oxford, a most painful conviction that he was far below the evangelical standard. He had then, as this letter sufficiently shows, a large measure of "the spirit of bondage unto fear;" and that after which his perplexed heart panted, was the "spirit of adoption," by which he might "cry, Abba, Father."

During the summer of this year, 1732, Mr. Wesley visited London, where he formed an acquaintance with several respectable and pious persons. He also made two journeys to Epworth. The latter of these was in order to meet the whole family, which had assembled, upon the father's request, once more before their final separation by death. These and other journeys he performed on foot, partly, no doubt, to avoid what he considered needless expense, that he might, according to his rule, have the more to distribute in charity, and partly to accustom himself to fatigue and hardship. "In these excursions he constantly preached on the Lord's day; so that he might now be called, in some degree, an itinerant preacher." In the following year he again visited Epworth, Manchester, and some other places; but his occasional absence had a bad effect upon the still persecuted society at Oxford, whose members shrunk from the storm, and took the opportunity of his being away to shake off the strictness of the rules. The five-and-twenty communicants at St. Mary's, he informs his father, had shrunk to five. Still his courage was unshaken, and he exerted himself the more, upon his return, to repair the loss. Toward the end of the year, his exertions of mind and body, with an excess of abstemiousness, greatly affected his health, and induced spitting of blood. His state was such as greatly to alarm his friends; but the vigor of his constitution triumphed; and this attack of disease served to impress him the more deeply with eternal things, and to give renewed ardor to his endeavors after universal holiness, and to his plans for the religious benefit of his fellow-creatures.

A considerable trial to his feelings now awaited him. The declining age of his father, who anxiously desired to provide for the spiritual wants of his parishioners in a suitable manner, joined with the wishes of the people of Epworth, and the concerns of the family, for which no provision, it seems, had been made, induced him to write to his son, to make interest for the next presentation to the living. Mr. Wesley, from his reluctance to leave Oxford, where he thought he should be far more useful, and where, according to his own convictions, he was placed in circumstances more conducive to his spiritual improvement, refused the proposal; and the most urgent letters of the different branches of the family were insufficient to bend his resolutions. His father wrote him a pathetic letter, in which every consideration was urged which might answer his objections, or move his feelings. His brother Samuel addressed him in a sterner mood, urging that he was not at liberty to resolve against undertaking a cure of souls, to which he was solemnly pledged by his ordination; and ridiculed his notion that he could not, so safely to himself, or so usefully to others, take the charge of a parish priest, as remain at Oxford. To all this he reiterates, that his own holiness and usefulness could be promoted no where so effectually as in his present station; that his retirement, his friends, and other advantages, were essential to his improvement; that he was inadequate to the charge of two thousand parishioners; and that he did not consider his ordination vows in the same light as his brother. On the last point, indeed, he was supported by the opinion of the bishop who ordained him, and whom he consulted on the question. These and other topics run through the correspondence, which, though it is not necessary to give entire, affords considerable insight into the state of Mr. Wesley's mind. His conduct in this matter has been criticised as unfeeling, without considering that the kindness of his general character is a sufficient pledge, that the refusal of the urgent request of a venerable father, and a beloved mother whose widowhood would be unprovided for, must have been to him sufficiently painful. Dr. Southey thinks the correspondence not "creditable to his judgment," (Life of Wesley;) but it would be hard to prove that the leading consideration which influenced him, that he was more usefully employed in doing good at the very "fountain" from which the nation was to be so largely supplied with its clergy, than as a country parish priest, was not a very obvious truth. This conclusion, true or false, was at least a very plausible one, and as such concerned his conscience; and his disregard of his own temporal advantage, which certainly lay on the side of the Epworth rectory, and his merging all consideration of the interests of the family in the higher question of what he regarded as a duty, might not appear instances of "good judgment" to worldly minds, and yet be so in reality.

His leading reason, drawn from his greater usefulness at Oxford, being strong in itself, that he, with his wonted decision of character, should stand firmly upon it, will create no surprise; but that some of his other reasons are less weighty may be granted. They show that he had more confidence in a certain class of means, to secure his religious safety, than in the grace of God. This was the natural effect of those notions of the efficacy of retirement, and self-denial, and "the wisdom of flight" from danger, which he had learned from Bishop Taylor; while the views he entertained of the necessity of exercising a minute personal superintendence over every individual committed to his charge, as being equally necessary to his own good conscience, and to their salvation, led him to regard a parish, containing two thousand souls, as too formidable and fearful an undertaking. His *religious* judgment was, indeed, as yet immature and perplexed; but, in reasoning from his own principles, his *natural* judgment showed its usual strength in the conclusions to which it conducted him. Whatever weakness there might be in the case was the result of the imperfect state of his religious experience, and of that dependence upon his own plans of attaining spirituality, to which it gave rise; but connecting him with that great work which he was designed afterward to effect, we must shut out also the doctrine of providence, if we do not see a higher hand than that of man in this determination—a hand which is not the less certainly employed, when it works its ends through the secret volitions, aversions, inclinations, and even prejudices of the human heart, than when it more sensibly and immediately interposes to hasten or retard our purposes. Mr. Wesley's father died in April, 1735. He had been manifestly ripening for his change; and in his last moments had the consolation of the presence of his two sons, John and Charles. "He had no fear of death; and the peace of God which he enjoyed appeared sometimes to suspend his bodily sufferings, and, when they recurred, to sustain his mind above them. When, as nature seemed spent, and his speech was failing, his son John asked him whether he was not near heaven, he answered, 'Yes, I am,' distinctly, and with a voice of hope and joy. After John had used the commendatory prayer, he said, 'Now you have done all:' these were his last words, and he passed away so peacefully and insensibly, that his children continued over him a considerable time in doubt whether or not the spirit was departed. Mrs. Wesley, who for several days, whenever she entered his chamber, had been carried out of it in a fit, recovered her fortitude now, and said her prayers were heard, for God had granted him an easy death, and had strengthened her to bear it." (Southey's Life.) Brighter views of the doctrine of faith had opened upon his mind, during his sickness, and shed their influence upon his last hours. This his sons afterward more clearly understood than at the time.*

About the middle of this year the trustees of the new colony of Georgia, who wished to send out clergymen both to administer to the spiritual wants of the colonists, and also to attempt the conversion of the Indians, directed

* In some of the biographical notices which have been published of this venerable man, he is represented of a harsh and stern character. On this point the late Miss Wesley observes, in a MS. letter before me, "I never understood this from any of his children, who idolized his memory, and spoke of his kindness. He certainly never forced his daughter to marry Wright, as it has been suggested." In the same letter, Miss Wesley also corrects the current anecdote respecting the Epworth clerk and the rector's wig, which, though laughable enough, implicates Mr. Wesley in an irreverent act, in the house of God, of which he was not capable. The clerk did appear one Sunday, in church, in the ill-befitting, cast-off wig of his master; and, to the disturbance of the gravity of the congregation, gave out the psalm,

"Like to an owl in ivy bush,
That fearsome thing am I."

But Mr. Wesley had no hand in selecting the psalm, which appears to have been purely accidental.

their attention to Mr. John Wesley, and some of his friends at Oxford, as peculiarly qualified, both by zeal and piety, and their habits of self-denial, for this service. After some delay, and consultation with his family, he accepted the offer; and thus, though Epworth could not draw him from Oxford, an enterprise of a missionary character, and presenting no temptations to ease and sloth, such as he feared in a parish at home, overcame his scruples. This itself is in proof that he had not resolved to remain in Oxford, in preference to accepting the living of Epworth, from selfish motives. In the question of usefulness, the balance before inclined to Oxford; and now that he thought a greater field for doing good opened in America, he yielded to that consideration. This mission was accompanied also with the certainty of great hardships and sufferings, which, according to his then defective, but most sincere views, were necessary to his perfection. His residence at Oxford now terminated, and this portion of his life may be properly concluded with some passages of a letter written by Mr. Gambold, a man of fine genius, as some of his poems show, and of eminent holiness; who, some years afterward, left the Church of England, and became a Moravian bishop. The letter was addressed to one of Mr. Wesley's relations, and contains a lively description of the character and proceedings of a friend, whom he did not then expect to see again on earth:

"About the middle of March, 1730, I became acquainted with Mr. Charles Wesley, of Christ Church. After some time, he introduced me to his brother John, of Lincoln College. 'For he is somewhat older,' said he, 'than I am, and can resolve your doubts better.' I never observed any person have a more real deference for another than he had for his brother; which is the more remarkable, because such near relations, being equals by birth, and conscious to each other of all the little familiar passages of their lives, commonly stand too close to see the ground there may be for such submission. Indeed, he followed his brother entirely; could I describe one of them, I should describe both. I shall, therefore, say no more of Charles, but that he was a man formed for friendship, who, by his cheerfulness and vivacity, would refresh his friend's heart; with attentive consideration, would enter into, and settle all his concerns as far as he was able; he would do any thing for him, great or small; and, by a habit of mutual openness and freedom, would leave no room for misunderstanding.

"The Wesleys were already talked of for some religious practices, which were first occasioned by Mr. Morgan, of Christ Church. From these combined friends began a little society. Mr. John Wesley was the chief manager, for which he was very fit; for he had not only more learning and experience than the rest, but he was blessed with such activity as to be always gaining ground, and such steadiness that he lost none. What proposals he made to any were sure to alarm them, because he was so much in earnest; nor could they afterward slight them, because they saw him always the same. What supported this uniform vigor was the care he took to consider well every affair before he engaged in it, making all his decisions in the fear of God, without passion, humor, or self-confidence. For though he had naturally a very clear apprehension, yet his exact prudence depended more on his humility and singleness of heart. He had, I think, something of authority in his countenance, yet he never assumed any thing to himself above his companions; any of them might speak their mind, and their words were as strictly regarded by him as his words were by them.

"Their undertaking included these several particulars: to converse with young students; to visit the prisons; to instruct some poor families; to take care of a school, and a parish workhouse. They took great pains with the younger members of the university, to rescue them from bad company, and encourage them in a sober, studious life. They would get them to breakfast, and over a dish of tea endeavor to fasten some good hint upon them. They would bring them acquainted with other well-disposed young men, give them assistance in the difficult parts of their learning, and watch over them with the greatest tenderness.

"Some or other of them went to the castle every day, and another most commonly to Bocardo. Whoever went to the castle was to read in the chapel to as many prisoners as would attend, and to talk apart to the man or men whom he had taken particularly in charge. When a new prisoner came, their conversation with him for four or five times was close and searching. If any one was under sentence of death, or appeared to have some intentions of a new life, they came every day to his assistance, and partook in the conflict and suspense of those who should now be found able, or not able, to lay hold on salvation. In order to release those who were confined for small debts, and to purchase books and other necessaries, they raised a little fund, to which many of their acquaintance contributed quarterly. They had prayers at the castle most Wednesdays and Fridays, a sermon on Sunday, and the sacrament once a month.

"When they undertook any poor family, they saw them at least once a week; sometimes gave them money, admonished them of their vices, read to them, and examined their children. The school was, I think, of Mr. Wesley's own setting up; however, he paid the mistress, and clothed some, if not all, the children. When they went thither, they inquired how each child behaved, saw their work, heard them read and say their prayers, or catechism, and explained part of it. In the same manner they taught the children in the workhouse, and read to the old people as they did to the prisoners.

"They seldom took any notice of the accusations brought against them for their charitable employments; but if they did make any reply, it was commonly such a plain and simple one, as if there was nothing more in the case, but that they had just heard such doctrines of their Savior, and had believed, and done accordingly.

"I could say a great deal of his private piety, how it was nourished by a continual recourse to God, and preserved by a strict watchfulness in beating down pride, and reducing the craftiness and impetuosity of nature to a childlike simplicity, and in a good degree crowned with divine love, and victory over the whole set of earthly passions. He thought prayer to be more his business than any thing else; and I have seen him come out of his closet with a serenity of countenance that was next to shining; it discovered what he had been doing, and gave me double hope of receiving wise directions, in the matter about which I came to consult him. In all his motions he attended to the will of God. He had neither the presumption nor the leisure to anticipate things whose season was not now; and would show some uneasiness whenever any of us, by impertinent speculations, were shifting off the appointed improvement of the present minute.

"Because he required such a regulation of our studies as might devote them all to God, he has been accused as one that discouraged learning. Far from that; for the first thing he struck at, in young men, was that indolence which will not submit to close thinking. He earnestly recommended to them a method and order in all their actions.

"If any one could have provoked him, I should; for I was very slow in coming into their measures, and very remiss in doing my part. I frequently contradicted his assertions; or, which is much the same, distinguished upon them. I hardly ever submitted to his advice at the time he gave it, though I relented afterward. He is now gone to Georgia as a missionary, where there is ignorance that aspires after divine wisdom, but no false learning that is got above it. He is, I confess, still living; and I know that an advantageous character is more decently bestowed on the deceased. But, beside that his condition is very like that of the dead, being unconcerned in all we say, I am not making any attempt on the opinion of the public, but only studying a private edification. A family picture of him his relations may be allowed to keep by them. And this is the idea of Mr. Wesley, which I cherish for the service of my own soul, and which I take the liberty likewise to deposit with you." (Whitehead's Life.)

This letter is honorable to Mr. Gambold's friendship; but he was not himself, at that time, of mature spiritual discernment, nor had Mr. Wesley opened the state of his heart to him with the freedom which we have seen in his letters to his mother. The external picture of the man is exact; but he is not inwardly that perfect Christian which Mr. Gambold describes, nor had he that abiding "interior peace." He was struggling with inward corruptions, which made him still cry, "O, wretched man that I am! who shall deliver me from the body of this death?" And he as yet put mortification, retirement, and contempt of the world, too much in the place of that divine atonement, the virtue of which, when received by simple faith, at once removes the sense of guilt, cheers the spirit by a peaceful sense of acceptance through the merits of Christ, and renews the whole heart after the image of God. He was, indeed, attempting to work out "his own salvation with fear and trembling;" but not as knowing that "it is God that worketh in us to will and to do of his good pleasure." He had not, in this respect, learned "to be nothing," that he might "possess all things."

CHAPTER III.

Mr. Wesley now prepared for Georgia, the place where, as he afterward said, "God humbled me, and proved me, and showed me what was in my heart." But he was not suffered to depart without remonstrances from friends which he answered calmly and at length, and the scoffs of the profane, to which he made but brief reply. "What is this, sir?" said one of the latter class to him; "are you turned Quixotte too? Will nothing serve you, but to encounter windmills?" To which he replied, "Sir, if the Bible be not true, I am as very a fool and madman as you can conceive; but if it be of God, I am sober-minded."

Mr. Charles Wesley, although in opposition to the opinion of his brother Samuel, agreed to accompany him to Georgia, and received holy orders. They were accompanied by Mr. Ingham, of Queen's College, and Mr. Delamotte. That Mr. Wesley considered the sacrifices and hardships of their mission in the light of means of religious edification to themselves, as well as the means of doing good to others, is plain from his own account: "Our end in leaving our native country was not to avoid want; God had given us plenty of temporal blessings; nor to gain the dung and dross of riches and honor; but singly this, to save our souls, to live wholly to the glory of God." These observations are sufficiently indicative of that dependence upon a mortified course of life, and that seclusion from the temptations of the world, which he then thought essential to religious safety.

Georgia is now a flourishing state, and the number of Methodist societies in it very considerable; a result not then certainly contemplated by the Wesleys, who labored there with little success, and quitted it almost in despair. The first settlers from England embarked in 1732, with Mr. James Oglethorpe at their head, who was also one of the trustees under the charter. This gentleman founded Savannah, and concluded a treaty with the Creek Indians. Wars with both Spaniards and Indians, however, subsequently arose, as well as domestic feuds; and in 1752 the trustees surrendered their charter to the king, and it was made a royal government. It was, therefore, in the infancy of the colony that the Wesleys commenced their labors.

That they should experience trouble, vexation, and disappointment, was the natural result both of the circumstances in which they were placed, and their own religious habits and views. A small colony, and especially in its infancy, is usually a focus of faction, discontent, and censoriousness. The colonists are often disappointed, uneasy in their circumstances, frustrated in their hopes, and impatient of authority. This was the case in Georgia; and although Mr. Oglethorpe upon the whole was a worthy governor, he was subject to prejudices, and prone to be misled by designing men. He certainly did not support the Wesleys with that steadiness and uniformity which were due to them;* and on the other hand they were not faultless, although their intentions were entirely upright. They had high notions of clerical authority; and their pastoral faithfulness was probably rigid and repulsive; for, in spite of the excellence of their own natural temper, an austere cast had been given to their piety. They stood firmly on little things, as well as great; and held the reins of ecclesiastical discipline with a tightness unsuitable to infant colonists especially, and which tended to provoke

* Oglethorpe's good opinion of the brothers was, however, shown by his anxiety to persuade Charles to return again to the colony, after he had visited England; and by the marked respect and even reverence with which at a future period he treated John.

resistance. Their integrity of heart, and the purity of their intentions, came forth without a stain: they must also be allowed to have proceeded according to the best light they had; but they knew not yet "the love of Christ," nor how to sway men's hearts by that all-commanding and controlling motion; and they aimed at making men Christians, in the manner they sought that great attainment themselves—by a rigid and ascetic discipline.

On their passage, an exact plan for the employment of time was arranged, and observed; but the voyage is most remarkable for bringing Mr. Wesley acquainted with the members of the Moravian Church; for among the settlers taken out were twenty-six Germans of this communion. Mr. Wesley immediately began to learn German, in order to converse with them; and David Nichtman, the Moravian bishop, and two others, received lessons in English. On the passage they had several storms, in which Mr. Wesley felt that the fear of death had not been taken away from him, and concluded therefore that he was not fit to die; on the contrary, he greatly admired the absence of all slavish dread in the Germans. He says, "I had long before observed the great seriousness of their behavior. Of their humility they had given a continual proof, by performing those servile offices for the other passengers which none of the English would undertake; for which they desired and would receive no pay; saying it was 'good for their proud hearts, and their loving Savior had done more for them.' And every day had given them occasion of showing a meekness, which no injury could move. If they were pushed, struck, or thrown down, they rose again and went away; but no complaint was found in their mouth. There was now an opportunity of trying whether they were delivered from the spirit of fear, as well as from that of pride, anger, and revenge. In the midst of the Psalm wherewith their service began, the sea broke over, split the mainsail in pieces, covered the ship, and poured in between the decks, as if the great deep had already swallowed us up. A terrible screaming began among the English. The Germans calmly sung on. I asked one of them afterward, 'Was you not afraid?' He answered, 'I thank God, no.' I asked, 'But were not your women and children afraid?' He replied, mildly, 'No; our women and children are not afraid to die.'" (Journal.)

Thus he had the first glimpse of a religious experience which keeps the mind at peace in all circumstances, and vanquishes that feeling which a formal and defective religion may lull to temporary sleep, but can not eradicate—"the fear of death."

They landed on the 6th of February, 1736, on a small uninhabited island; from whence Mr. Oglethorpe proceeded to Savannah, and returned the next day, bringing with him Mr. Spangenberg, one of the Moravian pastors, already settled there.

"I soon found," says Mr. Wesley, "what spirit he was of, and asked his advice with regard to my own conduct. He said, 'My brother, I must first ask you one or two questions. Have you the witness within yourself? Does the Spirit of God bear witness with your spirit, that you are the child of God?' I was surprised, and knew not what to answer. He observed it, and asked, 'Do you know Jesus Christ?' I paused and said, I know he is the Savior of the world. 'True,' replied he, 'but do you know he has saved you?' I answered, I hope he has died to save me. He only added, 'Do you know yourself?' I said, I do. But I fear they were vain words." (Journal.)

Mr. Charles Wesley took charge of Frederica, and Mr. John of Savannah, where, the house not being ready, he took up his residence with the Germans, with whose spirit and conduct he became still more favorably impressed, and whose mode of proceeding in the election and ordination of a bishop carried him back, he says, to those primitive times "where form and state were not, but Paul, the tent-maker, and Peter, the fisherman, presided, yet with demonstration of the Spirit, and power."

Mr. Wesley had not been long at Savannah, before he heard from Charles of his troubles and opposition at Frederica. His presence among the licentious colonists, and the frequent reproofs he administered, made him an object of great hatred, and "plots were formed either to ruin him in the opinion of Oglethorpe, or to take him off by violence." (Whitehead's Life.) Oglethorpe was, for a time, successfully practiced upon, treated him with coldness, and left him to endure the greatest privations. He lay upon the ground in the corner of a hut, and was denied the luxury of a few boards for a bed. He was out of favor with the governor; even the servants on that account insulted him; and, worn out with vexation and hardships, he fell into a dangerous fever. In this state he was visited by his brother John, who prevailed upon him to break a resolution which "honor and indignation" had induced him to form, of "starving rather than ask for necessaries." Soon after this, Mr. Oglethorpe discovered the plots of which he had been the victim, and was fully reconciled to him. He then took charge of Savannah, while John supplied his place at Frederica; and in July, 1736, he was sent to England, charged with dispatches from Mr. Oglethorpe to the trustees and the board of trade, and, in December, arrived at Deal; thus terminating a service in which he had preached with great fidelity and zeal; but had met with very unworthy returns.

Of the two places, Savannah appears to have been more hopeful than Frederica; and as Mr. John Wesley did not find the door open for preaching to the Indians, he consulted with his companions in what manner they might be most useful to the flock at Savannah. It was agreed, 1.

To advise the more serious among them to form themselves into a little society, and to meet once or twice a week, in order to reprove, instruct, and exhort one another. 2. To select out of these a smaller number for a more intimate union with each other; which might be forwarded partly by their conversing singly with each, and inviting them all together to Mr. Wesley's house; and this, accordingly, they determined to do every Sunday in the afternoon. "Here," says Dr. Whitehead, "we see the first rudiments of the future economy of classes and bands."*

In this respect he probably learned something from the Moravians, and the whole plan fell in with his previous views of discipline and method. The character of his mind was eminently practical; he was in earnest, and he valued things just as they appeared to be adapted to promote the edification and salvation of those committed to his charge. A school was also established, and the children regularly catechised by Mr. Wesley, both in private and in church. Evening meetings for the more serious were also held at his house; so actively did he apply himself, not only to the public services of the sanctuary, but to every kind of engagement, by which he might make "full proof of his ministry." The religious state of his own mind, however, remained much the same. He saw another striking instance of the power of faith, in the peaceful and edifying death of one of the Moravians; and had another proof that he himself was not saved from "the fear which hath torment," in a severe storm of thunder and lightning. Both indicated to him that he had not

* There was, however, nothing new in this. Mr. Wesley had doubtless heard, in his visit to London, of the religious societies described by Dr. Woodward, which were encouraged by the more serious clergy, and held weekly private meetings for religious edification. It is probable that he had even attended such meetings in the metropolis. Wherever, indeed, a revival of serious religion has taken place, and ministers have been in earnest to promote it, we see similar means adopted, as by Baxter at Kidderminster, during his eminently-successful ministry there.

attained the state of "the sons of God," but his views were still perplexed and obscure. From a conversation which he had with some Indians who had visited Savannah, he concluded that the way was opened for him to preach among the Choctaws, and this he was desirous of attempting; but as Savannah would have been left without a minister, the governor objected, and his friends were also of opinion that he could not then be spared from the colony.

In his visits to Frederica he met with great opposition and much illiberal abuse; in Savannah he was, however, rapidly gaining influence, when a circumstance occurred which issued in his departure from Georgia altogether. He had formed an attachment to an accomplished young lady, a Miss Hopkey,* niece to the wife of Mr. Causton, the chief magistrate of Savannah, which she appears to have returned, or at least encouraged. The biographers of Mr. Wesley, Dr. Whitehead and Mr. Moore, differ as to the fact, whether this connection was broken off by him, or by the lady herself in consequence of his delays. The latter professes to have received the whole account from Mr. Wesley, and must, therefore, be presumed to be the best authority. From this statement it appears that Mr. Delamotte suspected the sincerity of the lady's pretensions to piety, and thought his friend, Mr. Wesley, whose confiding and unsuspecting heart prevented him at all times from being a severe judge of others, was likely to be the victim of artifices which he had not the skill or the inclination to discern. His remonstrances led Mr. Wesley to refer the question of his marriage with Miss Hopkey to the judgment of the elders of the Moravian Church, which he thought he was at liberty to do, since the acquaintance, though it had ripened into regard and thoughts of marriage, had not, it seems, proceeded to any thing deter-

* Incorrectly called Miss Causton by Mr. Wesley's biographers.

minate. The Moravians advised him to proceed no farther; and his conduct toward Miss Hopkey became cautious and distant, very naturally to her mortification, and perhaps pain. An entry in his journal shows that he had a considerable struggle with his own feelings, and that his sense of duty had exacted a great sacrifice from his heart. The lady soon afterward married a Mr. Williamson; but a hostile feeling toward him had been left in the minds of her friends, which the gossiping and censorious habits of a small colony would not fail to keep alive. Though Mr. Wesley did not certainly see her married to another with perfect philosophy, it was not in his generous nature to allow his former affection to turn into resentment, which was the fault subsequently charged upon him; and, as he soon saw many things in her to reprove, it is probable that he thought his escape a fortunate one. Perhaps, considering the singularity of his habits at that time, it was well for the lady also; which seems, indeed, jocosely intimated in a passage of a letter of his brother Samuel to him on the occasion: "I am sorry you are disappointed in one match, because you are unlikely to find another."

An opportunity for the manifestation of the secret prejudice which had been nourished by the friends of the niece of Mrs. Causton was afforded in about five months after her marriage. Mr. Wesley adhered to the rubric of the Church of England as to the administration of the sacrament, without respect of persons, and with a rigidness which was not at all common. He repelled those whom he thought unworthy; and when any one had neglected the ordinance, he required him to signify his name the day before he intended to communicate again. Some time after Mrs. Williamson's marriage, he discovered several things which he thought blamable in her conduct. These, as she continued to communicate, he mentioned to her, and she in return became angry. For reasons, therefore, which he stated to her in a letter, he repelled her from the communion. This letter was written by desire of Mr. Causton, who wished to have his reasons for repelling his niece in writing:

"At Mr. Causton's request I write once more. The rules whereby I proceed are these: 'So many as intend to partake of the holy communion shall signify their names to the curate, at least some time the day before.' This you did not do.

"'And if any of these have done any wrong to his neighbor by word or deed, so that the congregation be thereby offended, the curate shall advertise him, that in any wise he presume not to come to the Lord's table, till he hath openly declared himself to have truly repented.'

"If you offer yourself at the Lord's table on Sunday, I will advertise you, as I have done more than once, wherein you have done wrong: and when you have openly declared yourself to have truly repented, I will administer to you the mysteries of God." (Journal.)

The storm now broke forth upon him. A warrant was issued, and he was brought before the recorder and magistrates, on the charges of Mr. Williamson, 1. That he had defamed his wife. 2. That he had causelessly repelled her from the holy communion. Mr. Wesley denied the first charge; and the second being wholly ecclesiastical, he would not acknowledge the authority of the magistrate to decide upon it. He was, however, told that he must appear before the next court, to be held at Savannah.

The Causton family became now most active in their efforts to injure him. By them the reason why Mr. Wesley had repelled Mrs. Williamson from the Lord's table, was stated to be his resentment against her for having refused to marry him; which they knew to be contrary to the fact. Garbled extracts of his letters were read by Causton to those whom he could collect to hear them, probably in order to confirm this; and Mrs. Williamson was prevailed upon to swear to and sign a paper containing assertions and insinuations injurious to his character. (Journal.)

The calm courage of the man who was thus so violently and unjustly persecuted, was not, however, to be shaken. "I sat still at home," says Mr. Wesley, "and, I thank God, easy, having committed my cause to him, and remembered his word, 'Blessed is the man that endureth temptation; for when he is tried, he shall receive the crown of life, which the Lord hath promised to them that love him.'" (Journal.)

As the sitting of the court drew near, Causton used every art to influence the grand jury, and, when they met, gave them "a long and earnest charge, 'to beware of spiritual tyranny, and to oppose the new illegal authority which was usurped over their consciences.' Mrs. Williamson's affidavit was read; and he then delivered to them a paper, entitled, A list of grievances, presented by the grand jury for Savannah, this —— day of August, 1737. In the afternoon Mrs. Williamson was examined, who acknowledged that she had no objections to make against Mr. Wesley's conduct before her marriage. The next day Mr. and Mrs. Causton were also examined, when she confessed, that it was by her request Mr. Wesley had written to Mrs. Williamson on the 5th of July; and Mr. Causton declared, that if Mr. Wesley had asked his consent to have married his niece, he should not have refused it. The grand jury continued to examine these ecclesiastical grievances, which occasioned warm debates till Thursday, when Mr. Causton being informed they had entered on matters beyond his instructions, went to them, and behaved in such a manner, that he turned forty-two, out of the forty-four, into a fixed resolution to inquire into his whole behavior. They immediately entered on that business, and continued examining witnesses all day on Friday. On Saturday,

Mr. Causton finding all his efforts to stop them ineffectual, adjourned the court till Thursday, the first of September, and spared no pains, in the mean time, to bring them to another mind. September 1.—He so far prevailed, that the majority of the grand jury returned the list of grievances to the court, in some particulars altered, under the form of two presentments, containing ten bills, only two of which related to the affair of Mrs. Williamson, and only one of these was cognizable by that court, the rest being merely ecclesiastical. September 2.—Mr. Wesley addressed the court to this effect: 'As to nine of the ten indictments againt me, I know this court can take no cognizance of them; they being matters of an ecclesiastical nature, and this not an ecclesiastical court. But the tenth, concerning my speaking and writing to Mrs. Williamson, is of a secular nature; and this, therefore, I desire may be tried here, where the facts complained of were committed.' Little answer was made, and that purely evasive.

"In the afternoon he moved the court again, for an immediate trial at Savannah; adding, 'that those who are offended may clearly see whether I have done any wrong to any one; or whether I have not rather deserved the thanks of Mrs. Williamson, Mr. Causton, and of the whole family.' Mr. Causton's answer was full of civility and respect. He observed, 'Perhaps things would not have been carried so far had you not said, you believed if Mr. Causton appeared, the people would tear him to pieces; not so much out of love to you as out of hatred to him for his abominable practices.' If Mr. Wesley really spoke these words, he was certainly very imprudent, considering the circumstances in which he was placed. But we too often find in disputes, that the constructions of others on what has been said are reported as the very words we have spoken; which I suspect to have been the case here. Mr. Causton, however, sufficiently discovered the motives that influenced his conduct in this business.

"Twelve of the grand jurors now drew up a protest against the proceedings of the majority, to be immediately sent to the trustees in England. In this paper they gave such clear and satisfactory reasons, under every bill, for their dissent from the majority, as effectually did away all just ground of complaint against Mr. Wesley, on the subjects of the prosecution." (Whitehead's Life.)

"He attended the court held on November the 3d; and again at the court held on the 23d; urging an immediate hearing of his case, that he might have an opportunity of answering the allegations alleged against him. But this the magistrates refused, and at the same time countenanced every report to his disadvantage: whether it was a mere invention, or founded on a malicious construction of any thing he did or said. Mr. Wesley perceiving that he had not the most distant prospect of obtaining justice; that he was in a place where those in power were combined together to oppress him, and could any day procure evidence—as experience had shown—of words he had never spoken, and of actions he had never done; being disappointed, too, in the primary object of his mission—preaching to the Indians; he consulted his friends what he ought to do; who were of opinion with him, that by these circumstances Providence did now call him to leave Savannah. The next day he called on Mr. Causton and told him he designed to set out for England immediately." (Whitehead's Life.)

The magistrates made a show of forbidding him to leave the colony; but he embarked openly, after having publicly advertised his intention, no man interposing to prevent him; one leading object of these persecutions being to drive him away. His sermons had been too faithful, and his reproofs too poignant, to make his continuance desirable to the majority of an irreligious colony.*

The root of all this opposition no doubt lay in the enmity of his hearers to truth and holiness; but its manifestation might be occasioned in part by the strictness with which he acted upon obsolete branches of ecclesiastical discipline, and the unbending manner in which he insisted upon his spiritual authority. In the affair of Mrs. Williamson, he stands perfectly exculpated from the base motives which his enemies charged upon him; but in the first stages, it neither appears to have been managed with prudence, nor a proper degree of Christian courtesy. His enemies have sneered at his declaration, that, after he left Georgia, he discovered that he who went out to teach others Christianity was not a Christian himself; but had he been a Christian in that full, evangelical sense, which he meant; had he been that which he afterward became, not only would the exclusion of Mrs. Williamson from the sacrament have been effected in another manner, but his mission to Georgia would probably have had a very different result.

[* The affair above explained, and other matters respecting Mr. Wesley in Georgia, have been most unfairly and unjustly represented in various illiberal publications, and particularly in Lempriere's Biographical Dictionary and Hale's History of the United States. The injustice done to Mr. Wesley's memory in the latter work is the more especially reprehensible, as pains have been taken to introduce it extensively into "schools." In this way many a youthful mind becomes prepossessed with strong early prejudice against one of the most devoted and the most honored embassadors for Christ that has ever graced any age or nation, since the day of the holy apostles. The influence of such prejudices extends itself in after life as well to the Christian denomination generally of which that eminent man was, under God, the founder, as to his own memory. This the contrivers of such *school* publications well know; and it is this effect of such books particularly that greatly aggravates the injustice and the mischief, as it tends, in fact, seriously to impede the spread of the Gospel itself. In these circumstances it is with peculiar pleasure that we are now enabled to issue a Life of Wesley, which, as well from the celebrity of its eminent author and its own intrinsic excellence, as from its remarkable cheapness, will, we doubt not, have a most extensive circulation.—AMERICAN EDITOR.]

His preaching was defective in that one great point, which gives to preaching its real power over the heart—"Christ crucified;" and his spirit, although naturally frank and amiable, was not regenerated by that "power from on high," the first and leading fruits of which are meekness and charity.

In the midst of his trials, Mr. Wesley received very consolatory letters from his friends, both in England and in America; and there were many in Georgia itself who rightly estimated the character and the labors of a man who held five or six public services on the Lord's day, in English, Italian, and French, for the benefit of a mixed population, who spent his whole time in works of piety and mercy, and who distributed his income so profusely in charity that, for many months together, he had not "one shilling in the house." His health, while in America, continued good; and it is in proof of the natural vigor of his constitution, that he exposed himself to every change of season, frequently slept on the ground, under the dews of the night in summer, and in winter with his hair and clothes frozen to the earth. He arrived in London, February 3, 1738, and, notwithstanding his many exercises, reviewed the result of his American labors with some satisfaction: "Many reasons I have to bless God for my having been carried into that strange land contrary to all my preceding resolutions. Hereby I trust he hath in some measure 'humbled me, and proved me, and shown me what was in my heart.' Hereby I have been taught to 'beware of men.' Hereby God has given me to know many of his servants, particularly those of the Church of Hernhuth. Hereby my passage is open to the writings of holy men, in the German, Spanish, and Italian tongues. All in Georgia have heard the word of God; some have believed and began to run well. A few steps have been taken toward publishing the glad tidings both to the

African and American heathens. Many children have learned 'how they ought to serve God,' and to be useful to their neighbor. And those whom it most concerns have an opportunity of knowing the state of their infant colony, and laying a firmer foundation of peace and happiness to many generations."

CHAPTER IV.

The solemn review which Mr. Wesley made of the state of his religious experience, both on his voyage home and soon after his landing in England, deserves to be particularly noticed, both for general instruction, and because it stands in immediate connection with a point which has especially perplexed those who have attributed his charges against himself, as to the deficiency of his Christianity at this period, to a strange and fanatical fancy. By the most infallible of proofs, he tells us—that of his feelings—he was convinced of his having "no such faith in Christ" as prevented his heart from being troubled; and he earnestly prays to be "saved by such a faith as implies peace in life and death." "I went to America to convert the Indians; but O, who shall convert me! Who is he that will deliver me from this evil heart of unbelief? I have a fair summer religion; I can talk well, nay, and believe myself, while no danger is present; but let death look me in the face, and my spirit is troubled, nor can I say, 'To die is gain.'

'I have a sin of fear, that when I've spun
My last thread, I shall perish on the shore.'"

He thought, therefore, that a faith was attainable, which should deliver him entirely from guilty dread, and fill him with peace; but of this faith itself his notions were still confused. He manifestly regarded it, generally, as a principle of belief in the Gospel, which, by quickening his efforts to self-mortification and entire obedience, would raise him, through a renewed state of heart, into acceptance and peace with God. This error is common. It regards faith, not so much as the personal trust of a guilty and helpless sinner upon Christ for salvation and all the gifts of spiritual life, but as working out sanctifying effects in the heart and life, partly by natural, partly by supernatural process, and thus producing peace of conscience. But he goes on with this interesting history of his heart.

"I was early warned against laying too much stress on outward works, as the Papists do, or on faith without works, which, as it does not *include*, so it will never lead to true hope or charity." (Journal.)

Here he manifestly confounds the faith by which a man is justified, which certainly does not "include" in itself the moral effects of which he speaks, with the faith of a man who is in a justified *state*, which necessarily produces them because of that vital union into which it brings him with Christ, his Savior, by whom he is saved from the power and love, as well as from the guilt, of sin.

"I fell among some Lutheran and Calvinistic authors, whose confused and indigested accounts magnified faith to such an amazing size, that it quite hid all the rest of the commandments." (Journal.)

This is perhaps a proof that he did not understand these writers any more than he did the Moravians in Georgia, who failed to enlighten him on the subject of faith, although he saw that they in fact possessed a "peace through believing," which he had not, and yet painfully felt to be necessary. The writers he mentions probably represented faith only as necessary to justification; while he conceived them to teach that faith only is necessary to final salvation.

"The English writers, such as Bishop Beveridge, Bishop Taylor, and Mr. Nelson, a little relieved me from these well-meaning, wrong-headed Germans. Their accounts of Christianity I could easily see to be, in the main, consistent both with reason and Scripture." (Journal.)

Beveridge would have met his case more fully than either Taylor or Nelson, had he been in a state of mind to comprehend him; and still better would he have been instructed by studying, with as much care as he examined Taylor and Law, the Homilies of his own Church, and the works of her older divines.

The writings of the fathers then promised to give him farther satisfaction; but to them he at length took various exceptions. He finally resorted to the Mystic writers, "whose noble descriptions of union with God, and internal religion, made every thing else appear mean, flat, and insipid. But in truth they made good works appear so too, yea, and faith itself, and what not? These gave me an entire new view of religion, nothing like any I had before. But, alas! it was nothing like that religion which Christ and his apostles lived and taught. I had a plenary dispensation from all the commands of God; the form ran thus, 'Love is all; all the commands beside are only means of love; you must choose those which you feel are means to you, and use them as long as they are so.' Thus were all the bands burst at once. And though I could never fully come into this, nor contentedly omit what God enjoined, yet, I know not how, I fluctuated between obedience and disobedience. I had no heart, no vigor, no zeal in obeying, continually doubting whether I was right or wrong, and never out of perplexities and entanglements. Nor can I at this hour give a distinct account how or when I came a little back toward the right way; only my present sense is this—all the other enemies of Christianity are triflers; the Mystics are the most dangerous of its enemies. They stab it in the vitals; and its most serious professors are most likely to fall by them. May I praise Him who hath snatched me out of this fire likewise, by warning all others that it is set on fire of hell!" (Journal.)

He was, however, delivered from the errors of the Mystics, only to be brought back to the point from which he set out; but his humble conclusions from the whole shows that the end of this long and painful struggle was about to be accomplished: he was now brought fully to feel and confess his utter helplessness, and was not "far from the kingdom of God."

"And now," says he, "it is upward of two years since I left my native country, in order to teach the Georgia Indians the nature of Christianity; but what have I learned myself in the mean time? Why—what I least of all suspected—that I, who went to America to convert others, was never converted myself. 'I am not mad,' though I thus speak; but 'speak the words of truth and soberness;' if haply some of those who still dream may awake, and see, that as I am, so are they.

"Are they read in philosophy? So was I. In ancient or modern tongues? So was I also. Are they versed in the science of divinity? I too have studied it many years. Can they talk fluently upon spiritual things? The very same I could do. Are they plenteous in alms? Behold, I give all my goods to feed the poor.

"Do they give of their labor as well as their substance? I have labored more abundantly than they all. Are they willing to suffer for their brethren? I have thrown up my friends, reputation, ease, country; I have put my life in my hand, wandering into strange lands; I have given my body to be devoured by the deep, parched up with heat, consumed by toil and weariness, or whatever God shall please to bring upon me. But does all this—be it more or less, it matters not—make me acceptable to God? Does all I ever did, or can know, say, give, do, or suffer, justify me in his sight? yea, or the constant use of all the means of grace?—which, nevertheless, is meet, right, and our bounden duty—or that I know nothing of myself, that I am, as touching outward, moral righteousness, blameless? or, to come closer yet, the having a rational conviction of all the truths of Christianity? Does all this give a claim to the holy, heavenly, divine character of a Christian? By no means. If the oracles of God are true, if we are still to abide by 'the law and the testimony,' all these things, though when ennobled by faith in Christ they are holy, and just, and good, yet without it are 'dung and dross.'

"This, then, have I learned in the ends of the earth, that I am 'fallen short of the glory of God;' that my whole heart is 'altogether corrupt and abominable,' and, consequently, my whole life—seeing it can not be, that 'an evil tree' should 'bring forth good fruit;' that my own works, my own sufferings, my own righteousness, are so far from reconciling me to an offended God, so far from making any atonement for the least of those sins which 'are more in number than the hairs of my head,' that the most specious of them need an atonement themselves, or they can not abide his righteous judgment; that having the sentence of death in my heart, and having nothing in or of myself to plead, I have no hope but that of being justified freely 'through the redemption that is in Jesus;' I have no hope, but that if I seek I shall find the Christ, and 'be found in him, not having my own righteousness but that which is through the faith of Christ, the righteousness which is of God by faith.'

"If it be said that I have faith—for many such things have I heard from many miserable comforters—I answer, So have the devils—*a sort of faith;* but still they are strangers to the covenant of promise. So the apostles had even at Cana in Galilee, when Jesus first 'manifested forth his glory;' even then they, in a sort, 'believed on him;' but they had not then 'the faith that overcometh the world.' The faith I want is 'a sure trust and confidence in God, that, through the merits of Christ, my sins are forgiven, and I reconciled to the favor of God.' I want that faith which St. Paul recommends to all the world, especially in his Epistle to the Romans—that faith which enables every one that hath it to cry out, 'I live not; but Christ liveth in me; and the life which I now live, I live by faith in the Son of God, who loved me, and gave himself for me.' I want that faith which none has, without knowing that he hath it—though many imagine they have it, who have it not; for whosoever hath it is freed from sin; the whole 'body of sin is destroyed' in him: he is freed from fear, 'having peace with God through Christ, and rejoicing in hope of the glory of God.' And he is freed from doubt, 'having the love of God shed abroad in his heart, through the Holy Ghost, which is given unto him; which Spirit itself beareth witness with his spirit, that he is a child of God.'" (Journal.)

A spirit thus breathing after God, and anxious to be taught "the way of God more perfectly," could not be left in its darkness and solicitude. A few days after his arrival in London, he met with Peter Bohler, a minister of the Moravian Church. This was on February 7th, which he marks as "a day much to be remembered," because the conversation which he had with Bohler on the subject of saving faith, a subject probably brought on by himself, first opened his mind to true views on that subject, notwithstanding the objections with which he assaulted the statements of the Moravian teacher, and which caused Bohler more than once to exclaim, "My brother, that philosophy of yours must be purged away." At Oxford, whither he had gone to visit Charles, who was sick, he again met with his Moravian friend, "by whom," he says, "in the hand of the great God, I was clearly convinced of unbelief, of the want of that faith whereby alone we are saved with the full Christian salvation."

"He was now convinced that his faith had been too much separated from an evangelical view of the promises of a free justification, or pardon of sin, through the atonement and mediation of Christ alone, which was the reason why he had been held in continual bondage and fear." (Whitehead's Life.) In a few days he met Peter Bohler again—"who now," he says, "amazed me more and more, by the account he gave of the fruits of living faith, the holiness and happiness which he affirmed to attend it. The next morning I began the Greek Testament again, resolved to abide by 'the law and the testimony,' being confident that God would hereby show whether this doctrine was of God." (Journal.)

In a fourth conversation with this excellent man, he was still more confirmed in the view, "that faith is, to use the words of our Church, a sure trust and confidence which a man has in God, that, through the merit of Christ, his sins are forgiven, and he reconciled to the favor of God." Some of his objections to Bohler's statements on instantaneous conversion were also removed by a diligent examination of the Scriptures. "I had," he observes, "but one retreat left on this subject: Thus I grant God wrought in the first ages of Christianity; but the times are changed. What reason have I to believe he works in the same manner now? But, on Sunday, 22d, I was beat out of this retreat, too, by the concurring evidence of several living witnesses, who testified God had so wrought in themselves, giving them, in a moment, such a faith in the blood of his Son, as translated them out of darkness into light, and from sin and fear into holiness and happiness. Here ended my disputing. I could now only cry out, 'Lord, help thou my unbelief!' "

He now began to declare that doctrine of faith which he had been taught; and those who were convinced of sin gladly received it. He was also much confirmed in the truth by hearing the experience of Mr. Hutchens, of Pembroke College, and Mrs. Fox: "Two living witnesses," he says, "that God can, at least, if he does not always, give that faith whereof cometh salvation in a moment, as lightning falling from heaven." (Journal.)

Mr. Wesley and a few others now formed themselves into a religious society, which met in Fetter-lane. But although they thus assembled with the Moravians, they remained members of the Church of England; and afterward, when some of the Moravian teachers introduced new doctrines, Mr. Wesley and his friends separated from them, and formed that distinct community which has since been known as "The Methodist Society." The rules of the Fetter-lane Society were printed under the title of "Orders of a Religious Society, meeting in Fetter-lane; in obedience to the command of God by St. James, and by the advice of Peter Bohler, in 1738."

As yet Mr. Wesley had not attained the blessing for which he so earnestly sought, and now with clearer views. His language as to himself, though still that of complaint, was become, in truth, the language of a broken and a contrite heart. It was no longer in the tone of a man, disappointed as to the results of his own efforts, and thrown into distressing perplexity, as not knowing where to turn for help. He was now bowed in lowly sorrow before the throne; but he knew that it was "the throne of grace;" and his cry was that of the publican, "God be merciful to me a sinner." In a letter to a friend, he says:

"I feel what you say, though not enough; for I am

under the same condemnation. I see that the whole law of God is holy, just, and good. I know every thought, every temper of my soul, ought to bear God's image and superscription. But how am I fallen from the glory of God! I feel that 'I am sold under sin.' I know that I too deserve nothing but wrath, being full of all abominations, and having no good thing in me to atone for them, or to remove the wrath of God. All my works, my righteousness, my prayers, need an atonement for themselves. So that my mouth is stopped. I have nothing to plead. God is holy: I am unholy. God is a consuming fire: I am altogether a sinner, meet to be consumed.

"Yet I hear a voice—and is it not the voice of God?—saying, 'Believe and thou shalt be saved. He that believeth is passed from death unto life. God so loved the world, that he gave his only-begotten Son, that whosoever believeth on him should not perish, but have everlasting life.'" (Journal.)

In this state of mind he continued till May 24, 1738, and then gives the following account of his conversion:

"I think it was about five this morning, that I opened my Testament on those words, 'There are given unto us exceeding great and precious promises, that by these ye might be partakers of the Divine nature,' 2 Peter i, 4. Just as I went out, I opened it again on those words, 'Thou art not far from the kingdom of God.' In the afternoon I was asked to go to St. Paul's. The anthem was, 'Out of the deep have I called unto thee, O Lord: Lord, hear my voice. O let thine ears consider well the voice of my complaint. If thou, Lord, wilt be extreme to mark what is done amiss, O Lord, who may abide it? But there is mercy with thee; therefore thou shalt be feared. O Israel, trust in the Lord, for with the Lord there is mercy, and with him is plenteous redemption. And he shall redeem Israel from all his sins.'

"In the evening I went very unwillingly to a society in Aldersgate-street, where one was reading Luther's preface to the Epistle to the Romans. About a quarter before nine, while he was describing the change which God works in the heart through faith in Christ, I felt my heart strangely warmed. I felt I did trust in Christ, Christ alone for salvation: and an assurance was given me, that he had taken away my sins, even mine, and saved me from 'the law of sin and death.'

"I began to pray with all my might, for those who had in a more especial manner despitefully used me, and persecuted me. I then testified openly to all there, what I now first felt in my heart. But it was not long before the enemy suggested, 'This can not be faith, for where is thy joy?' Then was I taught, that peace and victory over sin are essential to faith in the Captain of our salvation; but that, as to the transports of joy that usually attend the beginning of it, especially in those who have mourned deeply, God sometimes giveth, sometimes withholdeth them, according to the counsels of his own will." (Journal.)

After this he had some struggles with doubt; but he proceeded from "strength to strength," till he could say, "Now I was always conqueror." His experience, nurtured by habitual prayer, and deepened by unwearied exertion in the cause of his Savior, settled into that steadfast faith and solid peace, which the grace of God perfected in him to the close of his long and active life.

His brother Charles was also made partaker of the same grace. They had passed together through the briers and thorns, through the perplexities and shadows of the legal wilderness, and the hour of their deliverance was not far separated. Bohler visited Charles in his sickness at Oxford, but the "pharisee within" was somewhat offended when the honest German shook his head at learning that his hope of salvation rested upon "his best endeavors." After his recovery, the reading of Halyburton's Life produced in him a sense of his want of that faith which brings "peace and joy in the Holy Ghost." Bohler visited him again in London, and he began seriously to consider the doctrine which he urged upon him. His convictions of his state of danger, as a man unjustified before God, and of his need of the faith whereof cometh salvation, increased, and he spent his whole time in discoursing on these subjects, in prayer, and reading the Scriptures. Luther on the Galatians then fell into his hands, and on reading the preface he observes:

"I marveled that we were so soon and entirely removed from him that called us into the grace of God, to another Gospel. Who would believe that our Church had been founded on this important article of justification by faith alone? I am astonished I should ever think this a new doctrine; especially while our Articles and Homilies stand unrepealed, and the key of knowledge is not yet taken away. From this time I endeavored to ground as many of our friends as came to see me in this fundamental truth—salvation by faith alone—not an idle, dead faith, but a faith which works by love, and is incessantly productive of all good works and all holiness." (Journal.)

"On Whitsunday, May 21st, he awoke in hope and expectation of soon attaining the object of his wishes, the knowledge of God reconciled in Christ Jesus. At nine o'clock his brother and some friends came to him and sung a hymn suited to the day. When they left him he betook himself to prayer. Soon afterward a person came and said, in a very solemn manner, 'Believe in the name of Jesus of Nazareth and thou shalt be healed of all thine infirmities.' The words went through his heart, and animated him with confidence. He looked into the Scripture, and read, 'Now Lord, what is my hope? truly my hope is even in thee.' He then cast his eye on these words, 'He hath put a new song into my mouth, even thanksgiving unto our God; many shall see it and fear, and put their trust in the Lord.' Afterward he opened upon Isaiah xl, 1: 'Comfort ye, comfort ye my people, saith our God; speak comfortably to Jerusalem, and cry unto her, that her warfare is accomplished, that her iniquity is pardoned, for she hath received of the Lord's hand double for all her sins.' In reading these passages of Scripture, he was enabled to view Christ as set forth to be a propitiation for his sins, through faith in his blood; and he received that peace and rest in God which he had so earnestly sought.

"The next day he greatly rejoiced in reading the 107th Psalm, so nobly descriptive, he observes, of what God had done for his soul. He had a very humbling view of his own weakness, but was enabled to contemplate Christ in his power to save to the uttermost all those who come to God by him." (Whitehead's Life.)

Such was the manner in which these excellent men, whom God had been long preparing for the great work of reviving Scriptural Christianity throughout these lands, were at length themselves brought "into the liberty of the sons of God." On the account thus given, a few observations may not be misplaced.

It is easy to assail with ridicule such disclosures of the exercises of minds impressed with the great concern of salvation, and seeking for deliverance from a load of anxiety in "a way which they had not known;" and flippantly to resolve all these shadowings of doubt, these dawnings of hope, and the joyous influence of the full day of salvation, as some have done, into fancy, nervous affection, or natural constitution. To every truly-serious mind, these will, however, appear subjects of a momentous character; and no one will proceed either safely or soberly to judge of them, who does not previously inquire into the doctrine of the New Testament on the subject of human salvation, and apply the principles which he may find there, authenticated by infallible inspiration, to the examination of such cases. If it be there declared that the state of man by nature, and so long as he remains unforgiven by his offended God, is a state of awful peril, then the all-absorbing seriousness of that concern for deliverance from spiritual danger, which was exhibited by the Wesleys, is a feeling becoming our condition, and is the only rational frame of mind which we can cultivate. If we are required to be of "a humble and broken spirit," and if the very root of a true repentance lies in a "godly sorrow" for sin, then their humiliations and self-reproaches were in correspondence with a state of heart which is enjoined upon all by an authority which we can not dispute. If the appointed method of man's salvation, laid down in the Gospel, be *gratuitous pardon through faith in the merits of Christ's sacrifice*, and if a method of seeking justification by works of moral obedience to the divine law be plainly placed by St. Paul in opposition to this, and declared to be vain and fruitless, then, if in this way the Wesleys sought their justification before God, we see how true their own statement must of necessity have been, that with all their efforts they could obtain no solid peace of mind, no deliverance from the enslaving fear of death and final punishment, because they sought that by imperfect works which God has appointed to be attained by faith alone. If it be said, that their case was not parallel to that of the self-righteous Jews, who did not receive the Christian religion, and, therefore, that the argument of the apostle does not apply to those who believe the Gospel, it will remain to be inquired, whether the circumstance of a mere belief in the Christian system, when added to works of imperfect obedience, makes any essential difference in the case; or, in other words, whether justification may not be sought by endeavors to obey the law, although the Judaism necessarily implied in it may be arrayed in the garb of Christian terms and phrases. If, indeed, by "works of the law" St. Paul had meant only the ceremonial observances of the Jewish Church, the case would be altered; but his Epistle to the Romans puts it beyond all doubt, that in his argument respecting justification he speaks of the moral law, since his grand reason to prove that by the works of the law no man can be justified, is, that "by the law is the knowledge of sin." That law is recognized and embodied in the New Testament, but its first office there is to give "the knowledge of sin," that men may be convinced, or, as St. Paul forcibly says, "slain" by it: and it stands there in connection with the atonement for sin made by the sacrifice upon the cross. Nor is the faith which delivers men from the condemnation of a law which has been broken, and never can be perfectly kept by man, a mere *belief* in the truth of the doctrine of Christ, but *reliance* upon his sacrifice, in which consists that personal act by which we become parties to the covenant of free and gratuitous justification; and which then only stands sure to us, because then only we accept the mercy of God, as exercised toward us through Christ, and on the prescribed conditions. If, therefore, in the matter of our justification, like the Wesleys before they obtained clearer light, and the divines who were their early guides, we change the office of the moral law, though we may still regard it as in some way connected with the Gospel, and call it by the general term of Christianity, of which it, in truth, forms the preceptive part, and resort to it, not that we may be convinced of the greatness of our sins, and of our utter inability to commend ourselves to a holy God, the requirements of whose law have never been relaxed, but as the means of qualifying ourselves, by efforts of obedience to it, for the reception of divine mercy, and acquiring a fitness and worthiness for the exercise of grace toward us, then we reject the perfection and suitableness of the atonement of Christ; we refuse to commit our whole case in the matter of our justification to that atonement, according to the appointment of God, and as much seek justification by works of the law as did the Jews themselves. Such was the case with the Wesleys, as stated by themselves. Theirs was not, indeed, a state of heartless formality, and self-deluding Pharisaism, aiming only at external obedience. It was just the reverse of this: they were awakened to a sense of danger, and they aimed, nay, struggled with intense efforts after universal holiness, inward and outward. But it was not a state of salvation: and if we find a middle state like this described in the Scriptures—a state in transit from dead formality to living faith and moral deliverance—the question with respect to the truth of their representations, as to their former state of experience, is settled. Such a middle state we see plainly depicted by the apostle Paul in the seventh chapter of the Epistle to the Romans. There the mind of the person described "consents to the law that it is good," but finds in it only greater discoveries of his sinfulness and danger; there the effort, too, is after universal holiness—"to will is present," but the power is wanting; every struggle binds the chain tighter; sighs and groans are extorted, till self-despair succeeds, and the true Deliverer is seen and trusted in: "O wretched man that I am! who shall deliver me from the body of this death?" I thank God through Jesus Christ my Lord.* The deliverance,

* "All the time I was at Savannah I was thus beating the air. Being ignorant of the righteousness of Christ, which, by a living faith in him, bringeth salvation 'to every one that believeth,' I sought to establish my own righteousness, and so labored in the fire all my days. I was now properly under the law; I knew that 'the law of God was spiritual;' 'I consented to it that it was good. Yea, I delighted in it after the inner man.'

also, in the case described by St. Paul, is marked with the same characters as that exhibited in the conversion of the Wesleys: "There is now no *condemnation* to them that are in Christ Jesus, who walk not after the flesh, but after the Spirit; for the law of the Spirit of life in Christ Jesus hath made me free from the law of sin and death;" "Therefore, being justified by faith, we have *peace* with God, through our Lord Jesus Christ." Every thing in the account of the change wrought in the two brothers, and several of their friends about the same time, answers, therefore, to the New Testament. Nor was their experience, or the doctrine upon which it was founded, new, although in that age of declining piety unhappily not common. The Moravian statement of justifying faith was that of all the Churches of the Reformation; and through Peter Bohler Mr. Wesley came first to understand the true doctrine of that Church of which he was a clergyman. His mind was never so fully imbued with the letter and spirit of that

Yet I was 'carnal, sold under sin.' Every day was I constrained to cry out, 'What I do, I allow not; for what I would I do not, but what I hate, that I do. To will is indeed present with me; but how to perform that which is good, I find not. For the good which I would I do not; but the evil which I would not, that I do. I find a law, that when I would do good, evil is present with me: even the law in my members warring against the law of my mind, and still bringing me into captivity to the law of sin.'

'In this state I was, indeed, fighting continually, but not conquering. Before, I had willingly served sin; now it was unwillingly; but still I served it. I fell and rose, and fell again. Sometimes I was overcome, and in heaviness: sometimes I overcame, and was in joy. For, as in the former state I had some foretastes of the terrors of the law, so had I in this of the comforts of the Gospel. During this whole struggle between nature and grace, which had now continued above ten years, I had many remarkable returns to prayer, especially when I was in trouble: I had many sensible comforts, which are indeed no other than short anticipations of the life of faith. But I was still under the law, not under grace, the state most who are called Christians are content to live and die in. For I was only striving with, not freed from, sin; neither had I 'the witness of the Spirit with my spirit.' And, indeed, could not; for 'I sought it not by faith, but, as it were, by the works of the law." (Wesley's Journal.)

Article in which she has so truly interpreted St. Paul as when he learned from him, almost in the words of the Article itself, that "we are justified by faith only;" and that this is "a most wholesome doctrine." For the joyous change of Mr. Wesley's feelings, upon his persuasion of his personal interest in Christ through faith, those persons who, like Dr. Southey, (Life of Wesley,) have bestowed upon it several philosophic solutions, might have found a better reason had they either consulted St. Paul, who says, "We *joy* in God, by whom we have received the reconciliation," or their own Church, which has emphatically declared that the doctrine of justification by faith is not only very wholesome, but also "very full of *comfort*."

CHAPTER V.

FROM this time Mr. Wesley commenced that laborious and glorious ministry, which directly or indirectly was made the instrument of the salvation of a multitude, not to be numbered till "the day which shall make all things manifest." That which he had experienced he preached to others, with the confidence of one who had "the witness in himself;" and with a fullness of sympathy for all who wandered in paths of darkness and distress, which could not but be inspired by the recollection of his own former perplexities.

At this period the religious and moral state of the nation was such as to give the most serious concern to the few remaining faithful. There is no need to draw a picture darker than the truth, to add importance to the labors of the two Wesleys, Mr. Whitefield, and their associates. The view here taken has often been drawn by pens unconnected with and hostile to Methodism.

The Reformation from Popery which so much promoted the instruction of the populace in Scotland, did much less for the people of England, a great majority of whose lower classes, at the time of the rise of Methodism, were even ignorant of the art of reading, in many places were semi-barbarous in their manners, and had been rescued from the superstitions of Popery, only to be left ignorant of every thing beyond a few vague and general notions of religion. Great numbers were destitute even of these; and there are still agricultural districts in the southern and western counties, where the case is not, even at this moment, much improved. A clergyman has lately asserted in print, that in many villages of Devonshire the only form of prayer still taught to their children by the peasantry, are the goodly verses handed down from their Popish ancestors,

> "Matthew, Mark, Luke, and John,
> Bless the bed that I lie on," etc.

The degree of ignorance on all Scriptural subjects, and of dull, uninquiring irreligiousness which prevails in many other parts, is well known to those who have turned their attention to such inquiries, and would be incredible to those who have not.* A great impression was made in many places by the zealous preachers who sprang forth at the Reformation; and, in the large towns especially, they turned many of the people "from darkness to light." But the great body of the Popish parish priests went round with the Reformation, without conviction, and performed the new service, as they performed the old, in order to hold fast their livings. As what was called Puritanism prevailed, more zealous preaching and more careful instruction were employed; and by such ministers as the two

* By far the greater number of the peasants in Hampshire and Berkshire, lately tried under the special commissions for riots and stack-burning were found unable to read.

thousand who were silenced by the act of uniformity, with many equally excellent men who conformed to the re-established Church, a great body of religious and well-instructed people were raised up; and, indeed, before the civil wars commenced the nation might be said to be in a state of hopeful moral improvement. These troubles, however, arose before the effect produced upon a state of society sunk very low in vice and ignorance could be widely extended; and the keen and ardent political feelings which were then excited, and the demoralizing effects of civil warfare, greatly injured the spirit of piety, by occupying the attention of men, and rousing their passions by other, and often unhallowed, subjects. The effect was as injurious upon the advocates of the old Church discipline as upon those of the new, and probably worse; because it did not meet in them, for the most part, with principles so genuine and active to resist it. In many of the latter Antinomianism and fanaticism became conspicuous; but in the former a total irreligion, or a lifeless formality, produced a haughty dislike of the spiritualities of religion, or a sneering contempt of them. The mischief was completed by the restoration of the Stuarts; for whatever advantages were gained by that event in a civil sense, it let in a flood of licentiousness and impiety, which swept away almost every barrier that had been raised in the public mind by the labors of former ages. Infidelity began its ravages upon the principles of the higher and middle classes; the mass of the people remained uneducated, and were Christians but in name and by virtue of their baptism; while many of the great doctrines of the Reformation were banished both from the universities and the pulpits. Archbishop Leighton complains that his "Church was a fair carcass without a spirit;" and Burnet observes, that in his time "the clergy had less authority, and were under more contempt, than those of any Church in Europe; for they were much the most remiss in their labors, and the least severe in their lives." Nor did the case much amend up to the period of which we speak. Dr. Southey says, that "from the Restoration to the accession of the House of Hanover the English Church could boast of its brightest ornaments and ablest defenders, men who have never been surpassed in erudition, in eloquence, or in strength and subtilty of mind." This is true; but it is equally so, that, with very few exceptions, these great powers were not employed to teach, defend, and inculcate the doctrines of that Church on personal religion as it is taught in her Liturgy, her Articles, and her Homilies, but what often was subversive of them; and the very authority, therefore, which such writers acquired by their learned and able works was in many respects mischievous. They stood between the people and the better divines of the earlier age of the Church, and put them out of sight; and they set an example of preaching which, being generally followed, placed the pulpit and the desk at perpetual variance, and reduced an evangelical liturgy to a dead form, which was repeated without thought, or so explained as to take away its meaning. A great proportion of the clergy, whatever other learning they might possess, were grossly ignorant of theology, and contented themselves with reading short unmeaning sermons, purchased or pilfered, and formed upon the lifeless theological system of the day. A little Calvinism remained in the Church, and a little evangelical Arminianism; but the prevalent divinity was Pelagian, or what very nearly approached it. Natural religion was the great subject of study, when theology was studied at all, and was made the test and standard of revealed truth. The doctrine of the *opus operatum* of the Papists, as to sacraments, was the faith of the divines of the older school: and a refined system of ethics, unconnected with Christian motives, and disjoined from the vital principles of religion in the heart, was the favorite theory of the modern. The body of the clergy neither knew nor cared about systems of any kind. In a great number of instances they were negligent and immoral; often grossly so. The populace of the large towns were ignorant and profligate; and the inhabitants of villages added to ignorance and profligacy brutish and barbarous manners. A more striking instance of the rapid deterioration of religious light and influence in a country scarcely occurs, than in our own, from the Restoration till the rise of Methodism. It affected not only the Church, but the dissenting sects in no ordinary degree. The Presbyterians had commenced their course through Arianism down to Socinianism; and those who held the doctrines of Calvin had, in too many instances, by a course of hot-house planting, luxuriated them into the fatal and disgusting errors of Antinomianism. There were indeed many happy exceptions; but this was the general state of religion and morals in the country, when the Wesleys, Whitefield, and a few kindred spirits came forth, ready to sacrifice ease, reputation, and even life itself, to produce a reformation.

Before Mr. Wesley entered upon the career which afterward distinguished him, and having no preconceived plan or course of conduct, but to seek good for himself, and to do good to others, he visited the Moravian settlements in Germany. On his journey he formed an acquaintance with several pious ministers in Holland and Germany; and at Marienbourn was greatly edified by the conversation of Count Zinzendorf, and others of the brethren, of whose views he did not, however, in all respects, even then approve. From thence he proceeded to Hernhuth, where he staid a fortnight, conversing with the elders, and observing the economy of that Church, part of which, with modifications, he afterward introduced among his own societies. The sermons of Christian David especially interested him;

and of one of them, on "the ground of our faith," he gives the substance; which we may insert, both as excellent in itself, and as it so well agrees with what Mr. Wesley afterward uniformly taught:

"The word of reconciliation which the apostles preached, as the foundation of all they taught, was, that 'we are reconciled to God, not by our own works, nor by our own righteousness, but wholly and solely by the blood of Christ.'

"But you will say, Must I not grieve and mourn for my sins? Must I not humble myself before my God? Is not this just and right? And must I not first do this before I can expect God to be reconciled to me? I answer, It is just and right. You must be humbled before God. You must have a broken and contrite heart. But then observe, this is not your own work. Do you grieve that you are a sinner? This is the work of the Holy Ghost. Are you contrite? Are you humbled before God? Do you indeed mourn, and is your heart broken within you? All this worketh the self-same Spirit.

"Observe again, this is not the foundation. It is not this by which you are justified. This is not the righteousness, this is no part of the righteousness, by which you are reconciled to God. You grieve for your sins. You are deeply humble. Your heart is broken. Well. But all this is nothing to your justification.* The remission of your sins is not owing to this cause, either in whole or in part. Nay, observe farther, that it may hinder your justification; that is, if you build any thing upon it; if you think, I must be so or so contrite: I must grieve more, before I can be justified. Understand this well. To think you must be more contrite, more humble, more grieved,

* "This is not guarded. These things do not merit our justification, but they are absolutely necessary in order to it. God never pardons the impenitent." (Wesley's Journal.)

more sensible of the weight of sin, before you can be justified, is, to lay your contrition, your grief, your humiliation for the foundation of your being justified: at least for a part of the foundation. Therefore, it hinders your justification; and a hinderance it is which must be removed, before you can lay the right foundation. The right foundation is, not your contrition—though that is not your own—not your righteousness, nothing of your own; nothing tha is wrought in you by the Holy Ghost; but it is something without you; namely, the righteousness and blood of Christ.

"For this is the word, 'To him that believeth on God that justifieth the ungodly, his faith is counted for righteousness.' See ye not, that the foundation is nothing in us? There is no connection between God and the ungodly. There is no tie to unite them. They are altogether separate from each other. They have nothing in common. There is nothing less or more in the ungodly, to join them to God. Works, righteousness, contrition? No. Ungodliness only. This, then, do, if you will lay a right foundation: go straight to Christ with all your ungodliness. Tell him, Thou whose eyes are as a flame of fire, searching my heart, seest that I am ungodly. I plead nothing else. I do not say, I am humble or contrite; but I am ungodly. Therefore, bring me to him that justifieth the ungodly. Let thy blood be the propitiation for me; for there is nothing in me but ungodliness.

"Here is a mystery. Here the wise men of the world are lost, are taken in their own craftiness. This the learned of the world can not comprehend. It is foolishness to them. Sin is the only thing which divides men from God. Sin—let him that heareth understand—is the only thing which unites them to God; that is, the only thing which moves the Lamb of God to have compassion upon them, and by his blood to give them access to the Father.

"This is the word of reconciliation which we preach. This is the foundation which never can be moved. By faith we are built upon this foundation; and this faith also is the gift of God. It is his free gift, which he now and ever giveth to every one that is willing to receive it. And when they have received this gift of God, then their hearts will melt for sorrow that they have offended him. But this gift of God lives in the heart, not in the head. The faith of the head, learned from men or books, is nothing worth. It brings neither remission of sins nor peace with God. Labor then to believe with your whole heart. So shall you have redemption through the blood of Christ. So shall you be cleansed from all sin. So shall ye go on from strength to strength, being renewed day by day in righteousness and all true holiness." (Journal.)

"I would gladly," says Mr. Wesley, "have spent my life here; but my Master calling me to labor in another part of his vineyard, I was constrained to take my leave of this happy place. O when shall this Christianity cover the earth, as the 'waters cover the sea!'" He adds in another place, "I was exceedingly comforted and strengthened by the conversation of this lovely people; and returned to England more fully determined to spend my life in testifying the Gospel of the grace of God." (Journal.)

He arrived in London in September, 1738. His future course of life does not appear to have been shaped out in his mind; no indication of this appears in any of his letters, or other communication: so little ground is there for the insinuation, which has been so often made, that he early formed the scheme of making himself the head of a sect. This, even those inconsistencies, considering him as a Churchman, into which circumstances afterward impelled him, sufficiently refute. That he was averse to settle as a parish minister is certain; and the man who regarded "the world as his parish" must have had large views of usefulness. That he kept in mind the opinion of the bishop who ordained him, that he was at liberty to decline settling as a parish priest, provided he thought that he could serve the Church better in any other way, is very probable; and if he had any fixed purpose at all, at this time, beyond what circumstances daily opened to him, and from which we might infer the path of duty, it was to attempt to revive the spirit of religion in the Church to which he belonged and which he loved, by preaching "the Gospel of the grace of God" in as many of her pulpits as he should be permitted to occupy. This was the course he pursued. Wherever he was invited, he preached the obsolete doctrine of salvation by grace through faith. In London great crowds followed him; the clergy generally excepted to his statement of the doctrine; the genteeler part of his audiences, whether they attended to the sermon or not, were offended at the bustle of crowded congregations; and soon almost all the churches of the metropolis, one after another, were shut against him. He had, however, largely labored in various parts of the metropolis in churches, rooms, houses, and prisons; and the effects produced were powerful and lasting. Soon after we find him in Oxford, employed in writing to his friends abroad, communicating the good news of a great awakening both in London and in that city. To Dr. Koker, of Rotterdam, he writes, October 13, 1738: "His blessed Spirit has wrought so powerfully both in London and Oxford, that there is a general awakening, and multitudes are crying out, What must we do to be saved? So that, till our gracious Master sendeth more laborers into his harvest, all my time is much too little for them." And to the Church at Hernhuth, he writes under the same date: "We are endeavoring here, also, by the grace which is given us, to be followers of you, as ye are of Christ. Fourteen were added to us since our return; so that we have now eight bands of men, consisting of fifty-six persons, all of whom seek for salvation only in the blood of Christ. As yet we have only two small bands of women, the one of three, the other of five persons. But here are many others who only wait till we have leisure to instruct them how they may most effectually build up one another in the faith and love of Him who gave himself for them.

"Though my brother and I are not permitted to preach in most of the churches in London, yet, thanks be to God! there are others left, wherein we have liberty to speak the truth as it is in Jesus. Likewise every evening, and on set evenings in the week, at two several places, we publish the word of reconciliation, sometimes to twenty or thirty, sometimes to fifty or sixty, sometimes to three or four hundred persons met together to hear it."

In December he met Mr. Whitefield, who had returned to London from America, "and they again took sweet counsel together." In the spring of the next year, he followed Mr. Whitefield to Boston, where he had preached with great success in the open air. Mr. Wesley first expounded to a little society,* accustomed to meet in Nicholas-street; and the next day he overcame his scruples,

* The "societies" which Mr. Wesley mentions in his journals as visited by him, for the purpose of expounding the Scriptures, in London and Bristol, were the remains of those which Dr. Woodward describes, in an account first published about the year 1698 or 1699. They began, about the year 1667, among a few young men in London, who, under Dr. Horneck's preaching, and the morning lectures in Cornhill, were brought, says Dr. Woodward, "to a very affecting sense of their sins, and began to apply themselves in a very serious way to religious thoughts and purposes." They were advised by their ministers to meet together weekly for "good discourse;" and rules were drawn up "for the better regulation of these meetings." They contributed weekly for the use of the poor, and stewards were appointed to take care of and to disburse their charities. In the latter part of the reign of James II, they met with discouragement; but on the accession of William and Mary they acquired new vigor. When Dr. Woodward wrote his account, there were about forty of these societies in activity, within the bills of mortality, a few in

and preached abroad, on an eminence near the city, to more than two thousand persons. On this practice he observes, that though till lately he had been so tenacious of every point relating to decency and order, that he should have thought the saving of souls almost a sin if it had not been done in a church, yet, "I have since seen abundant reason to adore the wise providence of God herein, making a way for myriads of people, who never troubled any church or were likely so to do, to hear that word which they soon found to be the power of God to salvation."

The manner in which he filled up his time may be seen from the following account of his weekly labors at this period, at or near Bristol. "My ordinary employment in public was now as follows: Every morning I read prayers and preached at Newgate. Every evening I expounded a portion of Scripture, at one or more of the societies. On Monday in the afternoon I preached abroad near Bristol.

the country, and nine in Ireland. Out of these societies about twenty associations arose, in London, for the prosecution and suppression of vice; and both these, and the private societies for religious edification, had for a time much encouragement from several bishops, and from the queen herself. By their rules they were obliged, at their weekly meetings, to discourse only on such subjects as tended to practical holiness, and to avoid all controversy; and beside relieving the poor, they were to promote schools, and the catechising of "young and ignorant persons in their respective families." These societies certainly opened a favorable prospect for the revival of religion in the Church of England; but, whether they were cramped by clerical jealousy lest laymen should become too active in spiritual concerns; or that from their being bound by their orders to prosecute vice by calling in the aid of the magistrate, their moral influence among the populace was counteracted; they appear to have declined from about 1710; and although several societies still remained in London, Bristol, and a few other places, at the time when Mr. Wesley commenced his labors, they were not in a state of growth and activity. They had, however, been the means of keeping the spark of piety from entire extinction. The sixth edition of Dr. Woodward's account of these societies was published in 1744; but from that time we hear no more of them; they either gradually died away, or were absorbed in the Methodist societies. This at least was the case with several of them in London and Bristol; and with that of St, Ives, in Cornwall.

On Tuesday at Bath and Two Mile Hill, alternately. On Wednesday at Baptist Mills. Every other Thursday, near Pensford. Every other Friday, in another part of Kingswood. On Saturday in the afternoon, and Sunday morning, in the Bowling Green. On Sunday at eleven near Hannam Mount, at two at Clifton, at five at Rose Green. And hitherto, as my day is, so is my strength." (Journal.)

During Mr. Wesley's visit to Germany, his brother Charles was zealously employed in preaching the same doctrines, and with equal zeal, in the churches in London; and in holding meetings for prayer and expounding the Scriptures. At this time he also visited Oxford, and was made useful to several of his old college friends. When his brother returned from Hernhuth, he met him with great joy in London, and they "compared their experience in the things of God." The doctrine of predestination, on which so many disputes have arisen in the Church, and which was soon to be warmly debated among the first Methodists, was soon after started at a meeting for exposition. Mr. Charles contented himself with simply protesting against it. He now first began to preach extempore. In a conference which the brothers had with the bishop of London, they cleared up some complaints as to their doctrine which he had received against them, and were upon the whole treated by him with liberality. He strongly disapproved, however, of their practice of rebaptizing persons who had been baptized by Dissenters, in which they exhibited the firm hold which their High Church feelings still retained upon their minds. His lordship showed himself, in this respect, not only more liberal, but better versed in ecclesiastical law and usage. The bishop at this, and at other interviews, guarded them strongly against Antinomianism, of which, however, they were in no danger. He was probably alarmed, as many had been, at the stress they laid on faith, not knowing the *necessary* connection of the faith they preached with universal holiness. Mr. Whitefield was at this time at Oxford, and pressed Charles earnestly to accept a college living; which, as Dr. Whitehead justly observes, "gives pretty clear evidence that no plan of itinerant preaching was yet fixed on, nor indeed thought of: had any such plan been in agitation among them, it is very certain Mr. Whitefield would not have urged this advice on Mr. Charles Wesley, whom he loved as a brother, and whose labors he highly esteemed." (Whitehead's Life.)

About this time some disputes took place, in the Fetter-lane Society, as to lay-preaching, and Mr. Charles Wesley, in the absence of his brother, declared warmly against it. He had, also, while Mr. John Wesley was still at Bristol, a painful interview at Lambeth, with the archbishop of Canterbury. His grace took no exceptions to his doctrine, but condemned the irregularity of his proceedings, and even hinted at proceeding to excommunication. This threw him into great perplexity of mind, till Mr. Whitefield, with characteristic boldness, urged him to preach "in the fields the next Sunday: by which step he would break down the bridge, render his retreat difficult or impossible, and be forced to fight his way forward." This advice he followed. "June 24th, I prayed," says he, "and went forth in the name of Jesus Christ. I found near a thousand helpless sinners waiting for the word in Moorfields. I invited them in my Master's words, as well as name: *Come unto me, all ye that labor and are heavy-laden, and I will give you rest.* The Lord was with me, even me, the meanest of his messengers, according to his promise. At St. Paul's, the psalms, lessons, etc., for the day, put new life into me; and so did the sacrament. My load was gone, and all my doubts and scruples. God shone on my path, and I knew this was his will concerning me. I walked to Kennington Common, and cried to multitudes upon multitudes, *Repent ye, and believe the Gospel.* The Lord was my strength, and my mouth, and my wisdom. O that all would therefore praise the Lord for his goodness!"

At Oxford, also, he had to sustain the severity of the dean on the subject of field-preaching; but he seized the opportunity of bearing his testimony to the doctrine of justification by faith, by preaching with great boldness before the university. On his return to London, he resumed field-preaching in Moorfields, and on Kennington Common. At one time it was computed that as many as ten thousand persons were collected, and great numbers were roused to a serious inquiry after religion. His word was occasionally attended with an overwhelming influence.

That great public attention should be excited by these extraordinary and novel proceedings, and that the dignitaries of the Church, and the advocates of stillness and order, should take the alarm at them, as "doubting whereunto this thing might grow," were inevitable consequences. A doctrine so obsolete, that on its revival it was regarded as new and dangerous, was now publicly proclaimed as the doctrine of the apostles and reformers; the consciousness of forgiveness of sins was professed by many, and enforced as the possible attainment of all; several clergymen of talents and learning, which would have given influence to any cause, endued with mighty zeal, and with a restless activity, instead of settling in parishes, were preaching in various churches and private rooms, and to vast multitudes in the open air, alternately in the metropolis, and at Bristol, Oxford, and the interjacent places. They alarmed the careless by bringing before them the solemnities of the last judgment; they explained the spirituality of that law, upon which the self-righteous trusted for salvation, and convinced them that the justification of man was by the grace of God alone through faith; and they roused the dozing adherents of mere forms, by teaching that true religion implies a change of the whole heart wrought by the Holy Ghost. With equal zeal and earnestness, they checked the pruriency of the Calvinistic system, as held by many Dissenters, by insisting that the law which can not justify, was still the rule of life, and the standard of holiness to all true believers; and taught that mere doctrinal views of evangelical truth, however correct, were quite as vain and unprofitable as Pharisaism and formality when made a substitute for vital faith, spirituality, and practical holiness. All this zeal was supported and made more noticeable, by the moral elevation of their character. Their conduct was scrupulously hallowed; their spirit, gentle, tender, and sympathizing; their courage, bold and undaunted; their patience, proof against all reproach, hardships, persecutions; their charities to the poor abounded to the full extent of all their resources; their labors were wholly gratuitous; and their wonderful activity, and endurance of the fatigues of rapid traveling, seemed to destroy the distance of place, and to give them a sort of ubiquity in the vast circuit which they had then adopted as the field of their labors. For all these reasons, they "were men to be wondered at," even in this the infancy of their career; and as their ardor was increased by the effects which followed, the conversion of great numbers to God, of which the most satisfactory evidence was afforded, it disappointed those who anticipated that their zeal would soon cool, and that, "shorn of their strength" by opposition, reproach, and exhausting labors, they would become "like other men."

An infidel or semi-Christian philosophy has its theories at hand to account for the appearance and conduct of such extraordinary men. If their own supposed "artifices," and the "temptation to place themselves at the head of a sect," will not solve the case, it then resorts "to the circumstances of the age," or to "that restless activity and ambition" which finds in them "a promising sphere of action, and is attracted onward by its first successes." Even many serious Churchmen of later times, who contend that the great men of the Reformation were raised up by divine Providence in mercy to the world, are kept by sectarian prejudices from acknowledging a similar providential leading in the case of the Wesleys, Whitefield, and Howell Harris, because the whole of the good effected has not rested within their own pale, and all the sheep collected out of the wilderness have not been gathered into their own fold. The sober Christian will, however, resort to the first principles of his own religion in order to form his judgment. He will acknowledge that the Lord of the harvest has the prerogative of "sending forth his laborers;" that men who change the religious aspect of whole nations can not be the offspring of chance, or the creation of circumstances; that, whatever there may be of personal fitness in them for the work, as in the eminent natural and acquired talents of St. Paul, and whatever there may be in circumstances to favor their usefulness, these things do not shut out the special agency of God, but make it the more manifest; since the first more strikingly marks his agency in preparing his own servants, and training his soldiers; and the second, his wisdom in choosing the times of their appearance, and the scenes of their labors, and thus setting before them "an open door, and effectual." Nor can it be allowed, if we abide by the doctrine of the Scriptures, that a real spiritual good could have been so extensively and uniformly effected, and "multitudes turned to the Lord," unless God had been with the instruments, seconding their labors, and "giving his own testimony to the word of his grace." The hand of God is equally conspicuous in connecting the leading events of their earlier history with their future usefulness. They were men "separated to the Gospel of God;" and every devout and grateful Christian will not cease to recognize in their appearance, labors, and successes, the mercy of God to a land where "truth had fallen in the streets," and the people were sitting in darkness, and in the shadow of death.

CHAPTER VI.

We left Mr. Wesley at Bristol, in the summer of 1739, to which scene of labor, after a visit to London, he again returned. Kingswood was mentioned in the account given by Mr. Wesley, in the preceding chapter, of his labors; and in this district, inhabited by colliers, and, from its rudeness, a terror to the neighborhood, the preaching of the two brothers and of Mr. Whitefield was eminently successful. The colliers were even proverbial for wickedness; but many of them became truly exemplary for their piety. These had been exhorted, it seems, to go to Bristol to receive the sacrament; but their numbers were so considerable that the Bristol clergy,* averse to the additional labor imposed upon them, repelled them from the communion, on the plea that they did not belong to their parishes.

The effect of the leaven which had been thus placed in this mass of barbarism was made conspicuous in the following year, in the case of a riot, of which Mr. Charles Wesley gives the following account. Being informed that

* Several of the Bristol clergy were at that time of a persecuting character. They induced a Captain Williams, the master of a vessel trading to Georgia, to make an affidavit of some statements to the disadvantage of Mr. Wesley in the affair of Mrs. Williamson; but they took care that he should set sail before they published it. This led to the publication of Mr. Wesley's first journal, as he states in the preface. In that journal he gave his own account of the matter, and they were silenced.

the colliers had risen, on account of the dearness of corn, and were marching for Bristol, he rode out to meet them, and talk with them. Many seemed disposed to return with him to the school which had been built for their children; but the most desperate rushed violently upon them, beating them, and driving them away from their pacific adviser. He adds, "I rode up to a ruffian, who was striking one of our colliers, and prayed him rather to strike me. He answered, 'No, not for all the world,' and was quite overcome. I turned upon another, who struck my horse, and he also sunk into a lamb. Wherever I turned, Satan's cause lost ground, so that they were obliged to make one general assault, and the violent colliers forced the quiet ones into the town. I seized one of the tallest, and earnestly besought him to follow me. Yes, he said, that he would, all the world over. I pressed about six into the service. We met several parties, and stopped and exhorted them to follow us; and gleaning some from every company, we increased as we marched on singing to the school. From one till three o'clock we spent in prayer, that evil might be prevented, and the lion chained. Then news was brought us that the colliers had returned in peace. They had walked quietly into the city, without sticks or the least violence. A few of the better sort of them went to the mayor, and told their grievance; then they all returned as they came, without noise or disturbance. All who saw it were amazed. Nothing could more clearly have shown the change wrought among them than this conduct on such an occasion. . . I found afterward that all our colliers to a man had been forced away. Having learned of Christ not to resist evil, they went a mile with those who compelled them, rather than free themselves by violence. One man the rioters dragged out of his sick bed, and threw him into the fish pond. Near twenty of Mr. Willis' men they had prevailed on, by threatening to fill up their pits, and bury them alive, if they did not come up and bear them company. . . It was a happy circumstance that they forced so many of the Methodist colliers to go with them; as these, by their advice and example, restrained the savage fury of the others. This undoubtedly was the true cause why they all returned home without making any disturbance."

To a gentleman who requested some account of what had been done in Kingswood, Mr. John Wesley wrote the following statement:

"Few persons have lived long in the west of England who have not heard of the colliers of Kingswood, a people famous, from the beginning hitherto, for neither fearing God nor regarding man; so ignorant of the things of God, that they seemed but one remove from beasts that perish, and therefore utterly without the desire of instruction, as well as without the means of it.

"Many last winter used tauntingly to say of Mr. Whitefield, 'If he will convert heathens, why does he not go to the colliers of Kingswood?' In the spring he did so. And as there were thousands who resorted to no place of public worship, he went after them into their own 'wilderness, to seek and save that which was lost.' When he was called away, others went into 'the highways and hedges, to compel them to come in.' And, by the grace of God, their labor was not in vain. The scene is already changed. Kingswood does not now, as a year ago, resound with cursing and blasphemy. It is no more filled with drunkenness and uncleanness, and the idle diversions that naturally lead thereto. It is no longer full of wars and fightings, of clamor and bitterness, of wrath and envyings. Peace and love are there. Great numbers of the people are mild, gentle, and easy to be entreated. They 'do not cry, neither strive;' and hardly is 'their voice heard in the streets,' or indeed in their own wood, unless when they are at their usual evening diversion, singing praise to God their Savior."

At this time Mr. Wesley visited Bath, where the celebrated Beau Nash, then Lord of the ascendant in that city, attempted to confront the field preacher.

"There was great expectation at Bath of what a noted man was to do to me there: and I was much entreated 'not to preach, because no one knew what might happen.' By this report I also gained a much larger audience, among whom were many of the rich and great. I told them plainly, the Scripture had concluded them all under sin, high and low, rich and poor, one with another. Many of them seemed to be not a little surprised, and were sinking apace into seriousness, when their champion appeared, and, coming close to me, asked by what authority I did these things. I replied, By the authority of Jesus Christ, conveyed to me by the [now] archbishop of Canterbury, when he laid his hands upon me, and said, 'Take thou authority to preach the Gospel.' He said, 'This is contrary to act of Parliament. This is a conventicle.' I answered, 'Sir, the conventicles mentioned in that act—as the preamble shows—are seditious meetings. But this is not such. Here is no shadow of sedition. Therefore, it is not contrary to that act.' He replied, 'I say it is. And, beside, your preaching frightens people out of their wits.' 'Sir, did you ever hear me preach?' 'No.' 'How then can you judge of what you never heard?' 'Sir, by common report. Common report is enough.' 'Give me leave, sir, to ask, Is not your name Nash?' 'My name is Nash.' 'Sir, I dare not judge of you by common report. I think it is not enough to judge by.' Here he paused awhile, and having recovered himself, asked, 'I desire to know what this people come here for?' On which one replied, 'Sir, leave him to me. Let an old woman answer him.' 'You, Mr. Nash, take care of your body. We take care of our souls, and for the good of our souls we come here.' He replied not a word, but walked away.

"As I returned, the street was full of people, hurrying to and fro, and speaking great words. But when any of them asked, 'Which is he?' and I replied, 'I am he,' they were immediately silent. Several ladies following me into Mr. Merchant's house, the servant told me there were some wanted to speak with me. I went to them, and said, 'I believe, ladies, the maid mistook; you only wanted to look at me.' I added, 'I do not expect that the rich and great should want either to speak with *me*, or to hear *me*, for I speak the plain truth; a thing *you* hear little of, and do not desire to hear.' A few more words passed between us, and I retired." (Journal.)

After visiting London, and preaching to vast multitudes in Moorfields, on Kennington Common, and other places, some of whom were strangely affected, and many effectually awakened to a sense of sin, in October Mr. Wesley had a pressing invitation to visit Wales, where, although the churches were shut against him, he preached in private houses, and in the open air, often during sharp frosts, and was gladly received by the people. "I have seen," says he, "no part of England so pleasant, for sixty or seventy miles together, as those parts of Wales I have been in, and most of the inhabitants are indeed ripe for the Gospel. I mean, if the expression seems strange, they are earnestly desirous of being instructed in it, and as utterly ignorant of it they are as any Creek or Cherokee Indians. I do not mean they are ignorant of the name of Christ; many of them can say both the Lord's Prayer and the Belief; nay, and some, all the Catechism; but take them out of the road of what they have learned by rote, and they know no more—nine in ten of those with whom I conversed—either of Gospel salvation, or of that faith whereby alone we are saved, than Chicali, or Tomo Chachi. Now, what spirit is he of who had rather these poor creatures should perish for lack of knowledge than that they should be saved, even by the exhortations of Howell Harris or an itinerant preacher? The word did not fall to the ground. Many repented, and believed the Gospel. And some joined together to strengthen each other's hands in God, and to provoke one another to love and to good works." (Journal.)

About this time he stated his doctrinal views in perhaps as clear a manner, though in a summary form, as at any period subsequently:

"A serious clergyman desired to know in what points we differed from the Church of England. I answered, To the best of my knowledge, in none; the doctrines we preach are the doctrines of the Church of England, indeed the fundamental doctrines of the Church clearly laid down, both in her Prayers, Articles, and Homilies.

"He asked, 'In what points then do you differ from the other clergy of the Church of England?' I answered, In none from that part of the clergy who adhere to the doctrines of the Church; but from that part of the clergy who dissent from the Church—though they own it not—I differ in the points following:

"First. They speak of justification, either as the same thing with sanctification, or as something consequent upon it. I believe justification to be wholly distinct from sanctification, and necessarily antecedent to it.

"Second. They speak of our own holiness or good works as the cause of our justification, or that for the sake of which, on account of which, we are justified before God. I believe, neither our own holiness nor good works are any part of the cause of our justification; but that the death and righteousness of Christ are the whole and sole cause of it, or that for the sake of which, on account of which, we are justified before God.

"Third. They speak of good works as a condition of justification, necessarily previous to it. I believe, no good work can be previous to justification, nor, consequently, a condition of it; but that we are justified—being till that hour ungodly, and therefore incapable of doing any good work—by faith alone; faith, without works; faith, though producing all, yet including no good works.

"Fourth. They speak of sanctification, or holiness, as if it were an outward thing; as if it consisted chiefly, if not wholly, in these two points: 1. The doing no harm; 2. The doing good, as it is called—that is, the using the means of grace, and helping our neighbor.

"I believe it to be an inward thing, namely, 'the life of God in the soul of man; a participation of the divine nature; the mind that was in Christ;' or, 'the renewal of our heart after the image of Him that created us.'

"Lastly. They speak of the new birth as an outward thing; as if it were no more than baptism, or, at most, a change from outward wickedness to outward goodness, from a vicious to what is called a virtuous life. I believe it to be an inward thing; a change from inward wickedness to inward goodness; an entire change of our inmost nature from the image of the devil, wherein we are born, to the image of God; a change from the love of the creature to the love of the Creator, from earthly and sensual to heavenly and holy affections; in a word, a change from the tempers of the spirits of darkness to those of the angels of God in heaven.

"There is, therefore, a wide, essential, fundamental, irreconcilable difference between us; so that if they speak the truth as it is in Jesus, I am found a false witness before God. But if I teach the way of God in truth, they are blind leaders of the blind." (Journal.)

Disputes having arisen between the Methodists and Moravians, who still formed one society at Fetter-lane, Mr.

Wesley returned to London. Over this society he professed to have no authority, and, as it appeared, had but little influence. Various new doctrines of a mystical kind, which he thought dangerous, had been introduced by several of the teachers; and it seems he foresaw a separation from them to be inevitable, for he had taken a place near Moorfields, which had been used as a foundery for casting cannon; and on this visit he preached in it to very numerous congregations. He was on this and other visits to London unsuccessful in settling the disputes which had arisen in the society; and in June, 1740, he again came to London, and spent upward of a month among them, occupied at intervals in the same attempt. His efforts being fruitless, he read to them the following paper:

"About nine months ago, certain of you began to speak contrary to the doctrine we had till then received. The sum of what you asserted is this: 1. That there is no such thing as weak faith: that there is no justifying faith, where there is ever any doubt or fear; or where there is not, in the full sense, a new, a clean heart. 2. That a man ought not to use those ordinances of God, which our Church terms means of grace, before he has such a faith as excludes all doubt and fear, and implies a new, a clean heart. 3. You have often affirmed, that to search the Scriptures, to pray, or to communicate, before we have this faith, is to seek salvation by works; and till these works are laid aside, no man can receive faith.

"I believe these assertions to be flatly contrary to the word of God. I have warned you hereof again and again, and besought you to turn back to the law and to the testimony. I have borne with you long, hoping you would turn. But as I find you more and more confirmed in the error of your ways, nothing now remains but that I should give you up to God. You that are of the same judgment follow me. . . I then," adds Mr. Wesley, "without saying any thing more, withdrew, as did eighteen or nineteen of the society."

Those who continued to adhere to him then met at the foundery, the whole number amounting to about seventy-two. The Moravian teacher Molther appears to have been the chief author of the novel opinions objected to by Mr. Wesley, whom, however, Peter Bohler thought Mr. Wesley misunderstood; which was not likely, as Mr. Charles Wesley mentions the same thing in his journal. Toward the Moravian Church at large, Mr. Wesley continued to feel an unabated affection; but as he was never a member of that Church, and maintained only a kind of co-fraternity with those of them who were in London, when these became infected with novel opinions, his departure from them, with such as were of the same mind as himself, and were also members of the Church of England, was a step of prudence and of peace. From a conversation which he had with Count Zinzendorf a short time afterward, and which he has published, it would seem that a refined species of Antinomianism had crept in among the Moravians; and that the Count was at that time by no means a teacher of the class of Peter Bohler. But, to affirm with Zinzendorf, that there is nothing but imputed righteousness, and to reject inherent righteousness—to insist upon all our perfection being *in* Christ, and to deny the Christian perfection or maturity which believers derive *from* him—was not in accordance with the Moravian Church, appears from the following extract from the authorized exposition of their doctrines by Spangenberg, which, as the perversions of these "wrong-headed men" have been mentioned, it would be unjust to the body of Moravians to withhold:

"Although this faith, which is so peculiar to all the children of God, that whoever has it not is no child of God, does no outward wonders and signs, raises none from the dead, removes no mountains, yet it does and performs other things, which are of much greater importance. What are those things? Answer: We through faith attain to the enjoyment of that which Christ hath by his sacrifice purchased for us. We are, (1.) Through faith in Jesus Christ, made free from the dominion of sin. Paul says, 'Sin shall not have dominion over you, for ye are not under the law, but under grace,' Rom. vi, 14.

"All those who believe in Jesus Christ are freed from the curse and condemnation of the law; they obtain forgiveness of sins, become the adopted children of God, and are sealed with the Holy Ghost. These are they, then, who are made free from the dominion of sin, because they are under grace. Now, when they are thus exhorted, 'Let not sin reign in your mortal body, that ye should obey it in the lusts thereof; neither yield ye your members as instruments of unrighteousness unto sin,' etc., Rom. vi, 12, 13, they can not say, O that is impossible for us; we are but sinful men; the flesh is weak, and the like; for they have Jesus Christ, who saveth his people from their sins; they have a Father in heaven, who heareth their prayer and supplication. The Holy Ghost dwells in their hearts, and strengthens them in all that is good. If they, therefore, do but rightly make use of the grace wherein through faith they stand, then sin can have no dominion over them. This is exactly what John says, 1st Epist. iii, 9, 'Whosoever is born of God, doth not commit sin'—he doth not let sin reign, or have the dominion in his mortal body, that he should obey it in the lusts thereof—'for his seed remaineth in him; and he can not sin, because he is born of God.' That is, his heart will comply with no such thing; for he loves our Savior, being a child of God, and a partaker of the Holy Ghost." (Exposition, pp. 215, 216.)

Not only Antinomian errors, but mystic notions of ceasing from ordinances and waiting for faith in *stillness*, greatly prevailed also among the Moravians in London at this time, and were afterward carried by them into many of the country Methodist societies in Yorkshire, Derbyshire, and other places. Of the effect at Nottingham, Mr. Wesley gives a curious account in his journal for June, 1743:

"In the afternoon we went on to Nottingham, where Mr. Howe received us gladly. At eight the society met, as usual. I could not but observe, 1. That the room was not half full, which used, till very lately, to be crowded within and without. 2. That not one person who came in used any prayer at all; but every one immediately sat down, and began either talking to his neighbor or looking about to see who was there. 3. That when I began to pray, there appeared a general surprise, no one suffering to kneel down, and those who stood, choosing the most easy, indolent posture which they conveniently could. I afterward looked for one of our hymn-books upon the desk—for I knew Mr. Howe had brought one from London—but both that and the Bible were vanished away. And in the room lay the Moravian Hymns and the Count's Sermons." (Journal.)

That incautious book, Luther on the Galatians, appears to have been the source of the Antinomianism of the Moravians; and their quietism they learned from Madame Guion, and other French mystic writers.

The Methodist society, as that name distinguishes the people who to this day acknowledge Mr. Wesley as their founder under God, was, properly speaking, as a society specially under his pastoral charge, collected in this year, (1740,) at the chapel in Moorfields, where he regularly preached, and where, by the blessing of God upon his and Mr. Charles Wesley's labors, the society rapidly increased. For this, and for the societies in Bristol, Kingswood, and other parts, he, in 1743, drew up a set of rules, which continue in force to the present time, and the observance of which was then, and continues to be, the condition of membership. They are so well known as to render it unnecessary to quote them. It may only be observed, that they enjoin no peculiar opinions, and relate entirely to moral conduct, to charitable offices, and to the observance of the ordinances of God. Churchmen or Dissenters, walking by these rules, might become and remain members of these societies, provided they held their doctrinal views and disciplinary prepossessions in peace and charity. The sole object of the union was to assist the members to "make their calling and election sure," by cultivating the religion of the heart, and a holy conformity to the laws of Christ. These rules bear the signature of John and Charles Wesley.

Mr. Wesley's mother about this time began to attend his ministry. She had been somewhat prejudiced against her sons by reports of their "errors" and "extravagances;" but was convinced, upon hearing them, that they spoke "according to the oracles of God." There is an interesting entry in Mr. Wesley's Journal respecting this venerable woman:

"September 3. I talked largely with my mother, who told me, that, till a short time since, she had scarce heard such a thing mentioned as the having forgiveness of sins now, or God's Spirit bearing witness with our spirit: much less did she imagine, that this was the common privilege of all true believers. 'Therefore,' said she, 'I never durst ask for it myself. But two or three weeks ago, while my son Hall was pronouncing those words, in delivering the cup to me, *The blood of our Lord Jesus Christ which was given for thee,* the words struck through my heart, and I knew God for Christ's sake had forgiven me all my sins.'

"I asked whether her father—Dr. Annesley—had not the same faith; and whether she had not heard him preach it to others. She answered, 'He had it himself, and declared a little before his death, that, for more than forty years, he had no darkness, no fear, no doubt at all of his being *accepted in the Beloved.*' But that, nevertheless, she did not remember to have heard him preach, no, not once, explicitly upon it: whence she supposed he also looked upon it as the peculiar blessing of a few, not as promised to all the people of God." (Journal.)

The extraordinary manner in which some persons were frequently affected under Mr. Wesley's preaching, as well as that of his coadjutors, now created much discussion, and to many gave great offense. Some were seized with trembling; others sunk down and uttered loud and piercing cries; others fell into a kind of agony. In some instances while prayer was offered for them, they rose up with a sudden change of feeling, testifying that they had "redemption through the blood of Christ, even the forgiveness of sins, according to the riches of his grace." Mr. Samuel Wesley, who denied the knowledge of the forgiveness of sins, treated these things, in a correspondence with his brother, alternately with sarcasm and serious severity, and particularly attacked the doctrine of assurance. In this controversy, Mr. John Wesley attaches no weight whatever to these outward agitations; but contends that he is bound to believe the profession made by many, who had been so affected, of an inward change, because that had been confirmed by their subsequent conduct and spirit. On the subject of assurance the disputants put forth their logical acuteness; but the result appears to have been upon the whole instructive to the elder brother, whose letters soften considerably toward the close of the dispute. Mr. Samuel Wesley died in the following November. The circumstances to which he objected, although he knew them only by report, and was too far removed from the scene to be an accurate judge, have since that time furnished ample subject for serious or satirical animadversion to many writers, and to none more than to Dr. Southey. (Life of Wesley.) A few general remarks upon this point may not, therefore, be here out of place. By this writer it is affirmed, that great importance was attached by Mr. Wesley to those emotions, and bodily affections, which occasionally occurred; and that the most visionary persons, and those whose pretended ecstasies, dreams, etc., were, at least in the early part of his ministry, the objects of his special respect, as eminently holy and favored. This is so far from the fact, that it is difficult to meet with a divine whose views of religion are more practical and definite. He did not deny that occasionally "God," even now, "speaketh in a dream, in a vision of the night," and that he may thus "open the ears of men to instruction, and command them to depart from iniquity;" he believed that, in point of fact, many indisputable cases of this kind have occurred in modern times; and in this belief he agreed with many of the wisest and the best of men. He has recorded some cases of what may be called ecstasy, generally without an opinion of his own, leaving every one to form his own judgment from the recorded fact. He unquestionably believed in special effusions of the influence of the Holy Spirit upon congregations and individuals, producing powerful emotions of mind, expressed in some instances by bodily affections; and he has furnished some facts on which Dr. Southey has exercised his philosophy with a success, probably, more satisfactory to himself than convincing to his readers. But that any thing extraordinary, either of bodily or mental affection, was with Mr. Wesley, at any time of his life, of itself, deemed so important as to be regarded as a mark of superior piety, is a most unfounded assumption. Those of his sermons which contain the doctrines which he deemed essential, his Notes on the New Testament, and the rules by which every member of his societies was required to be governed, are sufficiently in refutation of this notion. In them no reference is made to any thing visionary as a part, however small, of true religion; unless, indeed, all spiritual religion, changing the heart, and sanctifying the affections, be thought visionary. The rule of admission into his societies was "a desire to fly from the wrath to come;" but then the sincerity of this was to be evidenced by corresponding "fruits" in the conduct; and on this condition only, farther explained by detailed regulations, all of them simple and practical, were the members to remain in connection with him. These rules are the standing evidence, that, from the first formation of the Methodist societies, neither a speculative nor a visionary scheme of religion was the basis of their union. Had Mr. Wesley placed religion, in the least, in those circumstances, he would have set up a very different standard of doctrine in his sermons; and the rules of his societies would have borne an equivocal and mystic character.

That cases of real enthusiasm occurred at this and subsequent periods is indeed allowed. There are always nervous, dreamy, and excitable people to be found; and the emotion which was produced among those who were really so "pricked in the heart" as to cry with a sincerity equal to that which was felt by those of old, "What shall we do to be saved?" would often be communicated to such persons by natural sympathy. No one could be blamed for this; unless he had encouraged the excitement for its own sake, or taught the people to regard it as a sign of grace, which most assuredly Mr. Wesley never did. Nor is it correct to represent these effects, genuine and factitious together, as peculiar to Methodism. A great impression was made by the preaching of the Wesleys and Mr. Whitefield in almost all places where they went. Thousands in the course of a few years, and of those, too, who had lived in the greatest unconcern as to spiritual things, and were most ignorant and depraved in their habits, were recovered from their vices, and the moral appearance of whole neighborhoods was changed. Yet the effects were not without precedent even in those circumstances in which they have been thought most singular and exceptionable. Great and rapid results of this kind were produced in the first ages of Christianity, but not without "outcries," and strong corporeal as well as mental emotions, nay, and extravagances, too. By perversion, even condemnable heresies arose, and a rank and real enthusiasm; but will any man from this argue against Christianity itself, or asperse the labors and characters of those holy men who planted its genuine root in Asia, Africa, and Europe? Will he say, that as, through the corrupt nature of men, evil often accompanies good, one is to be confounded with the other, and that those great evangelists were the authors of the evil because they were the instruments of the benefit? Even in the decline of true piety in the Church of Christ, there were not wanting holy and zealous ministers to carry the tidings of salvation to the barbarous ancestors of European nations; and strong and effectual impressions were made by their faithful and powerful preaching upon the savage multitudes who surrounded them, accompanied with many effects similar to those which attended the preaching of the Wesleys and Whitefield; but all who went on these sacred missions were not enthusiasts; nor were all the conversions effected by them a mere exchange of superstitions. Such objectors might have known that like effects often accompanied the preaching of eminent men at the Reformation, and that many of the Puritan and Non-Conformist ministers had similar successes in large districts in our own country. They might have known that, in Scotland, and also among the grave Presbyterians of New England, previous to the rise of Methodism, such impressions had not unfrequently been produced by the ministry of faithful men, attended by very similar circumstances; and they might have been informed that, though on a smaller scale, the same results have followed the ministry of modern missionaries of different religious societies in various parts of the world. It may be laid down as a principle established by fact, that, whenever a zealous and faithful ministry is raised up, after a long spiritual death, the early effects of that ministry are not only powerful, but often attended with extraordinary circumstances; nor are such extraordinary circumstances necessarily extravagances because they are not common. If there be an explicit truth in Scripture, it is, that the success of the ministry of the Gospel, and the conversion of men, is the consequence of Divine influence; and if there be a well-ascertained fact in ecclesiastical story, it is, that no great and indisputable results of this kind have been produced but by men who have *acknowledged* this truth, and have gone forth in humble dependence upon that promised co-operation contained in the words, "And, lo, I am with you always, even to the end of the world." This fact, equally striking and notorious, is a strong confirmation that the sense of the sacred oracles on this point was not mistaken by them. The testimony of the word of God is, that, as to ministerial success, "God giveth the increase;" the testimony of experience is, that no success in producing true conversion has ever taken place in any Church, but when this co-operation of God has been acknowledged and sought by the agents employed in it.

The doctrine of Divine influence, as necessary to the conversion of men, being thus grounded on the evidence of Scripture, and farther confirmed by fact, it may follow, and that in perfect conformity with revelation, that such influence may be dispensed in different degrees at different periods. That it was more eminently exerted at the first establishment of Christianity than at some other periods, is certain; and that not only in extraordinary gifts—for though these might awaken attention and silence unbelief, we have the evidence of Scripture history to prove, that miracles can not of themselves convert men from vice—but in sanctifying energy, without which the heart is never brought to yield to the authority and will of God in its choice and affections. That in various subsequent periods there have been special dispensations of favor to nations, with reference to the improvement of their moral state, is clear from a fact which can not be denied, that eminently-holy and gifted men have been raised up at such periods for the benefit of the countries and the age in which they appeared, from whose exertions they have derived the highest moral advantages. For the reasons we have given, we can not refer the appearance of such men to chance, nor the formation of their characters to the circumstances and spirit of "stirring times." We leave these conclusions to the philosophy of the world; and recognize in the appearance of such instruments, the merciful designs and special grace of Him "who worketh all and in all." But the argument is, that if such men have really been the instruments of "turning many to righteousness," and that if the principles of our religion forbid us to believe that this can be done by any gifts or qualities in them, however lofty, then, according to the Scripture doctrine, they were "workers together with God," and the age in which they labored was distinguished by a larger effusion of the Holy Spirit upon the minds of men. Why this should occur at one time more eminently than at another, we pretend not to say; but even this notion, so enthusiastic probably to many, is still in conformity to the word of God, which declares that "the wind bloweth where it listeth," and that the influence of the Holy Spirit, like the atmosphere, is subject to laws not ascertainable by man; and if this effusion of his influence argue especial, though undeserved, favor to particular nations and ages, this is not more difficult to account for than that, at some periods and places, men of eminent usefulness should be sent into the world, when they do not appear in others, which being a mere matter of fact, leaves no room for cavil. This view likewise accords with what the Scriptures teach us to expect as to the future. For the accomplishment of the sublime consummation of the Divine counsels, agents of great efficiency and qualifications, we believe, will from time to time appear; but our hope does not rest on them, but on Him only who has explicitly promised to "pour out his Spirit upon all flesh," at once to give efficiency to instruments in themselves feeble, however gifted, and so "to order the unruly wills and passions of men, that they may be subdued and sanctified by the truth. If such effusions of Divine influence be looked for, and on such principles, as the means of spreading the power of Christianity generally, we may surely believe it quite accordant both with the spirit and letter of Scripture, that the same influence should often be exerted to preserve and to revive religion; and that if nations already Christian are to be the instruments of extending Christianity, not in name only, but in its spirit and sanctity into all the earth, they should be prepared for this high designation by the special exercise of the same agency turning them from what is merely formal in religion to its realities, and making them examples to others of the purifying grace of the Gospel of God our Savior. Let it then be supposed—no great presumption, indeed—that Christians have quite as good a foundation for these opinions as others can boast for that paltry philosophy by which they would explain the effects produced by the preaching of holy and zealous ministers in different ages; and we may conclude that such effects, as far as they are genuine, are the result of Divine influence; and, when numerous and rapid, of a Divine influence specially and eminently exerted, giving more than ordinary assistance to the minds of men in their religious concerns, and rendering the obstinate more inexcusable by louder and more explicit calls. Of the extraordinary circumstances which has usually accompanied such visitations, it may be said, that if some should be resolved into purely-natural causes, some into real enthusiasm, and—under favor of our philosophers—others into Satanic imitation, a sufficient number will remain, which can only be explained by considering them as results of a strong impression made upon the consciences and affections of men by an influence ascertained to be Divine, though usually exerted through human instrumentality, by its unquestionable effects upon the heart and life. Nor is it either irrational or unscriptural to suppose, that times of great national darkness and depravity, the case certainly of this country at the outset of Mr. Wesley and his colleagues in their glorious career, should require a strong remedy; and that the attention of a sleeping people should be roused by circumstances which could not fail to be noticed by the most unthinking. We do not attach primary importance to secondary circumstances; but they are not to be wholly disregarded. The Lord was not in the wind, nor in the earthquake, nor in the fire, but in the "still, small voice;" yet that "still, small voice" might not have been heard, except by minds roused from their inattention by the shaking of the earth, and the sounding of the storm.

If, however, no special and peculiar effusion of Divine influence on the minds of many of Mr. Wesley's hearers be supposed; if we only assume the exertion of that ordinary influence which, as we have seen, must accompany the labors of every minister of Christ to render them successful in saving men, the strong emotions often produced by the preaching of the founder of Methodism might be accounted for on principles very different from those adopted by many objectors. The multitudes to whom he preached were generally grossly ignorant of the Gospel; and he poured upon their minds a flood of light; his discourses were plain, pointed, earnest, and affectionate; the feeling produced was deep, piercing, and, in numberless cases, such as we have no right, if we believe the Bible, to attribute to any other cause than that inward operation of God with his truth which alone can render human means effectual. Many of those on whom such impressions were made retired in silence, and nurtured them by reflection. The "stricken deer" hastened into solitude, there to bleed, unobserved by all but God. This was the case with the majority; for visible and strong emotions were the occasional, and not the constant, results. At some seasons, indeed, effects were produced which, on Christian principles, we may hesitate not to say, can only be accounted for on the assumption that the influence was both Divine and special; at others, the impression was great; but yet we need assume nothing more than the ordinary blessing of God which accompanies "the word of his grace," when delivered in the fullness of faith and love, in order to account for it. But, beside those who were silently pierced, and whose minds were sufficiently strong to command their emotions, there were often many of a class not accustomed to put such restraints upon themselves. To a powerful feeling they offered but a slight resistance, and it became visible. To many people then, as now, this would appear extravagant; but on what principle can the genuineness of the impression be questioned? Only if no subsequent fruit appeared. For if a true conversion followed, then, if there be truth in religion itself, the "finger of God" must be acknowledged.

We have hitherto seen Mr. Wesley and Mr. Whitefield laboring together in harmony, and uniting in a common design to promote the revival of Scriptural Christianity through the land. But Mr. Wesley about this time being impressed with the strong tendency of the Calvinistic doctrines to produce Antinomianism, published a sermon against absolute predestination, at which Mr. Whitefield, who some time previously had embraced that notion, took offense. A controversy between them, embracing some other points, ensued, which issued in a temporary estrangement; and they labored from this time independently of each other, their societies in London, Kingswood, and other places, being kept quite separate.

A reconciliation, however, took place between Mr. Wesley and Mr. Whitefield in January, 1750, so that they preached in each other's chapels. The following entry on this subject appears in his journal: "Friday 19th. In the evening I read prayers at the chapel in West-street, and Mr. Whitefield preached a plain, affectionate discourse. Sunday 21. He read prayers, and I preached. Sunday 28. I read prayers, and Mr. Whitefield preached. How wise is God, in giving different talents to different preachers! So, by the blessing of God, one more stumbling-block is removed." (Journal.)

The following extract from Mr. Whitefield's will, is a pleasing instance of generous, truly-Christian feeling: "I leave a mourning ring to my honored and dear friends, and disinterested fellow-laborers, the Rev. Messrs. John and Charles Wesley, in token of my indissoluble union with them in heart and Christian affection, notwithstanding our difference in judgment about some particular points of doctrine." (Journal.)

Mr. Wesley, at Mr. Whitefield's own desire, preached his funeral sermon at the Tabernacle, Moorfields.

Several preachers were now employed by Mr. Wesley to assist in the growing work, which already had swelled beyond even his and his brother's active powers suitably to supply with the ministration of the word of God. Mr. Charles Wesley had discouraged this from the beginning, and even he himself hesitated; but with John, the promotion of religion was the first concern, and Church order the second, although inferior in consideration to that only. With Charles, these views were often reversed. Mr. Wesley, in the year 1741, had to caution his brother against joining the Moravians, after the example of Mr. Gambold, to which he was at that time inclined; and adds, "I am not clear, that brother Maxfield should not expound at Greyhound-lane; nor can I as yet do without him. Our clergymen have increased full as much as the preachers." Mr. Maxfield's preaching had the strong sanction of the countess of Huntingdon; but so little of design, with reference to the forming of a sect, had Mr. Wesley, in the employment of Mr. Maxfield, that, in his own absence from London, he had only authorized him to pray with the society, and to advise them as might be needful; and upon his beginning to preach, he hastened back to silence him. On this his mother addressed him, "John, you know what my sentiments have been. You can not suspect me of favoring readily any thing of this kind. But take care what you do with respect to that young man, for he is as surely called of God to preach as you are. Examine what have been the fruits of his preaching, and hear him also yourself." He took this advice, and could not venture to forbid him.

His defense of himself on this point we may pronounce irrefutable, and turns upon the disappointment of his hopes, that the parochial clergy would take the charge of those who in different places had been turned to God by his ministry, and that of his fellow-laborers.

"It pleased God," says Mr. Wesley, "by two or three ministers of the Church of England, to call many sinners to repentance, who, in several parts, were undeniably turned from a course of sin to a course of holiness.

"The ministers of the places where this was done ought to have received those ministers with open arms; and to have taken those persons who had just begun to serve God into their particular care, watching over them in tender love, lest they should fall back into the snare of the devil.

"Instead of this, the greater part spoke of those ministers, as if the devil, not God, had sent them. Some repelled them from the Lord's table; others stirred up the people against them, representing them, even in their public discourses, as fellows not fit to live—Papists, heretics, traitors—conspirators against their king and country.

"And how did they watch over the sinners lately reformed? Even as a leopard watcheth over his prey. They drove some of them from the Lord's table, to which, till now, they had no desire to approach. They preached all manner of evil concerning them, openly cursing them in the name of the Lord. They turned many out of their work, persuaded others to do so too, and harassed them in all manner of ways.

"The event was, that some were wearied out, and so turned back to the vomit again; and then these good pastors gloried over them, and endeavored to shake others by their example.

"When the ministers by whom God had helped them before, came again to those places, great part of their work was to begin again, if it could be begun again; but the relapsers were often so hardened in sin, that no impression could be made upon them.

"What could they do in a case of so extreme necessity, where so many souls lay at stake?

"No clergyman would assist at all. The expedient that remained was, to find some one among themselves who was upright of heart, and of sound judgment in the things of God; and to desire him to meet the rest as often as he could, in order to confirm them, as he was able, in the ways of God, either by reading to them, or by prayer, or by exhortation."

This statement may indeed be considered as affording the key to all that which, with respect to Church order, may be called irregularity in Mr. Wesley's future proceedings. God had given him large fruits of his ministry in various places; when he was absent from them, the people were "as sheep having no shepherd," or were rather persecuted by their natural pastors, the clergy; he was reduced, therefore, to the necessity of leaving them without religious care, or of providing it for them. He wisely chose the latter; but, true to his own principles, and even prejudices, he carried this no farther than the necessity of the case: the hours of service were in no instance to interfere with those of the Establishment, and at the parish church the members were exhorted to communicate. Thus a religious society was raised up within the national Church, and with this anomaly, that as to all its interior arrangements, as a society, it was independent of its ecclesiastical authority. The irregularity was, in *principle*, as great when the first step was taken as at any future time. It was a form of practical and partial separation, though not of theoretical dissent; but it arose out of a moral necessity, and existed for some years in such a state, that, had the clergy been disposed to co-operate in this evident revival and spread of true religion, and had the heads of the Church been willing to sanction itinerant labors among its ministers, and private religious meetings among the serious part of the people for mutual edification, the great body of Methodists might have been retained in communion with the Church of England.

On this matter, which was often brought before the leading and influential clergy, they made their own election. They refused to co-operate; they doubtless thought that they acted right; and, excepting the obloquy and persecution with which they followed an innocent and pious people, they perhaps did so; for a great innovation would have been made upon the discipline of the Church, for which, at that time at least, it was little prepared. But the clergy, having made their election, have no right, as some of them continue to do, to censure either the founders of Methodism or their people for making more ample provision for their spiritual wants. It was imperative upon the former to provide that pastoral care for the souls brought to God by their labors, which the Church could not or would not afford; and the people had a Christian liberty to follow that course which they seriously believed most conducive to their own edification, as well as a liberty by the very laws of their country. The violent clerical writers against Methodism have usually forgotten, that no man in England is bound to the national Church by any thing but moral influence; and that from every other tie he is set free by the laws which recognize and protect religious liberty. Mr. Wesley resisted all attempts at formal separation, still hoping that a more friendly spirit would spring up among the clergy; and he even pressed hard upon the consciences of his people to effect their uniform and constant attendance at their parish churches, and at the sacrament; but he could not long and generally succeed. Where the clergyman of a parish was moral or pious there was no difficulty; but cases of conscience were continually arising among his societies, as to the lawfulness of attending the ministry of the irreligious and profane clergymen, who were then and long afterward found throughout the land, and as to hearing, and training up children to hear, false and misleading doctrines, Pelagian, Antinomian, or such as were directed in some form against the religion of the heart as taught in the Scriptures, and in the services of the national Church. These cases exceedingly perplexed Mr. Wesley; and though he relaxed his strictness in some instances, yet, as he did not sufficiently yield to meet the whole case, and perhaps could not do it without adopting such an ecclesiastical organization of his societies as would have contradicted the principles to which, as to their relation to the Church, he had, perhaps, overhastily and peremptorily committed himself, the effect was, that long before his death, the attendance of the Methodists at such parish churches as had not pious ministers was exceedingly scanty; and as they were not permitted public worship among themselves in the hours of Church service, a great part of the Sabbath was lost to them, except as they employed it in family and private exercises. So also as to the Lord's supper; as it was not then administered by their own preachers, it fell into great and painful neglect. To meet the case in part, the two brothers, and a few clergymen who joined them, had public service in Church hours, in the chapels in London and some other places, and administered the Lord's supper to numerous communicants; a measure, which, like other inconsistencies of a similar kind, grew out of a sense of duty, warring with, and restrained by, strong prepossessions, and the very sincere but very unfounded hope just mentioned, that a more friendly spirit would be awakened among the clergy, and that all the sheep gathered out of the wilderness would at length be kindly welcomed into the national fold. As ecclesiastical irregularities, these measures stood, however, precisely on the same principle as those subsequent changes which have rendered the body of Methodists still more distinct and separate; a subject to which reference will again be made. The warmest advocates of Church Methodism among ourselves were never consistent Churchmen; and the Church writers, who have set up the example of Mr. Wesley against his more modern followers, have been wholly ignorant or unmindful of his history. Dr. Southey and others who have fancied a *plan* of separation in Mr. Wesley's mind from the beginning, though followed cautiously and with policy "step by step," have shown a better acquaintance with the *facts* of the progress of Methodism, though they have been most unjust to the pure and undesigning mind of its founder, who walked "step by step," it is true, but only as Providence by an arrangement of circumstances seemed to lead the way, and would make no change but as a necessity, arising from conscientious views of the prosperity of a spiritual work, appeared to dictate. Had he looked forward to the forming of a distinct sect, as an *honor*, he would have attempted to enjoy it in its fullness during his life; and had he been so skillful a *designer* as some have represented him, he would not have left a large body unprovided for, in many respects essential to its prosperity and permanence, at his death. He left his work unfinished, and knew that he should leave it in that state; but he threw the final results, in the spirit of a strong faith, upon the care of Him whose hands he had seen in it from the beginning.

CHAPTER VII.

We have now to follow these apostolic men into still more extended fields of labor, and to contests more formidable. They had sustained many attacks from the press, and some frowns from the authorities of the Church.

By mobs they had occasionally been insulted both in England and Wales. But in London, some riotous proceedings, of a somewhat violent character, now occurred at their places of worship. With respect to these, the following anecdote is curious, as it shows that Mr. Wesley's zeal was regarded with favor in a high quarter: "On the last day of 1742, Sir John Ganson called upon Mr. Wesley, and said, 'Sir, you have no need to suffer these riotous mobs to molest you, as they have done long. I and all the other Middlesex magistrates have orders from above to do you justice whenever you apply to us.' Two or three weeks after they did apply. Justice was done, though not with rigor, and from that time the Methodists had peace in London." (Whitehead's Life.)

In the discipline of Methodism, the division of the society into classes is an important branch. Each class is placed under a person of experience and piety, who meets the others once a week, for prayer, and inquiry into the religious state of each, in order to administer exhortation and counsel. The origin of these classes was, however, purely accidental. The chapel at Bristol was in debt; and it was agreed that each member of the society should contribute one penny a week to reduce the burden. The Bristol society was therefore divided into classes; and for convenience, one person was appointed to collect the weekly subscriptions from each class, and to pay the amount to the stewards. The advantage of this system, when turned to a higher purpose, at once struck the methodical and practical mind of Mr. Wesley: he therefore invited several "earnest and sensible men" to meet him; and the society in London was divided into classes like that of Bristol, and placed under the spiritual care of these tried and experienced persons. At first they visited each person, at his own residence, once a week; but the preferable mode of bringing each class together weekly was at length adopted. These meetings are not, as some have supposed, inquisitorial; but their business is confined to statements of religious experience, and the administration of friendly and pious counsel. Mutual acquaintance with each other is thus formed; the leader is the friend and adviser of all; and among the members, by their praying so often with and for each other, the true "fellowship of saints" is promoted. Opportunities are also thus afforded for ascertaining the wants of the poorer members, and obtaining relief for them; and for visiting the sick: the duty of a leader being to see his members once in the week, either at the meeting, or, if absent from that, at home. Upon this institution Mr. Wesley remarks, "Upon reflection, I could not but observe, this is the very thing which was from the beginning of Christianity. In the earliest times, those whom God had sent forth 'preached the Gospel to every creature.' The body of *hearers* were mostly either Jews or heathens. But as soon as any of these were so convinced of the truth as to forsake sin, and seek the Gospel of salvation, they immediately joined them together, took an account of their names, advised them to watch over each other and met these κατηχȣμενοι, *catechumens*, as they were then called, apart from the great congregation, that they might instruct, rebuke, exhort, and pray with them, and for them, according to their several necessities." (Journal.)

A current charge against Mr. Wesley, about this time, was, that he was a Papist; and from the frequent references to it in his journal, although it was treated by him with characteristic sprightliness, it appears to have been the occasion of much popular odium, arising from the fears entertained by the nation of the movements of the Pretender. In his journal, March, 1741, he says, "Calling on a person near Grosvenor Square, I found there was but too much reason here for crying out of the increase of Popery, many converts to it being continually made by the gentleman who preaches in Swallow-street three days in every week. Now, why do not the champions, who are continually crying out, 'Popery, Popery,' in Moorfields, come hither, that they may not always be fighting 'as one that beateth the air?' Plainly, because they have no mind to fight at all, but to show their valor without an opponent. And they well know they may defy Popery at the foundery without any danger of contradiction." And some time afterward, he remained in London, from whence all Papists had been ordered by proclamation to depart, a week longer than he intended, that he might not seem to plead guilty to the charge. The notion that the Methodists were Papists was also, in those times, the occasion of their being persecuted in several places in the country.

Mr. Wesley now extended his labors northward. He first accepted an invitation into Leicestershire, and has the following amusing anecdote in his journal: "I stopped a little at Newport Pagnell, and then rode on till I overtook a serious man, with whom I immediately fell into conversation. He presently gave me to know what his opinions were; therefore, I said nothing to contradict them. But that did not content him; he was quite uneasy to know whether I held the doctrine of decrees as he did. But I told him, over and over, we had better keep to practical things, lest we should be angry at one another; and so we did for two miles, till he caught me unawares, and dragged me into the dispute before I knew where I was. He then grew warmer and warmer; told me I was rotten at heart, and supposed I was one of John Wesley's followers. I told him, 'No! I am John Wesley himself!' Upon which he appeared,

Improvisum aspris veluti qui sentibus anguem
Pressit———

'as one who had unawares trodden on a snake,' and would gladly have run away outright. But being the better mounted of the two, I kept close to his side, and endeavored to show him his heart till we came into the street of Northampton." In this journey he visited Yorkshire. At Birstal and the neighborhood many persons had been awakened to a serious concern by the conversation and preaching of honest John Nelson, who had himself been brought to the knowledge of God in London, by attending the service at the foundery, and had returned to his friends in Yorkshire, chiefly moved by a strong desire to promote their salvation. The natural genius of this excellent man, who afterward suffered much persecution, and was barbarously treated by the magistrates and clergy, was admirably acute, and gave to his repartees a surprising power and convincingness. He greatly excelled in conversation on religious subjects; and his journal is one of the most interesting pieces of biography published among the Methodists. When Mr. Wesley reached Birstal he found that he had been the instrument of very extensive good, so that the moral aspect of the town had been changed. After preaching to a large congregation on Birstal Hill, and on the side of Dewsbury Moor, and encouraging Mr. Nelson in his endeavors to do good, Mr. Wesley proceeded to Newcastle upon Tyne, hoping to have the same fruit of his labors among the colliers of that district as he had seen among those of Kingswood. So true was this lover of the souls of men to his own advice to his preachers, "Go not only to those who need you, but to those who need you most."

On walking through the town, after he had taken some refreshment, he observes, "I was surprised; so much drunkenness, cursing, and swearing, even from the mouths of little children, do I never remember to have seen and heard before in so short a time." Sunday, May 30th, at seven in the morning, he walked down to Sandgate, the poorest and most contemptible part of the town, and standing at the end of the street with John Taylor, began to sing the hundredth psalm. "Three or four people," says he, "came out to see what was the matter, who soon increased to four or five hundred. I suppose there might be twelve or fifteen hundred before I had done preaching, to whom I applied these solemn words, 'He was wounded for our transgressions, he was bruised for our iniquities; the chastisement of our peace was upon him, and by his stripes we are healed.'"

In returning southward, he preached in various parts of Yorkshire; and visiting Epworth, where a small society of Methodists had been collected, and finding the use of the church denied him, he stood upon his father's tomb, and preached to a numerous congregation, who, as well as himself, appear to have been deeply impressed with the circumstance of the son speaking to them, as from the ashes of his father, on those solemn subjects on which that venerable parish priest had faithfully addressed them for so many years. This was Sunday, June 6, 1742, and on the Wednesday following, he humorously relates, "I rode over to a neighboring town, to wait upon a justice of peace, a man of candor and understanding; before whom, I was informed, their angry neighbors had carried a whole wagon load of these new heretics. But when he asked what they had done, there was a deep silence; for that was a point their conductors had forgot. At length one said, 'Why, they pretend to be better than other people; and, beside, they pray from morning to night.' Mr. S—— asked, 'But have they done nothing beside?' 'Yes, sir,' said an old man, 'an't please your worship, they have *convarted* my wife. Till she went among them, she had such a tongue; and now she is as quiet as a lamb.' 'Carry them back, carry them back,' replied the justice, 'and let them convert all the scolds in the town.'" (Journal.)

On the Sunday following he also preached at Epworth,

and remarks, "At six I preached for the last time in Epworth church-yard—being to leave the town the next morning—to a vast multitude gathered together from all parts, on the beginning of our Lord's Sermon on the Mount. I continued among them for near three hours; and yet we scarce knew how to part. O let none think his labor of love is lost, because the fruit does not immediately appear. Near forty years did my father labor here; but he saw little fruit of all his labor. I took some pains among this people, too, and my strength also seemed to be spent in vain. But now the fruit appeared. There were scarce any in the town, on whom either my father or I had taken any pains formerly, but the seed sown so long since now sprung up, bringing forth repentance and remission of sins." (Journal.)

The following remarks, on a sermon he heard at Painswick, occur in his journal about this time, and deserve notice: "I went to church at ten, and heard a remarkable discourse, asserting 'that we are justified by faith alone; but that this faith, which is the previous condition of justification, is the complex of all Christian virtues, including all holiness and good works in the very idea of it.'

"Alas! how little is the difference between asserting, either, 1. That we are justified by works, which is Popery barefaced—and indeed so gross that the sober Papists, those of the Council of Trent in particular, are ashamed of it—or, 2. That we are justified by faith and works, which is Popery refined or vailed—but with so thin a vail that every attentive observer must discern it is the same still—or, 3. That we are justified by faith alone, but by such a faith as includes all good works.* What a poor shift is this, 'I will not say we are justified by works, nor yet by faith and works, because I have subscribed articles and

* Although the faith which justifies does not *include* good works, it will, when it has justified us, *produce* and be *followed by* good works, because it brings us into vital union with Christ.

homilies which maintain just the contrary. No; I say we are justified by faith alone. But, then, by faith I mean works!' "

After visiting Bristol, he was recalled to London, to attend the last moments of his mother: "Friday, July 30th, about three in the afternoon, I went to my mother, and found her change was near. I sat down on the bedside. She was in her last conflict, unable to speak, but, I believe, quite sensible. Her look was calm and serene, and her eyes fixed upward, while we commended her soul to God. From three to four, the silver cord was loosening, and the wheel breaking at the cistern; and then, without any struggle, or sigh, or groan, the soul was set at liberty. We stood round the bed, and fulfilled her last request, uttered a little before she lost her speech, 'Children, as soon as I am released, sing a psalm of praise to God.' " (Journal.)

So decided a witness was this venerable and intellectual woman of the assurance of faith, a doctrine which she had learned from her sons more clearly to understand. To their sound views, on this Scriptural and important subject, the latter years of her life, and her death, gave a testimony which to them must have been, in the highest degree, delightful and encouraging. The following beautiful epitaph, written by her son Charles, was inscribed on her tombstone in Bunhill Fields:

"In sure and steadfast hope to rise,
And claim her mansion in the skies;
A Christian here her flesh laid down,
The cross exchanging for a crown.

True daughter of affliction, she,
Inured to pain and misery,
Mourn'd a long life of griefs and fears,
A legal night of seventy years.

The Father then reveal'd his Son,
Him in the broken bread made known:
She knew and felt her sins forgiven,
And found the earnest of her heaven.

Meet for the fellowship above,
She heard the call, 'Arise, my love!'
'I come,' her dying looks replied,
And lamb-like, as her Lord, she died."

The labors of Mr. Charles Wesley had been very extended and arduous during the early part of the year 1743, and, by the Divine blessing, eminently successful. From the west of England he proceeded to the colliers of Staffordshire, who had before been visited, and found that the society at Wednesbury had increased to more than three hundred, of whose religious state he speaks, in his journal, with strong feelings of joy. At Walsall, he preached on the market-house steps:

"The street was full of fierce Ephesian beasts—the principal men setting them on—who roared and shouted, and threw stones incessantly. At the conclusion a stream of ruffians was suffered to beat me down from the steps: I rose, and having given the blessing, was beat down again; and so a third time. When we had returned thanks to the God of our salvation, I then from the steps bid them depart in peace, and walked through the thickest of the rioters. They reviled us, but had no commission to touch a hair of our head."

He then proceeded to Birmingham, Nottingham, and then to Sheffield. Here the infant society was as a "flock among wolves; the minister having so stirred up the people, that they were ready to tear the Methodists in pieces. At six o'clock I went to the society house, next door to our brother Bennet's. Hell from beneath was moved to oppose us. As soon as I was in the desk, with David Taylor, the floods began to lift up their voice. An officer in the army contradicted and blasphemed. I took no notice of him, but sung on. The stones flew thick, striking the desk and the people. To save them, and the house from being pulled down, I gave out that I should preach in the street, and look them in the face. The whole army of the aliens followed me. The captain laid hold on me, and began rioting: I gave him for answer, 'A Word in Season, or Advice to a Soldier.' I then prayed, particularly for his majesty King George, and 'preached the Gospel with much contention.' The stones often struck me in the face. I prayed for sinners, as servants of their master, the devil; upon which the captain ran at me with great fury, threatening revenge for abusing, as he called it, 'the king, his master.' He forced his way through the brethren, drew his sword, and presented it to my breast. I immediately opened my breast, and fixing my eye on his, and smiling in his face, calmly said, 'I fear God, and honor the king.' His countenance fell in a moment, he fetched a deep sigh, and putting up his sword, quietly left the place. He had said to one of the company, who afterward informed me, 'You shall see if I do but hold my sword to his breast, he will faint away.' So, perhaps, I should had I only his principles to trust to; but if at that time I was not afraid, no thanks to my natural courage. We returned to our brother Bennet's, and gave ourselves up to prayer. The rioters followed, and exceeded in outrage all I have seen before. Those at Moorfields, Cardiff, and Walsall, were lambs to these. As there is no 'king in Israel,' I mean no magistrate in Sheffield, every man doeth as seemeth good in his own eyes." The mob now formed the design of pulling down the society house, and set upon their work, while Mr. Charles Wesley and the people were praying and praising God within. "It was a glorious time," says he, "with us; every word of exhortation sunk deep, every prayer was sealed, and many found the Spirit of glory resting upon them." The next day the house was completely pulled down, not one stone being left upon another. He then preached again in the street, somewhat more quietly than before; but the rioters became very noisy in the evening, and threatened to pull down the house where he lodged. He went out to them and made a suitable exhortation, and they soon after separated, and peace was restored.

At five the next morning, he took leave of the society in these words, "Confirming the souls of the disciples, and exhorting them to continue in the faith, and that we must through much tribulation enter into the kingdom of God." He observes, "Our hearts were knit together, and greatly comforted: we rejoiced in hope of the glorious appearing of the great God, who had now delivered us out of the mouth of the lions. David Taylor had informed me, that the people of Thorpe, through which we should pass, were exceedingly mad against us. So we found them as we approached the place, and were turning down the lane to Barley Hall. The ambush rose, and assaulted us with stones, eggs, and dirt. My horse flew from side to side, till he found his way through them. They wounded David Taylor in the forehead, and the wound bled much. I turned back, and asked, what was the reason that a clergyman could not pass without such treatment. At first the rioters scattered, but their captain rallying them, answered with horrible imprecations and stones. My horse took fright, and turned away with me down a steep hill. The enemy pursued me from afar, and followed shouting. Blessed be God, I received no hurt, only from the eggs and dirt. 'My clothes, indeed, abhorred me,' and my arm pained me a little from a blow I received at Sheffield." (Journal.)

Such was the calm heroism with which these admirable men prosecuted their early labors, shrinking from no danger, and firmly trusting their lives in the hands of God. Proceeding to Leeds, Mr. Charles Wesley preached "to thousands," before Mr. Shent's door, and found the people "prepared for the Lord." The clergy of Leeds treated him with respect and deference, and obliged him to assist at the sacrament; such, indeed, was their kindness, that he began to fear the gleam of sunshine "more than the stones at Sheffield." He then went on to Newcastle, where he not only abounded in public labors, but, as the society had rapidly increased, he instituted a strict investigation into their spiritual state, accurately distinguishing between animal emotions and the true work of God in the heart, and leading all to try themselves by the only infal lible rule—their conformity to the word of God. So unjust are the insinuations, that the founders of Methodism allowed excited affections to pass as admitted proofs of a change of heart. On this visit to Newcastle, Mr. Charles Wesley remarks in his journal, that, since he had preached the Gospel, he had never had greater success than at this time at Newcastle. Soon after, his brother laid the foundation of a place for the public worship of the society, the size of which greatly startled some of the people, as they doubted whether money could be raised to finish it. "I was of another mind," he observes, "nothing doubting, but as it was begun for the Lord's sake, he would provide what was needful for finishing it." Many pecuniary difficulties arose in the completion of this work; but he received timely supplies of money, sometimes from very unexpected quarters. During this year new societies were formed in the western, midland, and northern counties, while those before collected continued greatly to increase.

In the latter end of this year, (1743,) Mr. Wesley appointed in London visitors of the sick, as a distinct office in his society. He says, "It was not long before the stewards found a great difficulty with regard to the sick. Some were ready to perish before they knew of their illness. And when they did know, it was not in their power—being persons generally employed in trade—to visit them so often as they desired. When I was apprised of this, I laid the case at large before the whole society, showed how impossible it was for the stewards to attend all that were sick in all parts of the town; desired the leaders of the classes would more carefully inquire, and more constantly inform them, who were sick; and asked, Who among you is willing, as well as able, to supply this lack of service?

"The next morning many willingly offered themselves. I chose six and forty of them, whom I judged to be of the most tender, loving spirit, divided the town into twenty-three parts, and desired two of them to visit the sick in each division.

"It is the business of a visitor of the sick,

"1. To see every sick person within his district thrice a week. 2. To inquire into the state of their souls, and advise them as occasion may require. 3. To inquire into their disorders, and procure advice for them. 4. To relieve them if they are in want. 5. To do any thing for them, which he (or she) can do. 6. To bring in his account weekly to the steward." "Upon reflection, I saw how exactly in this also we had copied after the primitive Church. What were the ancient deacons? What was Phebe the deaconess, but such a visitor of the sick?

"I did not think it needful to give them any particular rules besides those that follow:

"1. Be plain and open in dealing with souls. 2. Be mild, tender, patient. 3. Be cleanly in all you do for the sick. 4. Be not nice."

The same year was remarkable in the life of Mr. Wesley, for his escape from one of the most dangerous of his encounters with deluded and infuriated mobs. It was first incited by a sermon preached in Wednesbury church, by the clergyman. "I never," says Mr. Wesley, "heard so wicked a sermon, and delivered with such bitterness of voice and manner." While Mr. Wesley was at Bristol, he heard of the effect produced by this charitable address of the minister to his parishioners, who was assisted in stirring up the persecution against the society, as was very frequent in those days, by the neighboring magistrates—full of what they called Churchmanship and loyalty. At Wednesbury, Darlaston, and West Bromwich, the mobs were stimulated to abuse the Methodists in the most outrageous manner; even women and children were beaten, stoned, and covered with mud; their houses broken open, and their goods spoiled and carried away."* Mr. Wesley hastened to comfort and advise this harassed people as soon as the intelligence reached him, and preached at noon at Wednesbury without molestation; but in the afternoon the mob surrounded the house. The result will best be given from his own account, which displays at once his own admirable presence of mind and the singular providence of God:

"I was writing at Francis Ward's in the afternoon when the cry arose that the mob had beset the house We prayed that God would disperse them: and so it was one went this way and another that, so that in half an hour not a man was left. I told our brethren, Now is the time to go; but they pressed me exceeding'y to stay So, that I might not offend them, I sat down, though I foresaw what would follow. Before five the mob surrounded the house again, and in greater numbers than ever. The cry of one and all was, 'Bring out the minister, we will have the minister.' I desired one to take the captain by the hand and bring him into the house. After a few sentences interchanged between us, the lion was become a lamb. I desired him to go, and bring one or

* The descendants of some of these persecuted people still remain. and show, one a cupboard, another some other piece of furniture, the only article saved from the wreck, and preserved with pious care, as a monument of the sufferings of their ancestors.

two of the most angry of his companions. He brought in two, who were ready to swallow the ground with rage; but in two minutes they were as calm as he. I then bade them make way, that I might go out among the people. As soon as I was in the midst of them, I called for a chair, and asked, 'What do any of you want with me?' Some said, 'We want you to go with us to the justice.' I replied, 'That I will with all my heart.' I then spoke a few words, which God applied; so that they cried out with might and main, 'The gentleman is an honest gentleman, and we will spill our blood in his defense.' I asked, 'Shall we go to the justice to-night, or in the morning?' Most of them cried, 'To-night, to-night!' on which I went before, and two or three hundred followed, the rest returning whence they came.

"The night came on before we had walked a mile, together with heavy rain. However, on we went to Bentley Hall, two miles from Wednesbury. One or two ran before, to tell Mr. Lane they had brought Mr. Wesley before his worship. Mr. Lane replied, 'What have I to do with Mr. Wesley? Go and carry him back again.' By this time the main body came up, and began knocking at the door. A servant told them Mr. Lane was in bed. His son followed, and asked what was the matter. One replied, 'Why, an't please you, they sing psalms all day; nay, and make folks rise at five in the morning: and what would your worship advise us to do?' 'To go home,' said Mr. Lane, 'and be quiet.'

"Here they were at a full stop, till one advised to go to Justice Persehouse, at Walsall. All agreed to this: so we hastened on, and about seven came to his house. But Mr. Persehouse also sent word that he was in bed. Now they were at a stand again; but at last they all thought it the wisest course to make the best of their way home. About fifty of them undertook to convey me; but we had not gone a hundred yards, when the mob of Walsall came pouring in like a flood, and bore down all before them. The Darlaston mob made what defense they could; but they were weary, as well as outnumbered; so that, in a short time, many being knocked down, the rest went away, and left me in their hands.

"To attempt speaking was vain; for the noise on every side was like the roaring of the sea. So they dragged me along till we came to the town, where seeing the door of a large house open, I attempted to go in; but a man catching me by the hair, pulled me back into the middle of the mob. They made no more stop till they had carried me through the main street, from one end of the town to the other. I continued speaking all the time to those within hearing, feeling no pain or weariness. At the west end of the town, seeing a door half open, I made toward it, and would have gone in; but a gentleman in the shop would not suffer me, saying they would pull the house to the ground. However, I stood at the door and asked, 'Are you willing to hear me speak?' Many cried out, 'No, no! knock his brains out; down with him; kill him at once.' Others said, 'Nay, but we will hear him first.' I began asking, 'What evil have I done? Which of you have I wronged in word or deed?' and continued speaking for above a quarter of an hour, till my voice suddenly failed. Then the floods began to lift up their voice again; many crying out, 'Bring him away! bring him away!'

"In the mean time my strength and my voice returned, and I broke out aloud into prayer. And now the man, who just before headed the mob, turned and said, 'Sir, I will spend my life for you; follow me, and not one soul here shall touch a hair of your head.' Two or three of his fellows confirmed his words, and got close to me immediately. At the same time the gentleman in the shop cried out, 'For shame, for shame; let him go.' An honest butcher, who was a little farther off, said it was a shame they should do thus; and pulled back four or five, one after another, who were running on the most fiercely. The people, then, as if it had been by common consent, fell back to the right and left; while those three or four men took me between them, and carried me through them all: but on the bridge the mob rallied again; we therefore went on one side, over the mill-dam, and thence through the meadows, till, a little before ten, God brought me safe to Wednesbury; having lost only one flap of my waistcoat, and a little skin from one of my hands.

"From the beginning to the end I found the same presence of mind as if I had been sitting in my own study. But I took no thought for one moment before another; only once it came into my mind, that if they should throw me into the river, it would spoil the papers that were in my pocket. For myself, I did not doubt but I should swim across, having but a thin coat and a light pair of boots.

"The circumstances that follow I thought were particularly remarkable: 1. That many endeavored to throw me down while we were going down hill, on a slippery path, to the town; as well judging, that if I was once on the ground I should hardly rise any more. But I made no stumble at all, nor the least slip, till I was entirely out of their hands. 2. That although many strove to lay hold on my collar or clothes to pull me down, they could not fasten at all; only one got fast hold of the flap of my waistcoat, which was soon left in his hand. 3. That a lusty man just behind struck at me several times with a large oaken stick, with which if he had struck me once on the back part of my head, it would have saved him all farther trouble; but every time the blow was turned aside, I know not how. 4. That another came rushing through the press, and raising his arm to strike, on a sudden let it drop, and only stroked my head, saying, 'What soft hair he has!' 5. That I stopped exactly at the mayor's door, as if I had known it, which the mob doubtless thought I did, and found him standing in the shop; which gave the first check to the madness of the people. 6. That the very first men whose hearts were turned were the heroes of the town, the captains of the rabble on all occasions; one of them having been a prize-fighter at the bear gardens. 7. That from first to last I heard none give a reviling word, or call me by any opprobrious name whatever. But the cry of one and all was, 'The preacher! the preacher! the parson! the minister!' 8. That no creature, at least within my hearing, laid any thing to my charge, either true or false; having in the hurry quite forgot to provide themselves with an accusation of any kind. And, lastly, they were utterly at a loss what they should do with me; none proposing any determinate thing, only, 'Away with him; kill him at once.'

"When I came back to Francis Ward's, I found many of our brethren waiting upon God. Many also whom I had never seen before, came to rejoice with us; and the next morning as I rode through the town, in my way to Nottingham, every one I met expressed such a cordial affection, that I could scarce believe what I saw and heard."

At Nottingham he met with Mr. Charles Wesley, who has inserted in his journal a notice of the meeting, highly characteristic of the spirit of martyrdom in which both of them lived:

"My brother came, delivered out of the mouth of the lions! His clothes were torn to tatters; he looked like a soldier of Christ. The mob of Wednesbury, Darlaston, and Walsall, were permitted to take and carry him about for several hours, with a full intent to murder him; but his work is not yet finished, or he had been now with the souls under the altar." Undaunted by the usage of John, Charles immediately set out for Wednesbury, to encourage the societies.

In this year Mr. Wesley made his first journey into Cornwall, where his brother, led by the same sympathies to communicate the Gospel to the then rude and neglected miners of that extreme part of the kingdom, as had induced him to visit the colliers of Kingswood, Staffordshire, and the north, had preceded him. Here he had preached in various places, sometimes amidst mobs, "as desperate as that at Sheffield." Mr. Wesley followed in August, and came to St. Ives, where he found a small religious society, which had been formed upon Dr. Woodward's plan. They gladly received him, and formed the nucleus of the Methodist societies in Cornwall, which from this time rapidly increased. In this visit he spent three weeks, preaching in the most populous parts of the mining district, with an effect which still continues to be felt. In no part of England has Methodism obtained more influence than in the west of Cornwall. It has become, in fact, the leading profession of the people, and its moral effects upon society may be looked upon with the highest satisfaction and gratitude. Nor were the Cornish people ungrateful to the instrument of the benefit. When he was last in the country, in old age, the man who had formerly slept on the ground for want of a lodging, and picked blackberries to satisfy his hunger, and who had narrowly escaped with his life from a desperate mob at Falmouth, passed through the towns and villages as in a triumphal march, while the windows were crowded with people, anxious to get a sight of him, and to pronounce upon him their benedictions.

Between this visit and that of the next year, a hot persecution, both of the preachers and people, broke forth. The preaching house of St. Ives was pulled to the ground: one of the preachers was impressed and sent for a soldier, as were several of the people: while being stoned, covered with dirt, and abused, was the treatment which many others of them met with from day to day. But, notwithstanding this, they who had been eminent for hurling, fighting, drinking, and all manner of wickedness, continued eminent for sobriety, piety, and meekness. The impressment of the preachers for soldiers by the magistrates was not, however, confined to Cornwall. About the same time John Nelson and Thomas Beard were thus seized, and sent for soldiers, for no other crime, either committed or pretended, than that of calling sinners to repentance. The passive heroism of John Nelson is well known. Thomas Beard, also, was "nothing terrified by his adversaries;" but his body after a while sunk under affliction. He was then lodged in the hospital of Newcastle, where he still praised God continually. His fever increasing, he was let blood: his arm festered, mortified, and was cut off; two or three days after which, God signed his discharge, and called him to his eternal home.

The riots in Staffordshire, also, still continued. "The mob of Walsall, Dalaston, and Wednesbury, hired for the purpose by their superiors, broke open their poor neighbors' houses at their pleasure by day and by night; extorting money from the few that had it, taking away or destroying their victuals and goods, beating and wounding their bodies, insulting the women, and openly declaring they would destroy every Methodist in the country. Thus his Majesty's peaceable and loyal subjects were treated for eight months, and were then publicly branded in the Whitehall and London Evening Post, for rioters and incendiaries!" (Whitehead's Life.)

Several other instances of the brutal maltreatment of the preachers occurred in these early periods, which ended in disablement, or premature death. The persecution at St. Ives, Mr. Wesley observes, "was owing in great measure to the indefatigable labors of Mr. Hoblin, and Mr. Simmons, gentlemen worthy to be had in everlasting remembrance for their unwearied endeavors to destroy heresy.

Fortunati ambo! Siquid mea pagina possit,
Nulla dies unquam memori vos eximet ævo.

"Happy both! Long as my writings, shall your fame remain."

In August, 1744, Mr. John Wesley preached for the last time before the university of Oxford. Mr. Charles Wesley was present, and observes in his journal: "My brother bore his testimony before a crowded audience, much increased by the races. Never have I seen a more attentive congregation; they did not suffer a word to escape them. Some of the heads of colleges stood up the whole time, and fixed their eyes upon him. If they can endure sound doctrine, like his, he will surely leave a blessing behind him. The vice-chancellor sent after him, and desired his notes, which he sealed up and sent immediately."

His own remarks upon this occasion are, "I am now clear of the blood of those men. I have fully delivered my own soul. And I am well pleased that it should be the very day on which, in the last century, near two thousand burning and shining lights were put out at one stroke. Yet what a wide difference is there between their case and mine! They were turned out of house and home, and all that they had; whereas I am only hindered from preaching in one place, without any other loss, and that in a kind of honorable manner; it being determined, that, when my next turn to preach came, they would pay another person to preach for me. And so they did twice or thrice, even to the time I resigned my fellowship." (Journal.)

Mr. Wesley had at this time a correspondence with Rev. James Erskine, from whom he learned that several pious ministers and others, in Scotland, duly appreciated his character, and rejoiced in the success of his labors, notwithstanding the difference of their sentiments. Mr. Erskine's letter indeed contains a paragraph which breathes a liberality not very common in those days, and which may be useful in the present, after all our boastings of enlarged charity: "Are the points which give the different denominations—to Christians—and from whence proceed separate communities, animosities, evil speakings, surmises, and, at least, coolness of affection, aptness to misconstrue, slowness to think well of others, stiffness in one's own conceits, and overvaluing one's own opinion, etc.: are these points—at least among the far greatest part of Protestants—as important, as clearly revealed, and as essential, or as closely connected with the essentials of practical Christianity, as the loving of one another with a pure heart fervently, and not forsaking, much less refusing, the assembling of ourselves together, as the manner of some was, and now of almost all is?" (Journal.)

In a subsequent letter this excellent man expresses an ardent wish for union among all those of different denominations and opinions who love the Lord Jesus Christ; and on such a subject he was speaking to a kindred mind; for no man ever set a better example of Christian charity, and no where is the excellence and obligation of that temper more forcibly drawn and inculcated than in his most interesting sermon on "A Catholic Spirit." With such a testimony and example before them, his followers would be the most inexcusable class of Christians were they to indulge in that selfish sectarianism with which he was so often unjustly charged; and for which they, though not faultless in this respect, have also been censured more frequently and indiscriminately than they have merited. It would scarcely be doing justice to this part of Mr. Wesley's character not to insert an extract from the sermon alluded to:

"Is thy heart right with God? If it be, give me thy hand. I do not mean, 'Be of my opinion.' You need not. I do not expect or desire it. Neither do I mean, 'I will be of your opinion.' I can not. It does not depend on my choice; I can no more think, than I can see or hear, as I will. Keep you your opinion: I mine; and that as steadily as ever. You need not endeavor to come over to me, or bring me over to you. I do not desire you to dispute those points, or to hear or speak one word concerning them. Let all opinions alone on one side and the other. Only 'give me thine hand.'

"I do not mean, 'Embrace my modes of worship; or, I will embrace yours.' This, also, is a thing which does not depend either on your choice or mine. We must both act as each is fully persuaded in his own mind. Hold you fast that which you believe is most acceptable to God, and I will do the same. I believe the episcopal form of Church government to be Scriptural and apostolical. If you think the Presbyterian or Independent is better, think so still, and act accordingly. I believe infants ought to be baptized, and that this may be done either by dipping or sprinkling. If you are otherwise persuaded, be so still, and follow your own persuasion. It appears to me, that forms of prayer are of excellent use, particularly in the great congregation. If you judge extemporary prayer to be of more use, act suitable to your own judgment. My sentiment is, that I ought not to forbid water, wherein persons may be baptized; and, that I ought to eat bread and drink wine, as memorials of my dying Master. However, if you are not convinced of this, act according to the light you have. I have no desire to dispute with you one moment upon any of the preceding heads. Let all these smaller points stand aside. Let them never come into sight. 'If thine heart be as my heart,' if thou love God and all mankind, I ask no more: 'Give me thy hand.'

"I mean, first, love me. And that not only as thou lovest all mankind, not only as thou lovest thine enemies, or the enemies of God, those that hate thee, that 'despitefully use thee, and persecute thee:' not only as a stranger, as one of whom thou knowest neither good nor evil. I am not satisfied with this. No; 'if thine heart be right, as mine with thy heart,' then love me with a very tender affection, as a friend that is closer than a brother, as a brother in Christ, a fellow-citizen of the New Jerusalem, a fellow-soldier engaged in the same warfare, under the same Captain of our salvation. Love me as a companion in the kingdom and patience of Jesus, and a joint-heir of his glory.

"Love me—but in a higher degree than thou dost the bulk of mankind—with the love that is 'long-suffering and kind;' that is patient, if I am ignorant or out of the way, bearing and not increasing my burden; and is tender, soft, and compassionate still; that 'envieth not,' if at any time it please God to prosper me in this work even more than thee. Love me with the love that 'is not provoked' either at my follies or infirmities, or even at my acting—if it should sometimes so appear to thee—not according to the will of God. Love me so as to 'think no evil' of me, to put away all jealousy and evil surmising. Love me with the love that 'covereth all things;' that never reveals either my faults or infirmities, that 'believeth all things,' is always willing to think the best, to put the fairest construction on all my words and actions; that 'hopeth all things;' either that the thing related was never done, or not done with such circumstances as are related; or at least, that it was done with a good intention, or in a sudden stress of temptation. And hope to the end, that whatever is amiss will, by the grace of God, be corrected, and whatever is wanting supplied, through the riches of his mercy in Christ Jesus." (Sermons.)

And then, having shown how a catholic spirit differs from practical and speculative latitudinarianism and indifference, he concludes: "A man of a catholic spirit is one who, in the manner above mentioned, 'gives his hand' to all whose 'hearts are right with his heart.' One who knows how to value and praise God for all the advantages he enjoys, with regard to the knowledge of the things of God, the true Scriptural manner of worshiping him; and, above all, his union with a congregation fearing God and working righteousness. One who, retaining these blessings with the strictest care, keeping them as the apple of his eye, at the same time loves as friends, as brethren in the Lord, as members of Christ and children of God, as joint partakers now of the present kingdom of God, and fellow-heirs of his eternal kingdom, all, of whatever opinion, or worship, or congregation, who believe in the Lord Jesus Christ, who love God and man, who, rejoicing to please and fearing to offend God, are careful to abstain from evil, and zealous of good works. He is the man of a truly-catholic spirit, who bears all these continually upon his heart—who, having an unspeakable tenderness for their persons, and longing for their welfare, does not cease to commend them to God in prayer, as well as to plead their cause before men—who speaks comfortably to them, and labors by all his words to strengthen their hands in God. He assists them to the uttermost of his power in all things, spiritual and temporal. He is ready 'to spend and be spent for them;' yea, 'to lay down his life for their sake.'" (Sermons.)

The first CONFERENCE was held in June, 1744. The societies had spread through various parts of the kingdom; and a number of preachers, under the name of assistants and helpers, the former being superintendents of the latter, had been engaged by Mr. Wesley in the work. Some clergymen, also, more or less co-operated to promote these attempts to spread the flame of true religion, and were not yet afraid of the cross. These circumstances led to the distribution of different parts of the kingdom into circuits, to which certain preachers were for a time appointed, and were then removed to others. The superintendence of the whole was in the two brothers, but particularly in Mr. John Wesley. The annual conferences afforded, therefore, an admirable opportunity of conversing on important points and distinctions of doctrine, that all might "speak the same thing" in their public ministrations, and of agreeing upon such a discipline as the new circumstances in which the societies were placed might require. The labors of the preachers for the ensuing year were also arranged, and consultation was held on all matters connected with the promotion of the work of God, in which they were engaged. Every thing went on, however, not on preconceived plan, but "step by step," as circumstances suggested, and led the way. To the great principle of *doing good* to the souls of men, every thing was subordinated; not excepting even their prejudices and fears, as will appear from the minutes of the first conference, which was held in London, as just stated, in 1744. The ultimate separation of the societies from the Church, after the death of the first agents in the work, was at that early period contemplated as a *possibility,* and made a subject of conversation; and the resolution was, "We do and will do all we can to prevent those consequences which are supposed to be likely to happen after our death; but we can not, in good conscience, neglect the present opportunity of saving souls while we live, for fear of consequences which may possibly, or probably, happen after we are dead." To this principle Mr. Wesley was "faithful unto death," and it is the true key to his public conduct. His brother, after some years, less steadily adhered to it; and most of the clergymen, who attached themselves to Mr. Wesley in the earlier periods of Methodism, found it too bold a position, and one which exposed them to too severe a fire, to be maintained by them. It required a firmer courage than theirs to hold out at such a post; but the founder of Methodism never betrayed the trust which circumstances had laid upon him.

CHAPTER VIII.

THE year 1745 was chiefly spent by Mr. Charles Wesley in London, Bristol, and Wales. In the early part of the next year, he paid a visit to a society raised up by Mr. Whitefield at Plymouth, and from thence proceeded into Cornwall, where he preached in various places with great success; but in some of them amidst much persecution. He reviewed this journey with great thankfulness, because of the effects which had been produced by his ministry; and at the close of it he wrote the hymn beginning with the stanza,

"All thanks be to God,
Who scatters abroad
Throughout every place,
By the least of his servants, his savor of grace:
Who the victory gave
The praise let him have,
For the work he hath done;
All honor and glory to Jesus alone!"

On his return to London, through the introduction of Mr. E. Perronet, a pious young man, he visited the Rev. Vincent Perronet, the venerable vicar of Shoreham, in Kent, a very holy and excellent clergyman, of whose wise and considerate counsels the Wesleys afterward frequently availed themselves, in all matters which involved particular difficulty. The name of Wesley was, however, it seems, every-where become a signal for riot; for being invited to perform service in Shoreham church, "as soon," says he, "as I began to preach, the wild beasts began roaring, stamping, blaspheming, ringing the bells, and turning the church into a bear garden. I spoke on for half an hour, though only the nearest could hear. The rioters followed us to Mr. Perronet's house, raging, threatening, and throwing stones. Charles Perronet hung over me to intercept the blows. They continued their uproar after we got into the house." (Journal.)

Mr. E. Perronet returned with him to London, and accompanied him on a tour to the north. On the way, they visited Staffordshire, which was still riotous and persecuting; and Mr. Charles Wesley's young friend had a second specimen of the violent and ignorant prejudice with which these modern apostles were followed. The mob beset the house at Tippen Green, and, beating at the door, demanded entrance. "I sat still," says he, "in the midst of them for half an hour, and was a little concerned for E. Perronet, lest such rough treatment, at his first setting out, should daunt him. But he abounded in valor, and was for reasoning with the wild beasts before they had spent any of their violence. He got a deal of abuse thereby, and not a little dirt, both of which he took very patiently. I had no design to preach; but being called upon by so unexpected a congregation, I rose at last, and read, 'When the Son of man shall come in his glory, and all the holy angels with him, then shall he sit on the throne of his glory.' While I reasoned with them of judgment to come, they grew calmer by little and little. I then spoke to them, one by one, till the Lord had disarmed them all. One who stood out the longest, I held by the hand, and urged the love of Christ crucified, till, in spite of both his natural and diabolical courage, he trembled like a leaf. I was constrained to break out into prayer for him. Our leopards were all become lambs; and very kind we were at parting. Near midnight the house was clear and quiet. We gave thanks to God for our salvation, and slept in peace." (Journal.)

Proceeding onward to Dewsbury, he met with an instance of clerical candor, which, as it was rare in those times, deserves to be recorded: "The minister did not condemn the society unheard, but talked with them, examined into the doctrine they had been taught, and its effects on their lives. When he found that as many as had been affected by the preaching were evidently reformed, and brought to church and sacrament, he testified his approbation of the work, and rejoiced that sinners were converted to God." (Whitehead's Life.)

After visiting Newcastle, he went, at the request of Mr. Wardrobe, a dissenting minister, to Hexham, where the following incidents occurred: "I walked directly to the market-place, and called sinners to repentance. A multitude of them stood staring at me, but all quiet. The Lord opened my mouth, and they drew nearer and nearer, stole off their hats, and listened; none offered to interrupt, but one unfortunate esquire who could get no one to second him. His servants and the constables hid themselves; one he found, and bid him go and take me down. The poor constable simply answered, "Sir, I can not have the face to do it, for what harm does he do?' Several Papists attended, and the Church minister who had refused me his pulpit with indignation. However, he came to hear with his own ears. I wish all who hang us first would, like him, try us afterward.

"I walked back to Mr. Ord's through the people, who acknowledged, 'It is the truth, and none can speak against it.' A constable followed, and told me, 'Sir Edward Blacket orders you to *disperse* the town'—depart, I suppose he meant—'and not raise a disturbance here.' I sent my respects to Sir Edward, and said, if he would give me leave, I would wait upon him and satisfy him. He soon returned with an answer that Sir Edward would have nothing to say to me; but if I preached again, and raised a disturbance, he would put the law in execution against me. I answered that I was not conscious of breaking any law of God or man; but if I did, I was ready to suffer the penalty; that, as I had not given notice of preaching again at the Cross, I should not preach again at that place, nor cause a disturbance any where. I charged the constable, a trembling, submissive soul, to assure his worship that I reverenced him for his office's sake. The only place I could get to preach in was a cockpit, and I expected Satan would come and fight me on his own ground. 'Squire Roberts, the justice's son, labored hard to raise a mob, for which I was to be answerable; but the very boys ran away from him, when the poor 'Squire persuaded them to go down to the cockpit and cry fire. I called, in words then first heard in that place, 'Repent and be converted, that your sins may be blotted out.' God struck the hard rock, and the waters gushed out. Never have I seen a people more desirous of knowing the truth at the first hearing. I passed the evening in conference with Mr. Wardrobe. O that all our dissenting ministers were like-minded, then would all dissensions cease forever! November 28th, at six, we assembled again in our chapel, the cockpit. I imagined myself in the Pantheon, or some heathen temple, and almost scrupled preaching there at first; but we found 'the earth is the Lord's, and the fullness thereof.' His presence consecrated the place. Never have I found a greater sense of God than while we were repeating his own prayer. I set before their eyes Christ crucified. The rocks were melted, and gracious tears flowed. We knew not how to part. I distributed some books among them, which they received with the utmost eagerness, begging me to come again, and to send our preachers to them." (Journal.)

After preaching in various parts of Lincolnshire, and the midland counties, Mr. Charles Wesley returned to London; but soon, with unwearied spirit, in company with Mr. Minton, he set off for Bristol, taking Devizes by the way, where he had as narrow an escape for his life as his brother had experienced at Wednesbury. An account of these distinguished ministers of Christ would be imperfect without a particular notice of a few of their greatest perils. They show the wretched state of that country which they were the appointed instruments of raising into a higher *moral* and *civil* condition, and they illustrate their own character. Each of the brothers might truly say with an apostle, and his coadjutors, "We have not received the spirit of fear, but of power, [courage,] of love, and of a sound mind." They felt, too, that they "received" it; for, with them, "boasting was excluded" by that "law of faith" which led them in all things to trust in and to glorify God. The account is taken from Mr. Charles Wesley's journal. The Devizes mob had this peculiarity, that it was led on not only by the curate, but by two dissenters! thus "Herod and Pilate were made friends:"

"February 25th—a day never to be forgotten. At seven o'clock I walked quietly to Mrs. Philips', and began preaching a little before the time appointed. For three-quarters of an hour, I invited a few listening sinners to Christ. Soon after Satan's whole army assaulted the house. We sat in a little ground room, and ordered all the doors to be thrown open. They brought a hand engine and began to play into the house. We kept our seats, and they rushed into the passage; just then, Mr. Borough, the constable, came, and seizing the spout of the engine, carried it off. They swore if he did not deliver it they would pull down the house. At that time they might have taken us prisoners; we were close to them, and none to interpose; but they hurried out to fetch the larger engine. In the mean time we were advised to send for the mayor; but Mr. Mayor was gone out of town, in the sight of the people, which gave great encouragement to those who were already wrought up to a proper pitch by the curate, and the gentlemen of the town, particularly Mr. Sutton and Mr. Willy, dissenters, the two leading men. Mr. Sutton frequently came out to the mob to keep up their spirits. He sent word to Mrs. Philips, that if she did not turn that fellow out to the mob, he would send them to drag him out. Mr. Willy passed by again and again, assuring the rioters he would stand by them, and secure them from the law, do what they would.

"The rioters now began playing the larger engine, which broke the windows, flooded the rooms, and spoiled the goods. We were withdrawn to a small upper room in the back part of the house, seeing no way to escape their violence, as they seemed under the full power of the old murderer. They first laid hold on the man who kept the society house, dragged him away, and threw him into the horse pond, and, it was said, broke his back. We gave ourselves to prayer, believing the Lord would deliver us; how, or when, we saw not, nor any possible way of escaping; we, therefore, stood still to see the salvation of God. Every now and then some or other of our friends would venture to us, but rather weakened our hands, so that we were forced to stop our ears and look up. Among the rest, the mayor's maid came, and told us her mistress was in tears about me, and begged me to disguise myself in woman's clothes, and try to make my escape. Her heart had been turned toward us by the conversion of her son, just on the brink of ruin. God laid his hand on the poor prodigal, and instead of running to sea, he entered the society. The rioters without continued playing their engine, which diverted them for some time; but their number and fierceness still increased; and the gentlemen supplied them with pitchers of ale, as much as they would drink. They were now on the point of breaking in, when Mr. Borough thought of reading the proclamation; he did so at the hazard of his life. In less than an hour, of above a thousand wild beasts, none were left but the guard. Our constable had applied to Mr. Street, the only justice in town, who would not act. We found there was no help in man, which drove us closer to the Lord; and we prayed with little intermission the whole day.

"Our enemies at their return made their main assault at the back door, swearing horribly they would have me if it cost them their lives. Many seeming accidents concurred to prevent their breaking in. The man of the house came home, and instead of turning me out as they expected, took part with us, and stemmed the tide for some time. They now got a notion that I had made my escape, and ran down to the inn, and played the engine there. They forced the innkeeper to turn out our horses, which he immediately sent to Mr. Clark's, which drew the rabble and their engine thither. But the resolute old man charged and presented his gun till they retreated. Upon their revisiting us, we stood in jeopardy every moment. Such threatenings, curses, and blasphemies, I have never heard. They seemed kept out by a continual miracle. I remembered the Roman senators, sitting in the forum, when the Gauls broke in upon them, but thought there was a fitter posture for Christians, and told my companion they should take us off our knees. We were kept from all hurry and discomposure of spirit by a Divine power resting upon us. We prayed and conversed as freely as if we had been in the midst of our brethren, and had great confidence that the Lord would either deliver us from the danger, or in it. In the hight of the storm, just when we were falling into the hands of the drunken, enraged multitude, Mr. Minton was so little disturbed that he fell fast asleep.

"They were now close to us on every side, and over our heads untiling the roof. A ruffian cried out, 'Here they are, behind the curtain.' At this time we fully expected their appearance, and retired to the furthermost corner of the room, and I said, 'This is the crisis.' In that moment, Jesus rebuked the winds and the sea, and there was a great calm. We heard not a breath without, and wondered what was become of them. The silence lasted for three-quarters of an hour, before any one came near us; and we continued in mutual exhortation and prayer, looking for deliverance. I often told my companions, 'Now God is at work for us; he is contriving our escape; he can turn these leopards into lambs; can command the heathen to bring his children on their shoulders, and make our fiercest enemies the instruments of our deliverance.' About three o'clock Mr. Clark knocked at the door, and brought with him the persecuting constable. He said, 'Sir, if you will promise never to preach here again, the gentlemen and I will engage to bring you safe out of town.' My answer was, 'I shall promise no such thing; setting aside my office, I will not give up my birthright, as an Englishman, of visiting what place I please of his Majesty's dominions.' 'Sir,' said the constable, 'we expect no such promise, that you will never come here again; only tell me that it is not your present intention, that I may tell the gentlemen, who will then secure your quiet departure.' I answered, 'I can not come again at this time, because I must return to London a week hence. But, observe, I make no promise of not preaching here when the door is opened; and do not you say that I do.'

"He went away with this answer, and we betook ourselves to prayer and thanksgiving. We perceived it was the Lord's doings, and it was marvelous in our eyes. The hearts of our adversaries were turned. Whether pity for us, or fear for themselves, wrought strongest, God knoweth; probably the latter, for the mob were wrought up to such a pitch of fury that their masters dreaded the consequence, and therefore went about appeasing the multitude, and charging them not to touch us in our departure.

"While the constable was gathering his posse, we got our things from Mr. Clark's, and prepared to go forth. The whole multitude were without, expecting us, and saluted us with a general shout. The man Mrs. Naylor had hired to ride before her was, as we now perceived, one of the rioters. This hopeful guide was to conduct us out of the reach of his fellows. Mr. Minton and I took horse in the face of our enemies, who began clamoring against us; the gentlemen were dispersed among the mob, to bridle them. We rode a slow pace up the street, the whole multitude pouring along on both sides, and attending us with loud acclamations. Such fierceness and diabolical malice I have not before seen in human faces. They ran up to our horses as if they would swallow us, but did not know which was Wesley. We felt great peace and acquiescence in the honor done us, while the whole town were spectators of our march. When out of sight we mended our pace, and about seven o'clock came to Wrexall. The news of our danger was got thither before us; but we brought the welcome tidings of our deliverance. We joined in hearty prayer to our Deliverer, singing the hymn,

'Worship, and thanks, and blessings,' etc.

"February 26th, I preached at Bath, and we rejoiced

like men who take the spoil. We continued our triumph at Bristol, and reaped the fruit of our labors and sufferings."

Amidst such storms, more or less violent, were the foundations of that work laid, the happy results of which tens of thousands now enjoy in peace. But even the piety which could hazard such labors and dangers for the sake of "seeking and saving the lost," and the heroic devotedness which remained constant under them, has not been able to win the praise of prejudiced writers on the subject of Methodism. Dr. Southey (Life of Wesley) has little sympathy with the sufferings which a persecuted people were doomed in many places so callously to endure; and he finds in the heroism of their leaders a subject of reproach and contempt rather than of that admiration which, had they occupied some poetical position, he had doubtless expressed as forcibly and nobly as any man.

Mr. Whitefield, he tells us, had "a great longing to be persecuted," though the quotation from one of his letters, on which he justifies the aspersion, shows nothing more than a noble defiance of suffering, should it occur in the course of what he esteemed his duty. Similar sarcasms have been cast by infidels upon all who, in every age, have suffered for the sake of Christ; and, like those in which Dr. Southey has indulged, they were intended to darken the luster of that patient courage which sprang out of love to the Savior and the souls of men, by resolving it into spiritual pride, and a desire to render themselves conspicuous. Of John Nelson, one of Mr. Wesley's first lay coadjutors, who endured no ordinary share of oppression and suffering, as unprovoked and unmerited as the most modest and humble demeanor on his part could render it, Dr. Southey truly says, that "he had as high a spirit and as brave a heart as ever Englishman was blessed with;" yet even the narration of his wrongs, so scandalous to the magistracy of the day, and which were sustained by him in the full spirit of Christian constancy, is not dismissed without a sneer at this honest and suffering man himself. "To prison, therefore, Nelson was taken, to his *heart's content*." And so, because he chose a prison rather than violate his conscience, and endured imprisonments and other injuries, with the unbending feeling of a high and noble mind, corrected and controlled by "the meekness and gentleness of Christ," imprisonment was his desire, and the distinction which he is supposed to have derived from it, his motive! Before criticism so flippant and callous, no character, however sacred and revered, could stand. It might be applied with equal success to the persecutions of the apostles, and the first Christians themselves; to the confessors in the reign of Mary; and to the whole "noble army of martyrs."

The real danger to which these excellent men were exposed is, however, concealed by Dr. Southey. Whitefield's fears, or rather hopes of persecution, he says, "were suited to the days of Queen Mary, Bishop Gardiner, and Bishop Bonner; they were ridiculous or disgusting in the time of George the Second, Archbishop Potter, and Bishop Gibson." This is said because Mr. Whitefield thought that he might probably be called to "resist unto blood;" and our author would have it supposed, that all this was "safe boasting," in the reign of George the Second, and while the English Church had its Archbishop Potter and its Bishop Gibson. But not even in the early part of the reign of George the Third, and with other bishops in the Church as excellent as Potter and Gibson, was the anticipation groundless. The real danger was in fact so great from the brutality of the populace, the ignorance and supineness of the magistrates, and the mob-exciting activity of the clergy, one of whom was usually the instigator of every tumult, that every man who went forth on the errand of mercy in that day took his life in his hand, and needed the spirit of a martyr, though he was not in danger of suffering a martyr's death by regular civil or ecclesiastical process. Dr. Southey has himself in part furnished the confutation of his own suggestion, that little danger was to be apprehended, by the brief statements he has given of the hair-breadth escapes of the Wesleys, and of the sufferings of John Nelson. But a volume might be filled with accounts of outrages committed from that day to our own, in different places—for they now occasionally occur in obscure and unenlightened parts of the country—upon the persons of Methodist preachers, for the sole fault of visiting neglected places, and preaching the Gospel of salvation to those who, if Christianity be true, are in a state of spiritual darkness and danger. To be pelted with stones, dragged through ponds, beaten with bludgeons, rolled in mud, and to suffer other modes of ill treatment, was the anticipation of all the first preachers when they entered upon their work; and this was also the lot of many of their hearers. Some lives were lost, and many shortened; the most singular escapes are on record; and if the tragedy was not deeper, that was owing at length to the explicit declarations of George III on the subject of toleration, and the upright conduct of the judges in their circuits, and in the higher courts, when an appeal was made to the laws in some of the most atrocious cases. Assuredly, the country magistrates in general, and the clergy, were entitled to little share of the praise. Much of this is acknowledged by Dr. Southey; but he attempts to throw a part of the blame upon the Wesleys themselves. "Their doctrines of perfection and assurance" were, he thinks, among the causes of their persecution; and "their zeal was not tempered with discretion." With discretion, in his view of it, their zeal was not tempered. Such discretion would neither have put them in the way of persecution, nor brought it upon them; it would have disturbed no sinner and saved no soul; but they were not indiscreet in seeking danger, and provoking language never escaped lips in which the law of meekness always triumphed: and as for doctrines, the mobs and their exciters were then just as discriminating as mobs have ever been from the beginning of the world. They were usually stirred up by the clergy, and other persons of influence in the neighborhood, who were almost as ignorant as the ruffians they employed to assault the preachers and their peaceable congregations. The description of the mob at Ephesus, in the Acts of the Apostles, suited them as well as if they had been the original, and not the copy: "Some cried one thing, and some another; for the assembly was confused; and the most part knew not wherefore they were come together." They generally, however, agreed to pull down the preacher, and to abuse both him and his hearers, men, women, and even children; and that because "they troubled them about religion."

That immediate resort to God in prayer, which was practiced, in cases of "peril and danger," by these persecuted ministers, and their ascription of deliverances to the Divine interposition, as in the instances above given, have also been subjects of either grave rebuke or semi-infidel ridicule. It is not necessary to contend that every particular instance which, in the journals of the Wesleys, is referred to an immediate answer to prayer, was so in reality; because a few cases may reasonably appear doubtful. These, however, only prove that they cultivated the habit of regarding God in all things, and of gratefully acknowledging his hand in all the events of life; and if there was at any time any over-application of these excellent views and feelings, yet in minds so sober as to make the word of God, diligently studied, their only guide in all matters of practice, no injurious result could follow. But we must reject the Bible altogether, if we shut out a particular providence; and we reduce prayer to a real absurdity, unless we allow that its very ground and reason is special interposition. Why, for instance, should a Collect teach us to pray that "this day we may fall into no sin, neither run into any kind of danger," if we do not thereby place ourselves under a special protection of God, and if our interests must necessarily be dragged after the wheel of some general system of government? Divine interposition is, indeed, *ordinarily* invisible, and can be known only from general results; it impresses no mark of interruption or of quickened activity upon the general courses of things with which we may be surrounded; it works often unconsciously through our own faculties, and through the wills and purposes of others, as unconscious of it as we ourselves; yet even in this case, where the indevout see man only, the better instructed acknowledge God who "worketh all in all." But to say that the hand of God is never specially marked in its operations; that his servants who are raised up by him for important services shall never receive proofs of his particular care; that an entire trust in him in the most critical circumstances shall have no visible honor put upon it; that when we are "in all things" commanded to make our requests known to God, the prayers which, in obedience to that command, we offer to him in the time of trouble shall never have a special answer, is to maintain notions wholly subversive of piety, and which can not be held without rejecting, or reducing to unmeaningness, many of the most explicit and important declarations of holy Scripture. These were not the views entertained by the Wesleys; and in their *higher belief* they coincided with good men in all ages. They felt that they were about their Master's business, and they trusted in their Master's care, so long as it might be for his glory that they should be permitted to live. Nor for that were they anxious; desiring only, that while they lived they should "live to the Lord," and that when they died "they should die to him;" and that so "Christ might be magnified in their body, whether by life or by death."

The labors of Mr. John Wesley, during the same period of two years, may be abridged from his journal. In the first month of the year 1745, we find him at London, and at Bristol and its neighborhood. In February he made a journey, in the stormy and wintry weather of that season, to Newcastle, preaching at various intermediate places. The following extract shows the cheerful and buoyant spirit with which he encountered these difficulties:

"Many a rough journey have I had before; but one like this I never had, between wind and hail, and rain and ice, and snow, and driving sleet, and piercing cold. But it is past. Those days will return no more, and are therefore as though they had never been.

'Pain, disappointment, sickness, strife,
Whate'er molests or troubles life;
However grievous in its stay,
It shakes the tenement of clay,
When past, as nothing we esteem;
And pain, like pleasure, is a dream.'" (Journal.)

As a specimen of that cool and self-possessed manner which gave him so great a power over rude minds, we may take the following anecdote. A man at Newcastle had signalized himself by personal insults offered to him in the streets; and, upon inquiry, he found him an old offender in persecuting the members of the society by abusing and throwing stones at them. Upon this he sent him the following note:

"ROBERT YOUNG,—I expect to see you, between this and Friday, and to hear from you, that you are sensible of your fault. Otherwise, in pity to your soul, I shall be obliged to inform the magistrates of your assaulting me yesterday in the street.

"I am your real friend, JOHN WESLEY.

"Within two or three hours, Robert Young came, and promised a quite different behavior. So did this gentle reproof, if not save a soul from death, yet prevent a multitude of sins." (Journal.)

While at Newcastle, he drew up the following case:

"*Newcastle upon Tyne, March* 11, 1745–'46.

"I have been drawing up this morning a short state of the case between the clergy and us: I leave you to make any such use of it as you believe will be to the glory of God.

"1. About seven years since we began preaching *inward, present* salvation, as attainable by *faith alone.*

"2. For preaching *this doctrine* we were forbidden to preach in the churches.

"3. We then preached in *private houses,* as occasion offered; and when the houses could not contain the people, in the open air.

"4. For *this* many of the clergy *preached* or *printed* against us, as both heretics and schismatics.

"5. Persons who were convinced of sin begged us to advise them more particularly how to flee from the wrath to come. We replied, if they would all come at one time—for they were numerous—we would endeavor it.

"6. For *this* we were represented, both from the pulpit and the press—we have heard it with our ears, and seen it with our eyes—as introducing Popery, raising sedition, practicing both against Church and state; and all manner of evil was publicly said both of us and those who were accustomed to meet with us.

"7. Finding some truth herein, namely, that some of those who so met together walked disorderly, we immediately desired them not to come to us any more.

"8. And the more steady were desired to overlook the rest, that we might know if they walked according to the Gospel.

"9. But now several of the bishops began to speak against us, either in conversation or in public.

"10. On this encouragement several of the clergy stirred up the people to treat us as outlaws or mad dogs.

"11. The people did so, both in Staffordshire, Cornwall, and many other places.

"12. And they do still, wherever they are not restrained by their fear of the secular magistrate.

"Thus the case stands at present. Now, what can *we* do, or what can *you* our brethren do toward healing this breach? which is highly desirable; that we may withstand, with joint force, the still increasing flood of Popery, Deism, and immorality.

"Desire of *us* any thing we can do with a safe conscience, and we will do it immediately. Will *you* meet us here? Will you do what we desire of you so far as you can with a safe conscience?

"Let us come to particulars. Do you desire us, 1. To preach another, or to desist from preaching this, doctrine?

"We think you do not desire it, as knowing we *can not do this* with a safe conscience.

"Do you desire us, 2. To desist from preaching in private houses, or in the *open air?* As things are now circumstanced, this would be the same as desiring us not to preach at all.

"Do you desire us, 3. To desist from advising those who now meet together for that purpose? or, in other words, to dissolve our societies?

"We can not do this with a safe conscience; for we apprehend many souls will be lost thereby, and that God would require their blood at our hands.

"Do you desire us, 4. To advise them only one by one?

"This is impossible, because of their number.

"Do you desire us, 5. To suffer those who walk disorderly still to mix with the rest?

"Neither can we do this with a safe conscience; because *evil communications corrupt good manners.*

"Do you desire us, 6. To discharge those leaders of bands or classes—as we term them—who overlook the rest?

"This is, in effect, to suffer the disorderly walkers still to mix with the rest, which we dare not do.

"Do you desire us, lastly, to behave with reverence toward those who are overseers of the Church of God? and with tenderness, both to the character and persons of our brethren, the inferior clergy?

"By the grace of God, we can and will do this. Yea, our conscience beareth us witness, that we have already labored so to do, and that at all times and in all places.

"If you ask, what we desire of *you* to do, we answer: 1. We do not desire any of you to let us preach in your churches, either if you believe us to preach false doctrine, or if you have, upon any other ground, the least scruple concerning it. But we desire that any who believe us to preach true doctrine, and has no scruple at all in this matter, may not be either publicly or privately discouraged from inviting us to preach in his church.

"2. We do not desire that any one who thinks that we are heretics or schismatics, and that it is his duty to preach or print against us as such, should refrain therefrom, so long as he thinks it his duty—although in this case the breach can never be healed.

"But we desire that none will pass such a sentence, till he has calmly considered both sides of the question; that he would not condemn us unheard, but first read what we have written, and pray earnestly that God may direct him in the right way.

"3. We do not desire any favor, if either Popery, sedition, or immorality be proved against us.

"But we desire you will not credit, without proof, any of those senseless tales that pass current with the vulgar; that, if you do not credit them yourselves, you will not relate them to others—which we have known done—yea, that you will confute them, so far as ye have opportunity, and discountenance those who still retail them abroad.

"4. We do not desire any preferment, favor, or recommendation from those that are in authority, either in Church or state. But we desire,

"1. That if any thing material be laid to our charge, we may be permitted to answer for ourselves. 2. That you would hinder your dependents from stirring up the rabble against us, who are certainly not the proper judges of these matters; and 3. That you would effectually suppress, and thoroughly discountenance, all riots and popular insurrections, which evidently strike at the foundation of all government, whether of Church or state.

"Now these things you certainly can do, and that with a safe conscience; therefore, till these things are done, the continuance of the breach is chargeable on you and you only." (Works, vol. iii, pp. 329–331.)

It is evident from this paper that Mr. Wesley's difficulties, arising from his having raised up a distinct people, within the national Church, pressed upon him. He desired union and co-operation with the clergy, but his hope was disappointed; and, perhaps, it was much more than he could reasonably indulge. It shows, however, his own sincerity, and that he was not only led into his course of irregularity, but impelled forward in it, by circumstances which his zeal and piety had created, and which all his prejudices in favor of the Church could not control.

After spending some time in Newcastle and the neighboring places, he visited Lincolnshire, Yorkshire, Lancashire, and Cheshire. On his return southward he called at Wednesbury, long the scene of riot, and preached in peace. At Birmingham he had to abide the pelting of stones and dirt; and, on his return to London, he found some of the society inclined to Quakerism; but, by reading "Barclay's Apology" over with them, and commenting upon it, they were recovered. Antinomianism, both of Mystic and Calvinistic origin, also gave him trouble; but his testimony against it was unsparing. To erroneous opinions, when innocent, no man was more tender; but when they infected the conduct, they met from him the sternest resistance. "I would wish all to observe, that the points in question between us and either the German or English Antinomians are not points of opinion, but of practice. We break with no man for his opinion. We think and let think." (Journal.)

In the summer he proceeded to Cornwall, where Dr. Borlase, the historian of that country, in the plenitude of his magisterial authority, still carried on a systematic persecution against the Methodists. He had made out an order for Mr. Maxfield, who had been preaching in various places, to be sent on board a man-of-war, but the captain would not take him. A pious and peaceable miner, with a wife and seven children, was also apprehended under the Doctor's warrant, because he had said "that he knew his sins forgiven;" and this zealous anti-heretic finally made out a warrant against Mr. Wesley himself, but could find no one to execute it. From Cornwall, where his ministry had been attended with great effect, Mr. Wesley proceeded to Wales, and thence to Bristol.

Count Zinzendorf, about this time, directed the publication of an advertisement, declaring that he and his people had no connection with John and Charles Wesley; and concluded with a prophecy, that they would "soon run their heads against a wall." On this Mr. Wesley contents himself with coolly remarking, "We will not, if we can help it."

He now proceeded northward; and at Northampton called on Dr. Doddridge, from whom he had previously received several letters, breathing the most catholic spirit. At Leeds the mob pelted him and the congregation with dirt and stones; and the next evening, being "in higher excitement, they were ready," says he, "to knock out our brains for joy that the duke of Tuscany was emperor." On his arrival at Newcastle, the town was in the utmost consternation, news having arrived that the pretender had entered Edinburg. By the most earnest preaching, he endeavored to turn this season of alarm to the spiritual profit of the people, and the large congregations whom he addressed in the streets heard with solemn attention. He then visited Epworth, but speedily returned to Newcastle, judging, probably, that the place of anxiety and danger was his post of duty. Here he made an offer to the general, through one of the aldermen, to preach to the troops encamped near the town, whose dissolute language and manners greatly affected him; but he seems to have received no favorable answer; so, after preaching a few times near the camp, he returned southward, endeavoring, at Leeds, Birmingham, and other places, to turn the public agitation, arising from the apprehension of civil war, to the best account, by enforcing "repentance toward God, and faith in our Lord Jesus Christ."

Mr. Wesley had occasionally employed himself in writing and getting printed small religious tracts, many thousands of which were distributed. This was revived with vigor on his return to London this year; and he thus, by his example, was probably the first to apply, on any large scale, this important means of usefulness to the reformation of the people. In the form of those excellent institutions called "tract societies," the same plan has now long been carried on systematically, to the great spiritual advantage of many thousands. At this period he observes, adverting to the numerous small tracts he had written and distributed, "It pleased God hereby to provoke others to jealousy; insomuch that the lord mayor had ordered a large quantity of papers, dissuading from cursing and swearing, to be printed, and distributed to the train-bands. And this day, an 'Earnest Exhortation to Serious Repentance' was given at every church door in or near London, to every person who came out, and one left at the house of every householder who was absent from church. I doubt not but God gave a blessing therewith."*

In the early part of 1746, we find the following entry in Mr. Wesley's journal: "I set out for Bristol. On the road I read over Lord King's Account of the Primitive Church. In spite of the vehement prejudice of my education, I was ready to believe that this was a fair and impartial draught. But if so, it would follow, that bishops and presbyters are—essentially—of one order; and that originally every Christian congregation was a Church independent on all others!"

The truth is, that Lord King came in only to confirm

* Journal.—Previous to this we find him a tract writer and distributer; for he observes in the year 1742, "I set out for Brentford with Robert Swindels. The next day we reached Marlboro. When one in the room beneath us was swearing desperately, Mr. Swindels stepped down, and put into his hand the paper entitled *Swear not at all.* He thanked him, and promised to swear no more. And he did not while he was in the house." Mr. Wesley had already written tracts entitled, "A Word to a Smuggler," "A Word to a Sabbath-Breaker," "A Word to a Swearer," "A Word to a Drunkard," "A Word to a Street-Walker," "A Word to a Malefactor," and several others. He published these that his preachers and people might have them to give away to those who were guilty of these crimes, or in danger of falling into them. He considered this as one great means of spreading the knowledge of God. He also gave his early influence to the Sunday school system. Mr. Raikes began his Sunday school in Gloucester in 1784; and in January, 1785, Mr. Wesley published an account of it in his magazine, and exhorted his societies to imitate that laudable example.

him in views which he had for some time begun to entertain; and they were such as show, that though he was a Church of England man as to affection, which was strong and sincere as far as its doctrines and its liturgy were concerned, and though he regarded it with great deference as a legal institution, yet in respect to its ecclesiastical *polity* he was even then very free in his opinions. At the second conference, in 1745, it was asked, "Is Episcopal, Presbyterian, or Independent church government, most agreeable to reason?" The answer is as follows:

"The plain origin of Church government seems to be this: Christ sends forth a person to preach the Gospel: some of those who hear him, repent and believe in Christ: they then desire him to watch over them, to build them up in faith, and to guide their souls into paths of righteousness. Here, then, is an independent congregation, subject to no pastor but their own; neither liable to be controlled, in things spiritual, by any other man, or body of men whatsoever. But soon after, some from other parts, who were occasionally present while he was speaking in the name of the Lord, beseech him to come over and help them also. He complies, yet not till he confers with the wisest and holiest of his congregation; and, with their consent, appoints one who has gifts and grace to watch over his flock in his absence. If it please God to raise another flock, in the new place, before he leaves them, he does the same thing, appointing one whom God hath fitted for the work to watch over these souls also. In like manner, in every place where it pleases God to gather a little flock by his word, he appoints one in his absence to take the oversight of the rest, to assist them as of the ability which God giveth.

"These are deacons, or servants of the Church, and they look upon their first pastor as the common father of all these congregations, and regard him in the same light, and esteem him still as the shepherd of their souls. These congregations are not strictly independent, as they depend upon one pastor, though not upon each other.

"As these congregations increase, and the deacons grow in years and grace, they need other subordinate deacons, or helpers, in respect of whom they may be called presbyters or elders, as their father in the Lord may be called the bishop or overseer of them all."*

This passage is important, as it shows that from the first he regarded his preachers, when called out and devoted to the work, as, in respect of primitive antiquity and the universal Church, parallel to deacons and presbyters. He also then thought himself a Scriptural bishop. Lord King's researches into antiquity served to confirm these sentiments, and corrected his former notion as to a distinction of orders.

It should here be stated, that at these early conferences one sitting appears to have been devoted to conversation on matters of discipline, in which the propriety of Mr. Wesley's proceedings in forming societies, calling out preachers, and originating a distinct religious community, governed by its own laws, were considered; and this necessarily led to the examination of general questions of Church government and order. This will explain the reason why in the conferences which Mr. Wesley, his brother, two or three clergymen, and a few preachers held in the years 1744, 1745, 1746, and 1747, such subjects were discussed as are contained in the above extract and in those which follow. On these, as on all others, they set out with the principle of examining every thing "to the foundation."

[* It was in this relation, and from pressing necessity in circumstances of extreme emergency, that Mr. Wesley, assisted by other presbyters, ordained Dr. Coke, and through him Mr. Asbury, as superintendents, or bishops, of the American Methodist Churches.—AMERICAN EDIT.]

"Q. Can he be a spiritual governor of the Church who is not a believer, not a member of it?

"A. It seems not; though he may be a governor in outward things, by a power derived from the king.

"Q. What are properly the laws of the Church of England?

"A. The Rubrics: and to these we submit, as the ordinance of men, for the Lord's sake.

"Q. But is not the will of our governors a law?

"A. No, not of any governor, temporal or spiritual; therefore, if any bishop wills that I should not preach the Gospel, his will is no law to me.

"Q. But if he produce a law against your preaching?

"A. I am to obey God rather than man."

"Q. Is mutual consent absolutely necessary between the pastor and his flock?

"A. No question. I can not guide any soul, unless he consent to be guided by me; neither can any soul force me to guide him, if I consent not.

"Q. Does the ceasing of this consent on either side dissolve this relation?

"A. It must in the very nature of things. If a man no longer consent to be guided by me, I am no longer his guide—I am free. If one will not guide me any longer, I am free to seek one who will."

"Q. Does a Church in the New Testament always mean a single congregation?

"A. We believe it does; we do not recollect any instance to the contrary.

"Q. What instance or ground is there then in the New Testament for a national Church?

"A. We know none at all; we apprehend it to be a merely-political institution.

"Q. Are the three orders of bishops, priests, and deacons plainly described in the New Testament?

"A. We think they are, and believe they generally obtained in the Church of the apostolic age.

"Q. But are you assured that God designed the same plan should obtain in all Churches, throughout all ages?

"A. We are not assured of it, because we do not know it is asserted in Holy Writ.

"Q. If the plan were essential to a Christian Church, what must become of all foreign Reformed Churches?

"A. It would follow they are no part of the Church of Christ: a consequence full of shocking absurdity.

"Q. In what age was the divine right of Episcopacy first asserted in England?

"A. About the middle of Queen Elizabeth's reign: till then all the bishops and clergy in England continually allowed and joined in the ministrations of those who were not episcopally ordained.

"Q. Must there not be numberless accidental variations in the government of various Churches?

"A. There must, in the nature of things. As God variously dispenses his gifts of nature, providence, and grace, both the offices themselves, and the officers in each, ought to be varied from time to time.

"Q. Why is it that there is no determinate plan of Church government appointed in Scripture?

"A. Without doubt because the wisdom of God had a regard to that necessary variety.

"Q. Was there any thought of uniformity in the government of all Churches, till the time of Constantine?

"A. It is certain there was not, nor would there have been then had men consulted the word of God only."

Nothing, therefore, can be more clear, than that Mr. Wesley laid the ground-work of his future proceedings after much deliberation, at this early stage of his progress.

He felt that a case of necessity had arisen, calling upon him to provide a ministry and a government for the people who had been raised up; a necessity which rested upon the obvious alternative, that they must be either furnished with pastors of their own, or be left without sufficient aid in the affairs of their souls. This led him closely to examine the whole matter; and he saw that when the authority of Scripture alone was referred to in matters of Church arrangement and regulation, it enjoined no particular form of administration as binding, but left the application of certain great and inviolable principles to the piety and prudence of those whom God might honor as the instruments of usefulness to the souls of men. Here he took his stand; and he proceeded to call forth preachers, and set them apart, or *ordain them** to the sacred office, and to

* The act of setting apart ministers by Mr. Wesley, but without imposition of hands, is here called their *ordination*, although that term has not been generally in use among us; and may be objected to by those who do not consider that imposition of hands, however impressive as a form, and in most Churches the uniform practice, is still but a circumstance, and can not enter into the *essence* of ordination. That every religious society has the power to determine the mode in which "*the separation*" of its ministers "to *the Gospel of God*" shall be visibly notified and expressed, will only be questioned by those whom prejudice and a wretched bigotry have brought under their influence. What the body of Methodists now practice in this respect, will, however, be allowed to stand on clearer ground than the proceedings of Mr. Wesley, who still continued in communion with the Church. It has, therefore, been generally supposed that Mr. Wesley did not consider his appointment of preachers, without imposition of hands, as an *ordination* to the ministry; but only as an irregular employment of laymen in the spiritual office of merely expounding the Scriptures in a case of moral necessity. This, however, is not correct. They were not appointed to expound or preach merely, but were solemnly set apart to the pastoral office, as the minutes of the conferences show; nor were they regarded by him as *laymen*, except when in common parlance they were distinguished from the clergy of the Church; in which case he would have called any dissenting minister a layman. The first extract from the minutes of the conferences above given, sufficiently shows that as to the Church of Christ at large, and as to his own societies, he regarded the preachers, when fully devoted to the work, not as *laymen*, but as *spiritual* men, and *ministers;* men, as he says, "moved by the Holy Ghost" to preach the Gospel, and who after trial were ordained to

enlarge the work by their means, under the full conviction of his acting under as clear a Scriptural authority as could be pleaded by Churchmen for Episcopacy, by the Presbyterians for Presbytery, or by the Congregationalists for independency. Still he did not go beyond the *necessity*. He could make this Scriptural appointment of ministers and ordinances, without renouncing communion with the national Church, and therefore he did not renounce it. In these views Charles Wesley, too, who was at every one of the early conferences, concurred with him: and if he thought somewhat differently on these points afterward, it was Charles who departed from first principles, not John. So much for the accuracy of Dr. Whitehead, who constructed his Life of the two brothers upon just the opposite opinion!

The discipline which Mr. Wesley maintained in the

that and other branches of the pastoral office. In his sketch of the origin of church government in that extract, he clearly had in view the conformity between what had taken place in his own case, and that which must, in a great number of instances, have occurred in the earliest periods of Christianity; and while he evidently refers to himself as the father and bishop of the whole of the societies, he tacitly compares his "assistants" to the ancient "presbyters," and his "helpers" to the ancient "deacons." In point of fact, so fully did he consider himself, even in 1747—whether consistently or not, as a Churchman, let others determine, I speak only to the fact—as *setting apart* or *ordaining* to the ministry, that he appears to have had thoughts of adding imposition of hands to his usual mode of ordination, which was preceded by fasting and private prayer, and consisted of public examination, prayer, and appointment; and he only declines this for *prudential* reasons. "Why," says he, "do we not use more *form* in receiving a new laborer? 1. Because there is something of stateliness in it, and we would be little and inconsiderable. 2. Because we would not *make haste:* we desire barely to follow providence as it gradually opens." (Minutes of 1747.) Even this form, therefore, was regarded as what might in other circumstances be required. The bearing of these remarks upon some future ordinations of Mr. Wesley by imposition of hands, will be pointed out in its proper place.*

[* Among the American Methodists, ordination, by imposition of hands, has been uniformly practiced, from the time of the organization of the Methodist Episcopal Church in the year 1784. Our forms of ordination were prepared by Mr. Wesley himself, and are substantially the same as those used in the Church of England, and the Protestant Episcopal Church in this country.—AMERICAN EDIT.]

societies, was lenient and long-suffering; but where there was an evil at the root, he had an unsparing hand. In March, 1746, he came to Nottingham, and observes, "I had long doubted what it was which hindered the work of God here. But upon inquiry the case was plain. So many of the society were either triflers, or disorderly walkers, that the blessing of God could not rest upon them. So I made short work by cutting off all such at a stroke, and leaving only that little handful, who, as far as could be judged, were really in earnest to save their souls."

At Wednesbury and Birmingham he found that some Antinomian teachers, the offspring of that seed which before the recent revival of religion had been sown in various parts of the country, and who, in that concern about spiritual things which now prevailed, began more zealously to bestir themselves to mislead and destroy the souls of men, under pretense of preaching a purer Gospel, had troubled the societies. By personal conversation with some of these teachers, in the presence of the people, he drew out the odious extent to which they carried their notions of "Christian liberty;" and thus took an effectual method of exposing and confuting the deadly error.

Upon his return to London, it appeared that certain pretended prophets had appeared in the metropolis, and had excited the attention of many. He gratified his curiosity by going to visit one of them, and with good-humored sarcasm observes, that as "he aimed at talking Latin, and could not, he plainly showed that he did not understand his own calling." Sober Scotland has in our own day exhibited a similar fanaticism; and the gift of tongues, pretended by some persons there, appears to have proved quite as unsatisfactory an evidence of a divine commission, as in this case. In visiting Newgate he found a penitent and hopeful malefactor; and his journal affords a specimen of that originality of remark, which peculiar cases, often perplexing to others, called forth from him. "A real, deep work of God seemed to be already begun in his soul. Perhaps by driving him too fast, Satan has driven him to God—to that repentance which shall never be repented of." When he subsequently visited Dr. Dodd under condemnation, he is reported to have replied to his apologies for receiving him in the condemned cell, "Courage, brother, perhaps God saw that nothing else would do."

Bristol, Wales, Devonshire, and Cornwall, occupied Mr. Wesley's attention during the summer of 1746, and London, Bristol, and the places adjacent for the remainder of the year. About this time, also, he received various letters from the army abroad, giving an account of the progress of religion among the soldiers, and of the brave demeanor in battle of many of their Methodist comrades. These accounts appear to have given him great satisfaction, as showing the power of religion in new circumstances, and as affording him an answer to his enemies, who asserted that his doctrines had the effect of making men dastardly, negligent of duty, and disloyal. In the early part of the year 1747, we find him braving the snows of February in Lincolnshire; and in March he reached Newcastle, to supply the absence of his brother from that important station.

Among other excellences possessed by this great man, he was fond of smoothing the path of knowledge, to the diffusion of which he devoted much attention, and for which end he published many compendiums and brief treatises on its most important branches. In this respect, also, he was foremost to tread in a path which has been of late years vigorously pursued, and must be reckoned as one of the leaders of that class of wise and benevolent men, who have exerted themselves to extend the benefits of useful information from the privileged orders of society, into the middle and lower classes. "This week," says he,

"I read over, with some young men, a Compendium of Rhetoric, and a System of Ethics. I see not why a man of tolerable understanding may not in six months' time, learn more of solid philosophy than is commonly learned at Oxford in four—perhaps seven—years."

On his return from his labors in the north of England, he called at Manchester, which he had formerly several times visited in order to take counsel with his college friend Clayton, and Dr. Byrom, and had preached in the churches. He was now seen there in a new character. The small house which was occupied by the society could not contain a tenth part of the people, and he therefore walked to Salford Cross. "A numberless crowd of people partly ran before, partly followed after me. I thought it best not to sing, but looking round, asked abruptly, 'Why do you look as if you had never seen me before? Many of you have seen me in the neighboring church, both preaching and administering the sacrament.' I then gave out the text, *Seek ye the Lord while he may be found; call upon him while he is near.* None interrupted at all, or made any disturbance, till, as I was drawing to a conclusion, a big man thrust in, with three or four more, and bade them bring out the engine. Our friends desired me to remove into a yard just by, which I did, and concluded in peace."

From the north he proceeded through Nottingham and Staffordshire to London, and from thence to the west of England. The influence which his calm courage often gave him over mobs was remarkably shown on this journey. "Within two miles of Plymouth, one overtook and informed us that the night before all the dock was in an uproar; and that a constable, endeavoring to keep the peace, was beaten and much hurt. As we were entering the dock, one met us and desired we would go the back way; 'for,' said he, 'there are thousands of people waiting about Mr. Hyde's door.' We rode up straight into the midst of them. They saluted us with three hurras; after which I alighted, took several of them by the hand, and began to talk with them. I would gladly have passed an hour among them, and believe if I had, there had been an end of the riot; but the day being far spent—for it was past nine o'clock—I was persuaded to go in. The mob then recovered their spirits, and fought valiantly with the doors and windows. But about ten they were weary, and went every man to his own home. The next day I preached at four, and then spoke severally to a part of the society. About six in the evening I went to the place where I preached the last year. A little before we had ended the hymn came a lieutenant, a famous man, with his retinue of soldiers, drummers, and mob. When the drums ceased, a gentleman-barber began to speak; but his voice was quickly drowned in the shouts of the multitude, who grew fiercer and fiercer as their numbers increased. After waiting about a quarter of an hour, perceiving the violence of the rabble still increasing, I walked down into the thickest of them, and took the captain of the mob by the hand. He immediately said, 'Sir, I will see you safe home. Sir, no man shall touch you. Gentlemen, stand off. Give back. I will knock the first man down that touches him.' We walked on in great peace; my conductor every now and then stretching out his neck—he was a very tall man—and looking round, to see if any behaved rudely, till we came to Mr. Hyde's door. We then parted in much love. I staid in the street near half an hour after he was gone, talking with the people, who had now forgot their anger, and went away in high good-humor."

In Cornwall we have a specimen of his prompt and faithful habits of discipline.

"Wednesday, 8th, I preached at St. Ives, then at Sithney. On Thursday the stewards of all the societies met.

I now diligently inquired, what exhorters there were in each society? Whether they had gifts meet for the work? Whether their lives were eminently holy? And whether there appeared any fruit of their labor? I found upon the whole, 1. That there were no fewer than eighteen exhorters in the county. 2. That three of these had no gifts at all for the work, neither natural nor supernatural. 3. That a fourth had neither gifts nor grace, but was a dull, empty, self-conceited man. 4. That a fifth had considerable gifts, but had evidently made shipwreck of the grace of God. These, therefore, I determined immediately to set aside, and advise our societies not to hear them. 5. That J. B., A. L., and J. W., had gifts and grace, and had been much blessed in the work. Lastly. That the rest might be helpful when there was no preacher, in their own or the neighboring societies, provided they would take no step without the advice of those who had more experience than themselves."

In August he visited Ireland for the first time. Methodism had been introduced into Dublin by Mr. Williams, one of the preachers, whose ministry had been attended with great success, so that a considerable society had been already formed. Mr. Wesley was allowed to preach once at St. Mary's, "to as gay and senseless a congregation," he observes, "as I ever saw." This was not, however, permitted a second time; and he occupied the spacious yard of the meeting-house, both in the mornings and evenings, preaching to large congregations of both poor and rich. Among his hearers he had also the ministers of various denominations. The state of the Catholics excited his peculiar sympathy; and as he could have little access to them by preaching, he published an address specially for their use. In his journal he makes a remark on the religious neglect of this class of our fellow-subjects by Protestants, which contains a reproof, the force of which has, unhappily, extended to our own times: "Nor is it any wonder, that those who are born Papists, generally live and die such; when the Protestants can find no better ways to convert them, than penal laws and acts of Parliament." The chief perplexities which Ireland has occasioned to the empire are to be traced to this neglect; and the dangers which have often sprung up to the state from that quarter have been, and continue to be, its appropriate punishment. Mr. Wesley's visit, at this time, to Ireland was short; but he requested his brother to succeed him. Mr. Charles Wesley, therefore, accompanied by another preacher, Mr. Charles Perronet, one of the sons of the venerable vicar of Shoreham, arrived there in September. A persecution had broken out against the infant society in Dublin, and "the first news," says Mr. Charles Wesley, "we heard was, that the little flock stood fast in the storm of persecution, which arose as soon as my brother left them. The Popish mob broke open their room, and destroyed all before them. Some of them are sent to Newgate, others bailed. What will be the event we know not, till we see whether the grand jury will find the bill." He afterward states that the grand jury threw out the bill, and thus gave up the Methodists to the fury of a licentious mob. "God has called me to suffer affliction with his people. I began my ministry with, 'Comfort ye, comfort ye my people,' etc. I met the society, and the Lord knit our hearts together in love stronger than death. We both wept and rejoiced for the consolation. God hath sent me, I trust, to confirm these souls, and to keep them together in the present distress." (Whitehead's Life.)

Mr. Charles Wesley spent the winter in Dublin, being daily employed in preaching and visiting the people. In February he made an excursion into the country, where a few preachers were already laboring, and, in some places, with great success. Thus was the first active and systematic agency for the conversion of the neglected people of Ireland commenced by the Methodists; and, till of late years, it is greatly to be regretted that they were left to labor almost alone. From that time, however, not only was the spirit of religion revived in many Protestant parts of the country, and many Papists converted to the truth, but the itinerant plan, which was there adopted as in England, enabled the preachers to visit a great number of places where the Protestants were so few in numbers as not to be able to keep up regular worship, or to make head, when left to themselves, against Popish influence. A barrier was thus erected against the farther encroachments of Popery; and the light was kept burning in districts where it would otherwise have been entirely extinguished. The influence of the Methodist societies would, however, have been much more extensive, had not the large emigrations which have been almost constantly setting in from Ireland to America, borne away a greater number of their members in proportion than those of any other community. Mr. Charles Wesley spent part of the year 1748 in Ireland, and preached in several of the chief towns, and especially at Cork, with great unction and success.

CHAPTER IX.

The notices of the journeys and labors of these indefatigable ministers of Christ, given in the preceding chapter, afford but a specimen of the manner in which the foundations of the Methodist connection were carried out and firmly laid. Nor were the preachers under their direction, though laboring in more limited districts of country, scarcely less laboriously employed. At this period one of them writes from Lancashire to Mr. Wesley: "Many doors are opened for preaching in these parts, but can not be supplied for want of preachers. I think some one should be sent to assist me, otherwise we shall lose ground. My circuit requires me to travel one hundred and fifty miles in two weeks; during which time I preach publicly thirty-four times, beside meeting the societies, visiting the sick, and transacting other affairs." (Whitehead's Life.)

Of the preachers some were engaged in business, and preached at their leisure in their own neighborhoods; but still, zealous for the salvation of men, they often took considerable journeys. Others gave themselves up, for a time, to more extended labors, and then settled: but the third class, who had become the regular "assistants" and "helpers" of Mr. Wesley, were devoted wholly to the work of the ministry; and, after a period of probation, and a scrutiny into their character and talents at the annual conferences, were admitted, by solemn prayer, into what was called "full connection," which, as we have stated, was their ordination. No provision was, however, made at this early period for their maintenance. They took neither "purse nor scrip;" they cast themselves upon the providence of God, and the hospitality and kindness of the societies, and were by them, like the primitive preachers, "helped forward after a godly sort,"* on their journeys, to open new places, and to instruct those for whose souls "no man cared." It might be as truly said of them as of the first propagators of Christianity, they had "no certain dwelling-place." Under the severity of labor, and the wretched accommodations to which they cheerfully submitted, many a fine constitution was broken, and premature death was often induced.

The annual conferences have been mentioned; and that

* The want of a provision for their wives and families, in the early periods of Methodism, caused the loss of many eminent preachers, who were obliged to settle in independent congregations.

a correct view may be taken of the doctrines which at those meetings it was agreed should be taught in the societies, it will be necessary to go back to their commencement. At first every doctrine was fully sifted in successive "Conversations," and the great principles of a godly discipline were drawn out into special regulations, as circumstances appeared to require. After the body had acquired greater maturity, these doctrinal discussions became less frequent; a standard and a test being ultimately established in a select number of Mr. Wesley's doctrinal sermons, and in his "Notes on the New Testament." The free and pious spirit in which these inquiries were entered into was strikingly marked at the first conferences, in the commencing exhortation: "Let us all pray for a willingness to receive light, to know of every doctrine whether it be of God." The widest principle of Christian liberty was also laid down, as suited to the infant state of a society which was but just beginning to take its ground, and to assume the appearance of order.

"Q. 3. How far does each of us agree to submit to the judgment of the majority?

"A. In speculative things, each can only submit so far as his judgment shall be convinced; in every practical point, each will submit so far as he can, without wounding his conscience.

"Q. 4. Can a Christian submit any farther than this to any man, or number of men, upon earth?

"A. It is plain he can not; either to bishop, convocation, or general council. And this is that grand principle of private judgment on which all the Reformers at home and abroad proceeded: 'Every man must judge for himself; because every man must give an account of himself to God.'" (Minutes.)

Never, it may be affirmed, was the formation of any Christian society marked by the recognition of principles more liberal, or more fully in the spirit of the New Testament.

To some of the doctrinal conversations of the first conferences it is necessary to refer, in order to mark those peculiarities of opinion which distinguish the Wesleyan Methodists. It is, however, proper to observe that the clergymen and others who thus assembled did not meet to draw up formal articles of faith. They admitted those of the Church of England; and their principal object was to ascertain how several of the doctrines relative to experimental Christianity, which they found stated in substance in those articles, and farther illustrated in the Homilies, were to be understood and explained. This light they sought from mutual discussion, in which every thing was brought to the standard of the word of inspired truth.

Their first subject was *justification,* which they describe with great simplicity; not loading it with epithets, as in the systematic schools, nor perplexing it by verbal criticism. It is defined to be "pardon," or "reception into God's favor;" a view which is amply supported by several explicit passages of Scripture, in which the terms "pardon," "forgiveness," and "remission of sins," are used convertibly with the term "justification." To be "received into God's favor," according to these Minutes, is necessarily connected with the act of forgiveness, and is the immediate and inseparable consequence of that gracious procedure. The same may be said of *adoption;* which, in some theological schemes, is made to flow from regeneration, while the latter is held to commence previously to justification. In Mr. Wesley's views adoption, as being a *relative* change, is supposed to be necessarily involved in justification, or the pardon of sin; and regeneration to flow from both, as an inward, *moral* change arising from the powerful and efficacious work of the Holy Spirit who is in that moment given to believers.* To their definition of justification, the Minutes add, "It is such a state that, if we continue therein, we shall be finally saved;" thus making final salvation conditional, and justification a state which may be forfeited. All willful sin was held to imply a casting away of vital faith, and thereby to bring a man under wrath and condemnation; "nor is it possible for him to have justifying faith again without previously repenting." They also agree that faith is "the condition of justification;" adding, as the proof, "for every one that believeth not is condemned, and every one who believes is justified." In Mr. Wesley's sermon on justification by faith, the office of faith in justifying is thus more largely set forth:

"Surely the difficulty of assenting to the proposition, that faith is the *only condition* of justification, must arise from not understanding it. We mean thereby thus much, that it is the only thing, without which no one is justified; the only thing that is immediately, indispensably, absolutely requisite in order to pardon. As on the one hand, though a man should have every thing else, without faith, yet he can not be justified, so on the other, though he be supposed to want every thing else, yet if he hath faith, he can not be justified. For suppose a sinner of any kind or degree, in a full sense of his total ungodliness, of his utter inability to think, speak, or do good, and his absolute meetness for hell fire; suppose, I say, this sinner, helpless and hopeless, casts himself wholly on the mercy of God in Christ—which indeed he can not do but by the grace of God—who can doubt but he is forgiven in that moment?

* The connection of favor and adoption with *pardon*, arises from the very nature of that act. Pardon, or forgiveness, is release from the penalties and forfeitures incurred by transgression. Of those penalties, the loss of God's favor, and of filial relation to him, was among the most weighty. Pardon, therefore, in its nature, or at least in its natural consequences, implies a restoration to the blessings forfeited, for else the penalty would in part remain in force.

Who will affirm that any more is *indispensably required*, before that sinner can be justified?

"And at what time soever a sinner thus believes, be it in his early childhood, in the strength of his years, or when he is old and hoary-headed, God justifieth that ungodly one; God, for the sake of his Son, pardoneth and absolveth him, who had in him, till then, no good thing. Repentance, indeed, God hath given him before; but that repentance was neither more nor less than a deep sense of the want of all good, and the presence of all evil. And whatever good he hath or doeth from that hour, when he first believes in God through Christ, faith does not *find*, but *bring*. This is the fruit of faith. First, the tree is good, and then the fruit is good also."

Mr. Wesley's views of repentance in this passage will also be noted. Here, as at the first conference, he insists that repentance, which is conviction of sin, and works meet for repentance, go before justifying faith; but he held, with the Church of England, that all works, before justification, had "the nature of sin;" and that, as they had no root in the love of God, which can only arise from a persuasion of his being reconciled to us, they could not constitute a moral worthiness preparatory to pardon. That a true repentance springs from the grace of God is certain; but whatever fruits it may bring forth, it changes not man's *relation* to God. He is a sinner, and is justified *as such;* "for it is not a saint but a sinner that is forgiven, and under the notion of a sinner." God justifieth the ungodly, not the godly. (Sermons.) Repentance, according to his statement, is necessary to true faith; but faith alone is the direct and immediate instrument of pardon.

Those views of *faith*—of that faith by which a man, thus penitent, comes to God through Christ—which are expressed in the Minutes of this first conference, deserve a more particular consideration. Here, as in defining justification, the language of the schools, and of systematic, philosophizing divines, is laid aside, and a simple enunciation is made of the doctrine of the New Testament. "Faith in general is a divine, supernatural *elenchos*—evidence or conviction—of things not seen, that is, of past, future, or spiritual things. It is a spiritual sight of God, and the things of God." (Minutes.)

In this description, faith is distinguished from mere *belief*, or an intellectual conviction which the consideration of the evidences of the truth of Scripture may produce, and yet lead to no practical or saving consequence; and that there may be a sincere and undoubting belief of the truth, without producing any saving effect, is a point which our very consciousness may sufficiently assure us of; although, in order to support a particular theory on the subject of faith, this has sometimes been denied. *Trust* is constantly implied in the Scriptural account of acceptable and saving faith, and this is the sense in which it was evidently taken in the above definition; for its production in the heart is referred to supernatural agency, and it is made to result from, and to be essentially connected with, a demonstration of spiritual things—such a conviction, wrought by the teaching Spirit, as produces not merely a full *persuasion* but a full *reliance.* Six years before this time, Mr. Wesley, in a sermon before the university of Oxford, had more at large expressed the same views as to justifying faith: "Christian faith is not only an assent to the whole Gospel of Christ, but also a full reliance on the blood of Christ; a trust in the merits of his life, death, and resurrection; a recumbency upon him as our atonement and our life, as given for us, and living in us. It is a sure confidence which a man hath in God that, through the merits of Christ, his sins are forgiven, and he reconciled to the favor of God; and, in consequence hereof, a closing with him, and cleaving to him, as our 'wisdom, righteousness, sanctification, and redemption, or, in one word, our salvation." (Sermons.)

It will however be remarked, that, in order to support his view of the nature of justifying faith by the authority of the Church of England, Mr. Wesley has quoted her words from the Homily on Salvation in the latter part of the above extract; and he thereby involved the subject in an obscurity which some time afterward he detected and acknowledged. The incorrectness of the wording of the homily is indeed very apparent, although in substance it is sound and Scriptural. When that homily defines justifying faith to be "a sure trust and confidence which a man hath in God that his sins are forgiven, and he reconciled to the favor of God," it is clear that, by the founders of the English Church, saving faith was regarded not as mere *belief*, but as an act of *trust* and *confidence* subsequent to the discovery made to a man of his sin and danger, and the fear and penitential sorrow which are thereby produced. The *object* of that faith they make to be God, assuredly referring to God in the exercise of his mercy through the atonement and intercession of Christ; and the trust and confidence of which the homily speaks must be, therefore, taken to imply a distinct recognition of the merits of Christ, and a full reliance upon them. So far all is Scripturally correct, although not so fully expressed as could be desired. That from such a faith exercised in these circumstances, a "confidence," taking the word in the sense of persuasion or assurance, that "a man's sins are forgiven, and he reconciled to the favor of God," certainly *follows*, is the doctrine of Scripture; and the authority of the homily may therefore also be quoted in favor of that view of assurance at which Churchmen have so often stumbled, and to which they have so often scornfully referred as the fanatical invention of modern sectaries. There is, however, an error in the homily which lies not in its substance and general intent, but in this, that applies the same terms, "trust and confidence," both to God's mercy in Christ, which is its proper object, and to "the forgiveness of sins," which is the *consequence* of a sure trust and confidence in God as exercising mercy "through Christ," because it is that in order to which the trust or confidence is exercised. It follows, therefore, that either there is an error in the latter part of the statement itself—justifying faith not being a confidence that sin is forgiven, which is absurd, because it is the condition previously required in order to the forgiveness of sin—or otherwise, which is probable, that the term "confidence," in the mind of the writer of the homily, was taken in a different sense when applied to God, the object of trust, and to the forgiveness of sin; and, when referred to the latter, meant that persuasion of the fact of being forgiven which must be attributed to a secret assurance of remission and acceptance by the spirit of adoption, and which ordinarily closely follows, or is immediately connected with, justifying faith, but which is not of its essence. But "confidence" in this sense implies *filial confidence*, the trust of a child, of one already passed into the family of God, and hence this is rather the description of the habitual faith of a justified man than of the act by which a sinner is justified and adopted. Mr. Wesley therefore soon perceived that the definition of justifying faith in this homily needed some correction, and he thus expressed his views in 1747, in a letter to his brother:

"Is justifying faith a sense of pardon? *Negatur.*" It is denied.

"By justifying faith I mean that faith which whosoever hath not, is under the wrath and the curse of God. By a sense of pardon I mean a distinct, explicit assurance that my sins are forgiven.

"I allow, 1. That there is such an explicit assurance. 2. That it is the common privilege of real Christians.

3. That it is the common Christian faith, which purifieth the heart, and overcometh the world." * * * *

"But the assertion, that justifying faith is a sense of pardon, is contrary to reason: it is flatly absurd. For how can a sense of our having received pardon, be the condition of our receiving it?

"But does not our Church give this account of justifying faith? I am sure she does of saving or Christian faith: I think she does of justifying faith too. But to the law and to the testimony. All men may err: but the word of the Lord shall stand forever."

Mr. Wesley, however, still regarded that trust in the merits of Christ's death, in which justifying faith consists, as resulting from a supernatural conviction that Christ "*loved me*" as an individual, and "*gave himself for me.*" In this he placed the proof that faith is "the gift of God," a work of the Holy Spirit, as being produced along with this conviction, or immediately following it. From this supernatural conviction, not only that God was in Christ "reconciling the world unto himself," but that he died "for *my* sins," there follows an entire committal of the case of the soul to the merits of the sacrifice of Christ, in an act of *trust;* in that moment, he held, God pardons and absolves him that so believes or trusts, and that this, his pardon or justification, is then witnessed to him by the Holy Ghost. Nor can a clearer or simpler view of stating this great subject, in accordance with the Scriptures, be well conceived. The state of a penitent is one of various degrees of doubt, but all painful. He questions the love of God to him, from a deep sense of his sin, although he may allow that he loves all the world beside. Before he can fully rely on Christ, and the promises of the Gospel, he must have hightened and more influential views of God's love in Christ, and of his own interest in it. It is the office of the Holy Spirit "to take of the things of

Christ, and show them" to the humble mind. This office of the Spirit agrees with that ἔλεγχος or "divine conviction," of which Mr. Wesley speaks, and which shows, with the power of demonstrative evidence, the love of Christ to the individual himself in the *intention* of his sacrifice. From this results an entire and joyful acquiescence with the appointed method of salvation, and a full reliance upon it, followed, according to the promise of Scripture, with actual forgiveness, and the cheering testimony of the Spirit of adoption. Of this faith he allowed different degrees, yet the lowest degree saving; and also different degrees of assurance, and therefore of joy. He was careful to avoid binding the work of the Spirit to one rule, and to distinguish between that *peace* which flows from a comfortable persuasion of "acceptance through Christ," and those higher joys which may be produced by that more hightened assurance which God is pleased in many cases to impart. He taught that the essence of true justifying faith consists in the entire *personal* trust of the man of a penitent and broken spirit upon the merits of his Savior, as having died for *him;* and that to all who so believe, faith is "imputed for righteousness," or, in other words, pardon was administered.*

* That Mr. Wesley did not hold that assurance of personal pardon is of the essence of justifying faith is certain, from the remarks in his letter to his brother before quoted, in which he plainly states, that to believe that I am pardoned in order to pardon, is an absurdity and a contradiction. There will, however, appear some obscurity in a few other passages in his writings, unless we notice the sense in which he uses certain terms, a matter in which he never felt himself bound by the systematic phraseology of scholastic theologians. Thus there is an apparent discrepancy between the statement of his views as given above and the following passage in his sermon on the "Scripture Way of Salvation:"

"Taking the word in a more particular sense, faith is a Divine evidence and conviction, not only that 'God was in Christ, reconciling the world unto himself;' but also that *Christ loved* me, *and gave himself for* me. It is by faith—whether we term it the *essence* or rather a *property* thereof—that we *receive Christ*, that we receive him in all his offices, as Prophet,

The immediate fruits of justifying faith are stated in these Minutes to be "peace, joy, love; power over all outward sin, and power to keep down inward sin." Justifying faith, when lost, is not again attainable, except by repentance and prayer; but "no believer need come again into a state of doubt, or fear, or darkness; and that—ordinarily at least—he will not, unless by ignorance or unfaithfulness." Assaults of doubt or fear are, however, admitted, even after great confidence and joy; and "occasional heaviness of spirit before large manifestations of the presence and favor of God." To these views of doctrine may be added, that regeneration or the new birth is held to be concomitant with justification. "Good works

Priest, and King. It is by this that he is 'made of God unto us wisdom, and righteousness, and sanctification, and redemption.'

"'But is this the *faith of assurance*, or the *faith of adherence?*' The Scripture mentions no such distinction. The apostle says, 'There is one faith, and one hope of our calling,' one Christian, saving faith, 'as there is one Lord,' in whom we believe, and 'one God and Father of us all.' And it is certain, this faith necessarily implies an *assurance*—which is here only another word for *evidence*, it being hard to tell the difference between them—that *Christ loved* me, and *gave himself* for me. For 'he that believeth,' with the true living faith, 'hath the witness in himself:' 'The Spirit witnesseth with his spirit, that he is a child of God.' 'Because he is a son, God hath sent forth the Spirit of his Son into his heart, crying, Abba, Father;' giving him an assurance that he is so, and a childlike confidence in him. But let it be observed that, in the very nature of the thing, the assurance goes before the confidence. For a man can not have a childlike confidence in God till he know he is a child of God. Therefore, confidence, trust, reliance, adherence, or whatever else it be called, is not the first, as some have supposed, but the second branch or act of faith."

Yet in fact the only difficulty arises from not attending to his mode of stating the case, and his use of the term *assurance*. When he says that faith includes both adherence and assurance, it is obvious that he does not mean by assurance, the assurance of personal acceptance, which he distinctly, in the same passage, ascribes to the direct testimony of the Spirit of God; but the assurance that Christ "died for *me*," "for *my* sins," which special manifestation of God's love in Christ to me as an individual, producing an entire *trust* in the Divine sacrifice for sin, he attributes to a supernatural elenchos or conviction. This, however, he considers as a "conviction" in order to faith or trust; and then the act of personal and entire trust in this manifested love and goodness is succeeded by the

can not go before this faith; much less can sanctification, which implies a continued course of good works, springing from holiness of heart; but they follow after:" and the reason given for this is, that as salvation, which includes a present deliverance from sin, a restoration of the soul to its primitive health, the renewing of the soul after the image of God, all holy and heavenly tempers and conversation, is by faith, it can not precede faith, which is the appointed instrument of attaining it. To increase in all these branches of holiness, the exercise of faith in prayer, and the use of all the means appointed by God, are also necessary; a living faith being that which unites the soul to Christ, and secures the constant indwelling and influence of the Holy Spirit in the heart. Such a faith must, therefore, necessarily lead to universal holiness of heart

direct testimony of the Spirit of adoption, which he tells us gives a man "the assurance that he is a child of God, and a childlike confidence in him." And when he goes on so truly to state, that "in the very nature of the thing, the assurance goes before confidence," and that "confidence, trust, or reliance," is not the first but the second branch of faith, he evidently does not here mean that confidence and trust in the merit of Christ by which we are justified, but *filial trust and confidence in God* as our reconciled Father, which must necessarily be subsequent to the other. According to Mr. Wesley's views, the order of our passing into a *state* of justification and conscious reconcilement to God, is, 1. True repentance, which, however, gives us no worthiness, and establishes no claim upon pardon, although it so necessarily precedes justifying faith, that all trust even in the merits of Christ for salvation would be presumptuous and unauthorized without repentance; since, as he says, 'Christ is not even to be offered to the careless sinner." (Sermon on "the Law established through Faith.") 2. Supernatural *elenchos*, or assured conviction, that "Christ loved *me*, and *gave* himself for *me*," in the intention of his death; inciting to and producing full acquiescence with God's method of saving the guilty, and an entire personal trust in Christ's atonement for sin. Of this trust, actual justification is the result; but then follows, 3. The direct testimony of the Holy Spirit, giving assurance in different degrees, in different persons, and often in the same person, that I am a child of God; and, 4. Filial confidence in God. The *elenchos*, the *trust*, the *Spirit's witness*, and the *filial confidence* he ..eld, were frequently, but not always, so closely united as not to be distinguished as to *time*, though each is, from its *nature*, *successive* and *distinct*.

and life, and stands as an impregnable barrier against Pharisaism on the one hand, and the pollutions of Antinomianism on the other.

On another doctrine, in defense of which Mr. Wesley afterward wrote much, these early Minutes of Conference contain perhaps the best epitome of his views, and may be somewhat at length quoted.

"Q. 1. What is it to be sanctified?

"A. To be renewed in the image of God, in righteousness and true holiness.

"Q. 2. Is faith the condition, or the instrument, of sanctification?

"A. It is both the condition and instrument of it. When we begin to believe, then sanctification begins. And as faith increases, holiness increases, till we are created anew.

"Q. 3. What is implied in being a perfect Christian?

"A. The loving the Lord our God with all our heart, and with all our mind, and soul, and strength, Deut. vi, 5; xxx, 6; Ezek. xxxvi, 25–29.

"Q. 4. Does this imply that all inward sin is taken away?

"A. Without doubt: or how could he be said to be saved 'from all his uncleannesses?' Ezek. xxxvi, 29."

And again:

"Q. 1. How much is allowed by our brethren who differ from us, with regard to entire sanctification?

"A. They grant, 1. That every one must be entirely sanctified in the article of death.

"2. That, till then, a believer daily grows in grace, comes nearer and nearer to perfection.

"3. That we ought to be continually pressing after this, and to exhort all others so to do.

"Q. 2. What do we allow to them?

"A. We grant, 1, That many of those who have died

in the faith, yea, the greater part of those we have known, were not sanctified throughout, not made perfect in love, till a little before death.

"2. That the term 'sanctified' is continually applied by St. Paul to all that were justified—were true believers.

"3. That by this term alone, he rarely—if ever—means, saved from all sin.

"4. That, consequently, it is not proper to use it in this sense, without adding the word 'wholly, entirely,' or the like.

"5. That the inspired writers almost continually speak of or to those who were justified; but very rarely either of or to those who were wholly sanctified.

"6. That, consequently, it behooves us to speak in public almost continually of the state of justification; but more rarely, at least in full and explicit terms, concerning entire sanctification.

"Q. 3. What then is the point wherein we divide?

"A. It is this: whether we should expect to be saved from all sin, before the article of death.

"Q. 4. Is there any clear Scripture promise of this? that God will save us from *all* sin?

"A. There is: Psalm cxxx, 8, 'He shall redeem Israel from *all* his sins.'

"This is more largely expressed in the prophecy of Ezekiel: 'Then will I sprinkle clean water upon you, and you shall be clean; from *all* your filthiness and from *all* your idols will I cleanse you. I will also save you from *all* your uncleannesses,' chap. xxxvi, 25, 29. No promise can be more clear. And to this the apostle plainly refers in that exhortation, 'Having these promises, let us cleanse ourselves from all filthiness of flesh and spirit, perfecting holiness in the fear of God,' 2 Cor. vii, 1. Equally clear and express is that ancient promise, 'The Lord thy God will circumcise thine heart, and the heart of thy seed, to love the Lord thy God with all thy heart, and with all thy soul,' Deut. xxx, 6.

"Q. 5. But does any *assertion* answerable to this, occur in the New Testament?

"A. There does, and that laid down in the plainest terms. So St. John iii, 8, 'For this purpose the Son of God was manifested that he might destroy the works of the devil;' the works of the devil, without any limitation or restriction; but all sin is the work of the devil. Parallel to which is that assertion of St. Paul, Eph. v, 25, 27, 'Christ loved the Church, and gave himself for it—that he might present it to himself a glorious Church, not having spot or wrinkle, or any such thing, but that it should be holy and without blemish.'

"And to the same effect is his assertion in the eighth of Romans, (verses 3, 4,) 'God sent his Son—that the righteousness of the law might be fulfilled in us, walking not after the flesh, but after the Spirit.'

"Q. 6. Does the New Testament afford any farther ground for expecting to be saved from all sin?

"A. Undoubtedly it does, both in those prayers and commands which are equivalent to the strongest assertions.

"Q. 7. What prayers do you mean?

"A. Prayers for entire sanctification; which, were there no such thing, would be mere mockery of God. Such in particular are 1. 'Deliver us from evil;' or rather, 'from the evil one.' Now, when this is done, when we are delivered from all evil, there can be no sin remaining. 2. 'Neither pray I for these alone, but for them also which shall believe on me through their word; that they all may be one, as thou Father art in me, and I in thee; that they also may be one in us: I in them and thou in me, that they may be made perfect in one,' John xvii, 20, 21, 23. 3. 'I bow my knees unto the God and Father of our Lord Jesus Christ—that he would grant you—that ye, being rooted and grounded in love, may be able to comprehend with all saints, what is the breadth, and length, and hight, and to know the love of Christ which passeth knowledge, that ye might be filled with all the fullness of God,' Eph. iii, 14, 16–19. 4. 'The very God of peace sanctify you wholly. And I pray God, your whole spirit, soul, and body, be preserved blameless, unto the coming of our Lord Jesus Christ,' 1 Thess. v, 23.

"Q. 8. What command is there to the same effect?

"A. 1. 'Be ye perfect, as your Father which is in heaven is perfect,' Matt. v, 48.

"2. 'Thou shalt love the Lord thy God with all thy heart, and with all thy soul, and with all thy mind,' Matt. xxii, 37. But if the love of God fill all the heart, there can be no sin there.

"Q. 9. But how does it appear, that this is to be done before the article of death?

"A. First, from the very nature of a command, which is not given to the dead, but to the living.

"Therefore, 'Thou shalt love God with all thy heart,' can not mean, 'Thou shalt do this when thou diest, but while thou livest.'

"Secondly, from express texts of Scripture:

"1. 'The grace of God that bringeth salvation hath appeared to all men, teaching us, that having renounced [ἀρνησάμενοι] ungodliness and worldly lusts, we should live soberly, righteously, and godly in this present world: looking for—the glorious appearing of our Lord Jesus Christ; who gave himself for us, that he might redeem us from *all* iniquity; and purify unto himself a peculiar people, zealous of good works,' Tit. ii, 11–14.

"2. 'He hath raised up a horn of salvation for us—to perform the mercy promised to our fathers: the oath which he sware to our father Abraham, that he would grant unto us, that we, being delivered out of the hands of our enemies, should serve him without fear, in holiness and righteousness before him, all the days of our life,' Luke i, 69, etc.

"Q. 16. Does not the harshly preaching perfection, tend to bring believers into a kind of bondage or slavish fear?

"A. It does. Therefore we should always place it in the most amiable light, so that it may excite only hope, joy, and desire.

"Q. 17. Why may we not continue in the joy of faith, even till we are made perfect?

"A. Why indeed? since holy grief does not quench this joy: since, even while we are under the cross, while we deeply partake of the sufferings of Christ, we may rejoice with joy unspeakable.

"Q. 18. Do we not discourage believers from rejoicing evermore?

"A. We ought not so to do. Let them, all their life long, rejoice unto God, so it be with reverence. And even if lightness or pride should mix with their joy, let us not strike at the joy itself—this is the gift of God—but at that lightness or pride that the evil may cease, and the good remain.

"Q. 20. But ought we not to be *troubled* on account of the sinful nature which still remains in us?

"A. It is good for us to have a deep sense of this, and to be much ashamed before the Lord. But this should only incite us the more earnestly to turn to Christ every moment, and to draw light, and life, and strength from him, that we may go on, conquering and to conquer. And therefore, when the sense of our sin most abounds, the sense of his love should much more abound."

The doctrine of assurance, and the source of it, the testimony of the Holy Spirit, as the Spirit of adoption, are frequently referred to in these early doctrinal conversations. This however is more fully stated in Mr. Wesley's sermons; and the following extracts will be necessary to present his views on this subject in their true light:

"But what is *the witness of the Spirit?* The original word μαρτυρία may be rendered either—as it is in several places—*the witness*, or, less ambiguously, *the testimony*, or *the record:* so it is rendered in our translation, 1 John v, 11, 'This is the record,' the testimony, the sum of what God testifies in all the inspired writings, 'that God hath given unto us eternal life, and this life is in his Son.' The testimony now under consideration is given by the Spirit of God to and with our spirit. He is the person testifying. What he testifies to us is, 'that we are the children of God.' The immediate result of this testimony is, 'the fruit of the Spirit;' namely, 'love, joy, peace; long-suffering, gentleness, goodness.' And without these, the testimony itself can not continue; for it is inevitably destroyed, not only by the commission of any outward sin, or the omission of known duty, but by giving way to any inward sin: in a word, by whatever grieves the Holy Spirit of God.

"2. I observed many years ago, It is hard to find words in the language of men to explain the deep things of God. Indeed, there are none that will adequately express what the Spirit of God works in his children. But, perhaps, one might say—desiring any who are taught of God to correct, soften, or strengthen the expression—By the 'testimony of the Spirit' I mean, an inward impression on the soul, whereby the Spirit of God immediately and directly witnesses to my spirit, that I am a child of God; that 'Jesus Christ hath loved me, and given himself for me;' that all my sins are blotted out, and I, even I, am reconciled to God.

"3. After twenty years' farther consideration, I see no cause to retract any part of this. Neither do I conceive how any of these expressions may be altered, so as to make them more intelligible. I can only add, that if any of the children of God will point out any other expressions which are more clear, or more agreeable to the word of God, I will readily lay these aside.

"4. Meantime, let it be observed, I do not mean hereby, that the Spirit of God testifies this by any outward voice: no, nor always by an inward voice, although he may do this sometimes. Neither do I suppose that he always applies to the heart—though he often may—one or more texts of Scripture. But he so works upon the soul by his immediate influence, and by a strong, though inexplicable operation, that the stormy wind and troubled waves subside, and there is a sweet calm: the heart resting as in the arms of Jesus, and the sinner being clearly satisfied that all his 'iniquities are forgiven, and his sins covered.'

"5. Now, what is the matter of dispute concerning this? Not, whether there be a witness or testimony of the Spirit. Not, whether the Spirit does testify with our spirit, that we are the children of God. None can deny this without flatly contradicting the Scriptures, and charging a lie upon the God of truth. Therefore, that there is a testimony of the Spirit, is acknowledged by all parties.

"6. Neither is it questioned, whether there is an indirect witness or testimony that we are the children of God. This is nearly, if not exactly, the same with 'the testimony of a good conscience toward God,' and is the result of reason or reflection on what we feel in our own souls. Strictly speaking, it is a conclusion drawn partly from the word of God and partly from our own experience. The word of God says, Every one who has the fruit of the Spirit is a child of God. Experience or inward consciousness tells me that I have the fruit of the Spirit; and hence I rationally conclude, therefore, I am a child of God. This is likewise allowed on all hands, and so is no matter of controversy.

"7. Nor do we assert, that there can be any real testimony of the Spirit, without the fruit of the Spirit. We assert, on the contrary, that the fruit of the Spirit immediately springs from this testimony; not always, indeed, in the same degree, even when the testimony is first given; and much less afterward: neither joy nor peace is always at one stay. No, nor love: as neither is the testimony itself always equally strong and clear.

"8. But the point in question is, whether there be any *direct testimony* of the Spirit at all; whether there be any other testimony of the Spirit than that which arises from a consciousness of the fruit.

"1. I believe there is, because that is the plain, natural meaning of the text, 'the Spirit itself beareth witness with our spirit, that we are the children of God.' It is manifest here are two witnesses mentioned, who together testify the same thing, the Spirit of God and our own spirit. The late bishop of London, in his sermon on this text, seems astonished that any one can doubt of this, which appears upon the very face of the words. Now, '*the testimony of our own spirit*,' says the bishop, 'is one, which is the consciousness of our own sincerity;' or, to express the same thing a little more clearly, the consciousness of the fruit of the Spirit. When our spirit is conscious of this, of love, joy, peace, long-suffering, gentleness, goodness, it easily infers, from these premises, that we are the children of God.

"2. It is true, that great man supposes the other witness to be 'the consciousness of our own good works.' This, he affirms, is 'the testimony of God's Spirit.' But this is included in the testimony of our own spirit: yea, and in sincerity, even according to the common sense of the word. So the apostle, 'Our rejoicing is this, the testimony of our conscience, that in simplicity and godly sincerity we have our conversation in the world:' where it is plain sincerity refers to our words and actions, at least as much as to our inward dispositions. So that this is not another witness, but the very same that he mentioned before: the consciousness of our good works being only one branch of the consciousness of our sincerity. Consequently, here is only one witness still. If, therefore, the text speaks of two witnesses, one of these is not the consciousness of our good works, neither of our sincerity: all this being manifestly contained in 'the testimony of our spirit.'

"3. What, then, is the other witness? This might easily be learned, if the text itself were not sufficiently clear, from the verse immediately preceding. 'Ye have received, not the spirit of bondage, but the Spirit of adoption, whereby we cry, Abba, Father.' It follows, 'The Spirit itself beareth witness with our spirit, that we are the children of God.'

"4. This is farther explained by the parallel text, Gal. iv, 6: 'Because ye are sons, God hath sent forth the Spirit of his Son into your hearts, crying, Abba, Father.' Is not this something *immediate* and *direct*, not the result of reflection or argumentation? Does not this Spirit cry, 'Abba, Father,' *in our hearts*, the moment it is given, antecedently to any reflection upon our sincerity, yea, to any reasoning whatsoever? And is not this the plain, natural sense of the words, which strikes any one as soon as he hears them? All these texts, then, in their most obvious meaning, describe a direct testimony of the Spirit.

"5. That *the testimony of the Spirit of God* must, in the very nature of things, be antecedent to *the testimony of our own spirit,* may appear from this single consideration. We must be holy in heart and life, before we can be conscious that we are so. But we must love God before we can be holy at all, this being the root of all holiness. Now, we can not love God, till we know he loves us; 'we love him because he first loved us.' And we can not know his love to us, till his Spirit witnesses it to our spirit. Since, therefore, the testimony of his Spirit must precede the love of God and all holiness, of consequence it must precede our consciousness thereof."

A doctrine so often misrepresented and misunderstood could not be so properly stated as in Mr. Wesley's own words; and as many, and those even professing to be sober Christians, have, principally with reference to this doctrine, frequently opened upon this venerable man the full cry of enthusiasm and fanatical delusion, it may be proper to add a few explanatory and defensive remarks, and that not merely for the sake of justice to his opinions, but in support of a great doctrine of revelation, most intimately connected with the hope and comfort of man.

And, 1. The doctrine of assurance as held by the founder of Methodism was not the assurance of *eternal* salvation, as held by the Calvinistic divines, but that persuasion which is given by the Holy Spirit to penitent and believing persons, that they are '*now* accepted of God, pardoned, and adopted into God's family." It was an assurance, therefore, on the ground of which no relaxation of religious effort could be pleaded, and no unwatchfulness of spirit or irregularity of life allowed: for he taught, that only by the lively exercise of the same humble and obedient faith in the merits and intercession of Christ, this state of mind could be maintained, and it was made by him a motive—influential as our desire of inward peace can be influential—to vigilance and obedience.

2. This doctrine can not be denied without disconnecting religion from peace of mind, and habitual consolation. For if it is the doctrine of the inspired records, and of all orthodox Churches, that man is by nature prone to evil, and that in practice he violates that law under which, as a creature, he is placed, and is thereby exposed to

punishment; if also it is there stated, that an act of grace and pardon is promised on the conditions of repentance toward God and faith in our Lord Jesus Christ; if that repentance implies consideration of our ways, a sense of the displeasure of almighty God, contrition of heart, and consequently trouble and grief of mind, mixed, however, with hope, inspired by the promise of forgiveness, and which leads to earnest supplication for the actual pardon of sin so promised, it will follow from these premises, either that forgiveness is not to be expected till after the termination of our course of probation, that is, in another life; and that, therefore, this trouble and apprehension of mind can only be assuaged by the hope we may have of a favorable final decision on our case; or, that sin is, in the present life, forgiven as often as it is thus repented of, and as often as we exercise the required and specific acts of trust in the merits of our Savior; but that this forgiveness of our sins is not in any way made known to us: so that we are left, as to our feelings, in precisely the same state as if sin were not forgiven till after death, namely, in grief and trouble of mind, relieved only by hope; or, that when sin is forgiven by the mercy of God through Christ, we are, by some means, assured of it, and peace and satisfaction of mind take the place of anxiety and fear.

The first of these conclusions is sufficiently disproved by the authority of Scripture, which exhibits justification as a blessing attainable in this life, and represents it as actually experienced by true believers. "Therefore, being justified by faith, etc. . . There is *now* no condemnation to them who are in Christ Jesus. . . Whosoever believeth is justified from all things," etc. The quotations might be multiplied, but these are decisive. The notion, that though an act of forgiveness may take place, we are unable to ascertain a fact so important to us, is also irreconcilable with many texts in which the writers of the

New Testament speak of an experience, not confined personally to themselves, or to those Christians who were endowed with spiritual gifts, but common to all Christians. "Being justified by faith, we have *peace* with God. . . We joy in God, by whom we have received the *reconciliation*. . . Being reconciled unto God by the death of his Son. . . We have not received the spirit of bondage again unto fear, but the Spirit of adoption whereby we cry, Abba, Father." To these may be added innumerable passages which express the comfort, the confidence, and the joy of Christians; their "friendship" with God; their "access" to him; their entire union and delightful intercourse with him; and their absolute confidence in the success of their prayers. All such passages are perfectly consistent with deep humility and self-diffidence; but they are irreconcilable with a state of hostility between the parties, and with an unascertained, and only hoped-for, restoration of friendship and favor.

3. The services of the Church of which Mr. Wesley was a minister, may be pleaded also in support of his opinions on this subject. Those services, though, with propriety, as being designed for the use, not of true Christians only, but of mixed congregations, they abound in acts of confession, and the expressions of spiritual grief, exhibit also this confidence and peace, as objects of earnest desire and hopeful anticipation, and as blessings attainable in the present life. We pray to be made "children by adoption and grace;" to be "relieved from the fear of punishment by the comfort of God's grace;" not to be "left comfortless, but that God, the King of glory, would send to us the Holy Ghost to comfort us;" and that by the same Spirit having a right judgment in all things, "we may evermore rejoice in his holy comfort." In the prayer directed to be used for one troubled in mind or in conscience, we have also the following impressive petitions:

"Break not the bruised reed, nor quench the smoking flax. Shut not up thy tender mercies in displeasure, but make him to hear of joy and gladness, that the bones which thou hast broken may rejoice. Deliver him from the fear of the *enemy*, and *lift up the light of thy countenance upon him, and give him peace.*" Now, unless it be contended, that by these petitions we are directed to seek what we can never find, and always to follow that which we can never overtake, the Church, in the spirit of the New Testament, assumes that the forgiveness of sins, and the relief of the sorrows of the penitent state, are attainable, with those consequent comforts and joys which can only arise from some assurance of mind, by whatever means and in whatever degree communicated, that we have a *personal* interest in the general promise, and that *we* are reconciled to God by the death of his Son. For since the general promise is made to many who will never be benefited by it, it can not of itself be the ground of a settled religious peace of mind. As it is a promise of blessings to be *individually* experienced, unless I can have personal experience of them, it holds up to hope what can never come into fruition.*

* "Faith is not merely a speculative but a practical acknowledgment of Jesus as the Christ—an *effort and motion of the mind toward God;* when the sinner, convinced of sin, accepts with thankfulness the proffered terms of pardon, and in humble confidence applying individually to himself the benefit of the general atonement, in the elevated language of a venerable father of the Church, drinks of the stream which flows from the Redeemer's side. The effect is, that in a little he is filled with that perfect love of God which casteth out fear—he cleaves to God with the entire affection of the soul. And from this active, lively faith, overcoming the world, subduing carnal self, all those good works do necessarily spring, which God hath before ordained that we should walk in them." (Bishop Horsley's Sermons.)

"The purchase, therefore, was paid at once, yet must be *severally reckoned* to every soul whom it shall benefit. If we have not a hand to take what Christ's hand doth either hold or offer, what is sufficient in him can not be effectual to us. The spiritual hand, whereby we apprehend the sweet offer of our Savior, is faith, which, in short, is no other than an affiance in the Mediator. Receive peace and be happy: believe, and

An assurance, therefore, that those sins which were felt to "be a burden intolerable" are forgiven, and that all ground of that apprehension of future punishment which causes the penitent to "*bewail* his manifold sins" is removed by restoration to the favor of the offended God, must be allowed, or nothing would be more incongruous and indeed impossible, than the comfort, the peace, the rejoicing of spirit, which, in the Scriptures, are attributed to believers. If, indeed, self-condemnation, and the apprehension of danger, had no foundation but in the imagination, the case would be totally altered. Where there is no danger, delverance is visionary; and the joy it inspires is raving, and not reason. But if a real danger exists, and if we can not escape it except by an act of grace on the part of almighty God, we must have some evidence of his gracious interposition in our case, or the guilty gloom will abide upon us. The more sincere and earnest a person is in the affairs of his salvation, the more miserable he must become if there be no possibility of his knowing that the wrath of God no longer abideth upon him: then the ways of wisdom would be no longer "ways of pleasantness, and paths of peace."

4. Few real Christians, therefore, have ever denied the possibility of our becoming so persuaded of the favor and good-will of God toward us as to produce substantial comfort to the mind; but they have differed in opinion as to the means by which this is acquired. Some have said that

thou hast received. Thus it is that we have an interest in all that God hath promised, or Christ hath performed. Thus have we from God both forgiveness and love, the ground of all whether peace or glory." (Bishop Hall's Heaven upon Earth.)

"It is the property of saving faith, that it hath a force to appropriate, and make Christ our own. Without this, a general remote belief would have been cold comfort. 'He loved *me*, and gave himself for *me*,' saith St. Paul. What saith St. Chrysostom? 'Did Christ die only for St. Paul? No. *Non excludit, sed appropriat;*' he excludes no others, but he will secure himself." (Bishop Brownrigg's Sermon on Easter Day.)

we obtain it by *inference;* others, by *the direct inward testimony* of the Holy Spirit. The latter, as we have seen, was the opinion of Mr. Wesley; but he never failed to connect this doctrine with another, which, on the authority of St. Paul, he calls "the witness of our own spirit, . . . the consciousness of having received, in and by the Spirit of adoption, the *tempers* mentioned in the word of God, as belonging to his adopted children—a consciousness that we are inwardly conformed, by the Spirit of God, to the image of his Son, and that we *walk* before him in justice, mercy, and truth, *doing* the things which are pleasing in his sight." These two testimonies he never put asunder, although he assigned them distinct offices; and this can not be overlooked if justice be done to his opinions. In order to prevent presumption, he reminds his readers that the direct testimony of the Holy Spirit is subsequent to true repentance and faith; and on the other hand, to guard against delusion, he asks, "How am I assured that I do not mistake the voice of the Spirit? Even by the testimony of my own spirit, 'by the answer of a good conscience toward God:' hereby you shall know that you are in no delusion, that you have not deceived your own soul. The immediate fruits of the Spirit ruling in the heart are love, joy, peace, bowels of mercies, humbleness of mind, meekness, gentleness, long-suffering. And the outward fruits are the doing good to all men, and a uniform obedience to all the commands of God." Where, then, is the enthusiasm of the doctrine as thus stated? An enthusiastic doctrine is unsupported by the sacred records; but in confirmation of this we read, "The Spirit itself beareth witness with our spirit, that we are the children of God." Here the witnesses are the Spirit of God, and our own spirit; and the fact to which the testimony is given, is, that "we are the children of God. . . And because ye are sons, God hath sent forth the Spirit of his Son into your hearts, crying, Abba, Father!" To these passages may be added all those texts which speak of the inward intercourse of the Spirit of God with believers; of his dwelling in them, and abiding with them as the source of comfort and peace; and which, therefore, imply the doctrine. Nor can such passages be interpreted otherwise than as teaching the doctrine of assurance, conveyed immediately to the mind of true believers by the Holy Spirit, without allowing such principles of construction as would render the sense of Scripture uncertain, and unsettle the evidence of some of the most important doctrines of our religion.

It is true that a more "sober" and "less dangerous" method, as it has been called, of obtaining a comfortable assurance of our justification before God, has been insisted upon as equally consistent with the word of God; but, upon examination, it will be found delusive. This is what is termed a process of *inference*, and is thus explained. The question at issue is, "Am I a child of God?" The Scriptures declare that "as many as are led by the Spirit of God are the sons of God." I inquire, then, whether I have the Spirit of God; and, in order to determine this, I examine whether I have "the fruits of the Spirit." Now, "the fruits of the Spirit are love, joy, peace, gentleness, goodness, meekness, faith, temperance;" and having sufficient evidence of the existence of these fruits, I conclude that I have the Spirit of God, and am, therefore, a pardoned and accepted child of God. This is the statement. But, among these enumerated fruits of the Spirit, we find *love, joy,* and *peace,* as well as gentleness, goodness, meekness, fidelity, and temperance; and if it be said that no man has a right to assume that "he is so led by the Spirit of God," as to conclude that he is a child of God, who has only the affections of "peace and joy" to ground his confidence upon, we have as good a reason to affirm the same thing, if he has "meekness and temperance," without "love, and peace, and joy;" the love, the peace, and the joy being as much fruits of the Spirit as the moral qualities also enumerated.

But can "love," love to God as our *Father*—"peace," peace with God, as in a state of *friendship* with us—and "joy," "joy in God by whom we have received the *reconciliation*"—exist at all without a previous or concomitant assurance of the Divine forgiveness and favor? Surely nothing is so clear, that it is not possible to love God as a Father and a Friend, while he is still regarded as an offended Sovereign and a vengeful Judge; and that to feel a sense of his displeasure, and to be at "peace" with him, and to rejoice in him, are contradictions: and if so, the very ground of this inference, that we are in the Divine favor, and adopted into his family, is taken away. This whole inferential process proceeds upon dividing the undivided fruit of the Spirit, for which we have assuredly no authority; nor, indeed, have we any reason to conclude that we have *that* gentleness, *that* goodness, *that* meekness, etc., which the apostle describes, should the "love, joy, and peace," which he places among the leading fruits of the Spirit, be wanting. If, then, the whole undivided fruit of the Spirit be taken as the medium of ascertaining the fact of our forgiveness and adoption, and if it is even absurd to suppose that we can love God, while yet we feel him to be angry with us, and that we can rejoice and have peace, while the fearful apprehensions of the consequences of unremitted sin are not removed from our minds, then the only ground of our "love, joy, and peace" is pardon revealed and witnessed, directly and immediately, by the Spirit of adoption.*

* The *precedence* of the direct witness of the Spirit of God to the indirect witness of our own, and the dependence of the latter upon the former, are very clearly stated by three divines of great authority; to

The mind of Mr. Wesley was, also, too discriminating not to perceive, that, in the scheme of attaining assurance by inference from moral changes only, there was a total neglect of the offices explicitly ascribed to the Holy Spirit in the New Testament, and which on this scheme are unnecessary. These are clearly stated to be that of "*bearing witness*" with the spirits of believers, that they are the children of God; that of *the Spirit of adoption*, by which they call God *Father* in the special sense in which it is correlative to that sonship which we obtain only by a justifying faith in Christ; and that of a *Comforter*, promised to the disciples to abide with them "forever," that their "joy might be full."

whom I refer the rather, because many of their followers of the present day have become very obscure in their statements of this branch of Christian experience:

"St. Paul means that the Spirit of God gives such a testimony to us, that he being our guide and teacher, our spirit concludes our adoption of God to be certain. For our own mind, of itself, independent of the preceding testimony of the Spirit, [*nisi præeunte Spiritus testimonio,*] could not produce this persuasion in us. For while the Spirit witnesses that we are the sons of God, he, at the same time, inspires this confidence into our minds, that we are bold to call God our Father." (Calvin on Romans viii, 16.)

"Romans viii, 16, 'The Spirit itself beareth witness with our spirits that we are the sons of God:' the witness which our own spirits do give to our adoption is the *work and effect* of the Holy Spirit in us; if it were not, it would be false, and not confirmed by the testimony of the Spirit himself, who is the Spirit of truth. 'And none knoweth the things of God but the Spirit of God,' 1 Cor. ii, 11. If he declare not our sonship in us, and to us, we can not know it. How doth he then bear witness to our spirits? What is the distinct testimony? It must be some such act of his that evidenceth itself to be from him, *immediately*, to them that are concerned in it, that is, those to whom it is given." (Dr. Owen on the Spirit, sect. 9.)

"The Spirit of adoption doth not only excite us to call upon God as our Father, but it doth ascertain and assure us, as *before*, that we are his children. And this it doth not by any outward voice, as God the Father to Jesus Christ, nor by an angel, as to Daniel and the Virgin Mary, but by an inward and secret suggestion, whereby he raiseth our hearts to this persuasion, that God is our Father, and we are his children. *This is not the testimony of the graces and operations of the Spirit, but of the Spirit itself.*" (Poole on Romans viii, 16.)

Enough has been said on this subject to show that Mr. Wesley, on this doctrine, was neither rash nor inconsiderate, much less enthusiastic. It is grounded on no forced, no fanciful interpretation of Scripture; and it maintains, as of possible attainment, one of the most important and richest comforts of the human mind. It leaves no doubt as to a question which, while problematical, must, if we are earnest in seeking our salvation, be fatal to our peace; it supposes an intercourse between God and the minds of good men, which is, surely in the full and genuine spirit of the Christian religion, eminently called the "ministration of the Spirit;" and it is, as taught by him, vitally connected with sober, practical piety. That, like the doctrine of justification by faith alone, it is capable of abuse, is very true. Many have perverted both the one and the other. Faith with some has been made a discharge from duty; and with respect to the direct witness of the Spirit, fancy has, no doubt, been taken, in some instances, for reality. But this could never legitimately follow from the holy preaching of the founder of Methodism. His view of the doctrine is so opposed to license and real enthusiasm, to pride and self-sufficiency, that it can only be made to encourage them by so manifest a perversion, that it has never occurred except among those most ignorant of his writings. He never encouraged any to expect this grace but the truly penitent, and he prescribed to them "fruits meet for repentance." He believed that justification was always accompanied by a renewal of the heart, and as constantly taught, that the comfort "of the Holy Ghost" could remain the portion only of the humble and spiritual, and was uniformly and exclusively connected with a sanctifying and obedient faith. He saw that the fruits of the Spirit were "love, joy, peace," as well as "gentleness, goodness, meekness, and faith;" but he also taught that all who were not living under the constant influence of the latter would fatally deceive themselves by any pretensions to the former.

Such were the views of the first Methodists, on these important points, and such are the unchanged opinions of their successors to this day. They may be called *peculiarities*, because they differed in some respects from the same doctrines of justification, faith, assurance, and sanctification, when associated with various modifications of Calvinism; and although somewhat similar doctrines are found in many Arminian writers, yet in the theology of the Wesleys they derive life and vigor from the stronger views of the grace of God which were taught them by their Moravian and Calvinistic brethren.

No man more honestly sought truth than Mr. Wesley, and none more rigidly tried all systems by the law and the testimony. As to *authority* he was "a man of one book;" and whatever may be thought peculiar in his views, he drew from that source by the best application of his judgment.* He wanted not, however, authority of another

* The following beautiful and striking passage, illustrative of the above remark, is from the preface to his sermons:

"To candid, reasonable men, I am not afraid to lay open what have been the inmost thoughts of my heart. I have thought, I am a creature of a day, passing through life, as an arrow through the air. I am a spirit come from God, and returning to God: just hovering over the great gulf; till, a few moments hence, I am no more seen! I drop into an unchangeable eternity! I want to know one thing, the way to heaven: how to land safe on that happy shore. God himself has condescended to teach the way; for this very end he came from heaven. He hath written it down in a book! O give me that book! At any price, give me the book of God! I have it: here is knowledge enough for me. Let me be *homo unius libri*. [A man of one book.] Here then I am, far from the busy ways of men. I sit down alone! only God is here. In his presence, I read his book; for this end, to find my way to heaven. Is there a doubt concerning the meaning of what I read? Does any thing appear dark and intricate? I lift up my heart to the Father of lights. Lord, is it not thy word, 'If any man lack wisdom, let him ask of God?' Thou 'givest liberally, and upbraidest not.' Thou hast said, 'If any be willing to do thy will, he shall know.' I am willing to do: let me know thy will. I then search after and consider parallel passages of Scripture, 'comparing

kind for his leading opinions. On the article of justification he agreed with all the Reformed Churches; his notion of saving faith was substantially that of the divines of the best ages of the Reformation, and of still earlier times; nor was his doctrine of the direct witness of the Spirit to our adoption one as to which any exclusive peculiarity could be attributed to him, except that he more largely and zealously preached it than any other man in modern times. It was the doctrine of Luther, Calvin, Beza, Arminius, and others of equally eminent rank abroad and at home. We may add also that such prelates and divines as Hooper, Andrews, Hall, Hooker, Usher, Brownrigg, Wake, Pearson, Barrow, Owen, and Poole, have expressed it in terms as explicit, and with equal deference to the testimony of the word of God.

The minutes of the early conferences are not confined to doctrinal discussions; but we see in them the frame of the discipline of the body, growing up from year to year, and embodied in many copious directions and arrangements. The most important of these remain in force to this day, although some in a maturer state of the society have gone into disuse. This discipline need not particularly be specified, as being for the most part well known and established; but a few miscellaneous particulars may be selected from the minutes of several successive years, as being in some instances of great importance, and in others characteristic, and occasionally amusing.

The duty of obeying bishops was considered at the very first conference of 1744; and the conclusion is, that this obedience extends only to things indifferent; a rather strict narrowing up of canonical obedience, at this early

spiritual things with spiritual.' I meditate thereon, with all the attention and earnestness of which my mind is capable. If any doubt still remain, I consult those who are experienced in the things of God; and then, the writings, whereby, being dead, they yet speak. And what I thus learn, that I teach."

period. The establishment of "a seminary for laborers" was a subject of consideration at this conference also, but was postponed. The reasons why it was not afterward carried into effect appear to have been, the rapid spread of the work, and the consequent demand for additional preachers. Mr. Wesley also looked to Kingswood school as subsidiary to this design. In the mean time he enjoined the study of the Greek and Latin poets and historians, as well as the original Scriptures, upon the preachers; and a large course of theological and general reading. This shows his views of the subserviency of literature to usefulness in the ministry.*

No preaching was to be continued where societies were not raised up. It seems to have been a fixed maxim with the Wesleys, not to spend time in cultivating barren ground. No band ticket was to be given to the wearers of ruffles—a practice which, though then common, accorded not with their notions either of good taste or of the duty of economizing money in order to charity. Equal strictness was observed as to the dress of females. *Simplex munditiis* [plainness with neatness] was Mr. Wesley's classical rule; and the exclusive "ornament of a meek and quiet spirit," his Scriptural one. All who married unbelievers were to be expelled from society. The people were required not only to stand during singing, but while the text was read. This excellent custom now continues only in Ireland. Dram-drinking and

* As the subject of a seminary or college has been of late brought under discussion, it may be not uninteresting to those who have not access to the manuscript copies of the first minutes, extracts from which only are in print, to give the passages which relate to this subject from the complete minutes of 1744 and 1745. In the former year it is asked, "Can we have a seminary for laborers?" and the answer is, "If God spare us till another conference." The next year the subject was resumed, "Can we have a seminary for laborers yet?" Answer: "Not till God gives us a proper tutor." So that the institution was actually resolved upon, and delayed only by circumstances.

pawnbroking were also sins of exclusion: so that, in fact, the Methodist societies were the first temperance societies. Reading was enjoined as a religious duty, and every preacher was bound to circulate every new book published or recommended by Mr. Wesley; so anxious was he to spread useful knowledge through society, and to improve at once the intellects and hearts of his people. The officers of the society are said to be "clergymen, assistants, helpers, stewards, leaders of bands, leaders of classes, visitors of the sick, schoolmasters, and housekeepers." The last class will in the present day create a smile; but at that time their business was to reside in the houses built in several of the large towns, where both Mr. Wesley and the preachers took up their abode during their stay. They were elderly and pious women, who, being once invested with an official character, extended it sometimes from the *house* to the *church*, to the occasional annoyance of the preachers. As married preachers began to occupy the houses, they were at length dispensed with. Smuggling and the buying of uncustomed goods had frequent anathemas dealt out against them, and expulsion was the unmitigated penalty. Respect of persons was strictly forbidden to the preachers, who were also enjoined to be easy of access to all. Every preacher was to promise rather to break a limb than to disappoint a congregation. No preacher was to be continued who could not preach twice every day. He was to take care that only suitable tunes should be sung; and was advised to use in public only hymns of prayer and praise, not those descriptive of states of mind. Lemonade was to be taken after preaching, or candied orange peel, or a little warm ale; but egg and wine, and late suppers, are denounced as downright poison. The views entertained of a call to the ministry deserve quoting in full:

"Q. How shall we try those who think they are moved by the Holy Ghost, and called of God to preach?

"A. Inquire, 1. Do they know God as a pardoning God? Have they the love of God abiding in them? Do they desire and seek nothing but God? And are they holy in all manner of conversation?

"2. Have they *gifts*—as well as *grace*—for the work? Have they a clear, sound understanding? Have they a right judgment in the things of God? Have they a just conception of salvation by faith? And has God given them any degree of utterance? Do they speak justly, readily, clearly?

"3. Have they fruit? Are any truly convinced of sin, and converted to God, by their preaching?

"As long as these three marks concur in any, we believe he is called of God to preach."

The probation of the preachers was at first one year; but was afterward extended to four. The following minute of 1745 shows that Mr. Charles Wesley was never considered as co-ordinate with his brother in the government of the societies:

"Q. Should not my brother *follow* me step by step, and Mr. Meriton [another clergyman] him?

"A. As far as possible."

What Mr. Wesley was next to write, was a matter on which he asked the advice of the conference for several years. A little stock of medicines, to be dispensed to the poor, was ordered to be provided for London, Bristol, and Newcastle. It is not generally known that Mr. Wesley pursued a course of regular medical study, while at Oxford. Preachers were cautioned against giving out long hymns, and were exhorted to choose the tunes, that so they might be suitable to the hymn. Copies of the minutes of the conference were to be written out and given to each member present: when the number of preachers increased, printing was adopted.* In 1749 it seems to have been proposed that the societies every-where should be considered *one*, of which the London society should be the mother church. This, however, came to nothing. The societies, indeed, were one, but the center of union was first Mr. Wesley himself, then the conference of preachers. In the same year all chapels were directed to be built after the model of that of Rotherham, and the number of circuits, each very extensive, had increased to twenty-two. Regular funds for the support of the preachers, and for aiding worn-out preachers, began now to be established. A regular settlement of the chapels upon trustees had been enjoined in 1749; and in 1765 a person was appointed to be sent through England to survey the deeds, and supply wanting trustees. All chapel windows were to be sashed; no "tub pulpits" were to be allowed; and men and women were every-where to sit apart. The societies are warned against *little oaths*, such as "my life," "my honor," etc., and against "compliments," and unmeaning words. In general, many are reproved for *talking* too much, and *reading* too little. In 1776 all octagon chapels are directed to be built like that at Yarm; and all square ones like that at Scarboro. No Chinese paling was to be set up before any chapel; and the people are forbidden to crowd into the preachers' houses, as though they were coffee-houses. No leaders' meeting was to be held without the presence of a preacher, and the spirit of debating at all meetings was to be strictly guarded against.

* Perhaps not more than one or two manuscript copies of the complete minutes of the conferences from 1744 to 1747 are in existence. That which lies before me, and from which extracts have been made in the preceding pages, wants two or three of the first pages of the minutes of 1744. It was not written by Mr. Wesley, but is a copy corrected by his own hand in different places. This is mentioned, as several of the extracts will be new even to some of the senior preachers.

If bankrupts did not pay their debts when they are able, they were to be excluded the society. Sluts were to be kept out of the preachers' houses, and cleanliness was held to be next to godliness.

Thus, to a number of little things among many greater and weightier matters, the active mind, the taste, and the orderly habits of the founder of Methodism applied itself. Every thing was, however, kind and bland in his manner of injunction; and when he was disappointed as to the exact observance of his regulations, his displeasure was admirably proportioned to the weight of the case. No man generally knew better how to estimate the relative importance of things, and to give each its proper place and rank, although it would be to deny to him the infirmity of human nature to suppose that this rule of proportion was always observed. If little things were by him sometimes made great, this praise, however, he had without abatement, that he never made great things little.

The notices of the deaths of the preachers, year by year, in the early minutes, all bear the impress of the brevity and point of Mr. Wesley's style. The first time that the regular question, "What preachers have died this year?" appears, is in the minutes of 1777. A few sketches of character from this laconic obituary in different years, will illustrate his manner of keeping these annual records:

"Thomas Hosking, a young man, just entering on the work; zealous, active, and of an unblamable behavior. And Richard Burke, a man of faith and patience, made perfect through sufferings: one who joined the wisdom and calmness of age with the simplicity of childhood."

"Richard Boardman, a pious, good-natured, sensible man, greatly beloved of all that knew him. He was one of the two first that freely offered themselves to the service of our brethren in America. He died of an apoplectic fit, and preached the night before his death. It seems he might have been eminently useful, but good is the will of the Lord.

"Robert Swindells had been with us above forty years. He was an Israelite indeed. In all those years I never knew him to speak a word which he did not mean; and he always spoke the truth in love; I believe no one ever heard him speak an unkind word. He went through exquisite pain—by the stone—for many years; but he was not weary. He was still

'Patient in bearing ill, and doing well.'

"One thing he had almost peculiar to himself; he had no enemy! So remarkably was that word fulfilled, 'Blessed are the merciful; for they shall obtain mercy.'

"James Barry was for many years a faithful laborer in our Lord's vineyard. And as he labored much, so he suffered much; but with unwearied patience. In his death he suffered nothing, stealing quietly away in a kind of lethargy.

"Thomas Payne was a bold soldier of Jesus Christ. His temper was uncommonly vehement; but before he went hence, all that vehemence was gone, and the lion was become a lamb. He went away in the full triumph of faith, praising God with his latest breath.

"Robert Naylor, a zealous, active young man, was caught away by a fever, in the strength of his years. But it was in a good hour; for he returned to Him whom his soul loved, in the full assurance of faith.

"A fall from his horse, which was at first thought of little consequence, occasioned the death of John Livermore; a plain, honest man, much devoted to God, and determined to live and die in the best of services.

"John Prickard, a man thoroughly devoted to God, and an eminent pattern of holiness: and Jacob Rowell, a faithful old soldier, fairly worn out in his Master's service.

"Thomas Mitchell, an old soldier of Jesus Christ.

"John Fletcher, [vicar of Madeley,] a pattern of all holiness, scarce to be paralleled in a century; and J. Peacock, young in years, but old in grace; a pattern of all holiness, full of faith, and love, and zeal for God.

"Jeremiah Robertshaw, who was a good soldier of Jesus Christ, fairly worn out in his Master's service. He was a pattern of patience for many years, laboring under sharp, and almost continual pain, of meekness and gentleness to all men, and of simplicity and godly sincerity.

"Joshua Keighley, who was a young man deeply devoted to God, and greatly beloved by all that knew him. He was

> 'About the marriage state to prove,
> But death had swifter wings than love.'

"Charles Wesley, who, after spending fourscore years with much sorrow and pain, quietly retired into Abraham's bosom. He had no disease; but after a gradual decay of some months,

> 'The weary wheels of life stood still at last.'

His least praise was, his talent for poetry: although Dr. Watts did not scruple to say, that 'that single poem, *Wrestling Jacob*, was worth all the verses he himself had written.'

"John Mayly, worn out in the service of his Master: he suffered much in his last illness, and died triumphant in the Lord."

Thus neither his brother Charles, nor Mr. Fletcher, had a longer eulogy than any other preacher; so great was Mr. Wesley's love of brevity.

The "care of the Churches" now had come upon him, and was increasing; he had a responsibility to man as well as to God for the right management of a people whom his labors and those of his coadjutors had formed into a body distinct from the National Church, and indeed as to all ecclesiastical control separate from it, although, in part, the members were attendants on her services. He was most anxious that this people should be raised to the highest state of religious and moral excellence; that they should be exemplary in all the relations of life, civil and domestic; wise in the Scriptures; well-read in useful books; self-denying in their conduct almost to severity; and liberal in their charities, in order to which they were enjoined to abstain from all unnecessary indulgences, and to be plain and frugal in dress. They were expected to rise early to a religious service at five o'clock, and to attend some evening service, if possible, several times in the week; and, beside their own Sabbath meetings, to be punctual in observing the services of the Church. They were to add to all this the most zealous efforts to do good to the bodies and souls of those who were around them, and to persevere in all these things with an ardor and an unweariedness equal to his own. With these great objects so strongly impressed upon his mind, that he should feel compelled to superintend every part of the system he had put into operation, and attend to every thing great or little which he conceived to retard or accelerate its motion, was the natural consequence, and became with him matter of imperative conscience. A nobler object man could not propose to himself, than thus to spread the truth and the example of a living and practical Christianity through the land, and to revive the spirit of piety in a fallen Church, and among a neglected people; and he had sufficient proofs from the wonderful success which had followed, success, too, of the most unequivocal kind, because the hearts of "multitudes had been turned to the Lord," that he was in the path of duty, and that the work was of God; but the standard which he set up in his own mind, and in his rules, both for his preachers and people, was so high, that, in the midst of all those refreshing joys which the review of the work often brought, feelings of disappointment, and something like vexation, occasionally break forth in the minutes of his conferences. On the preachers in their circuits an activity, an occupation of time, and an attention to various duties had been enjoined, similar to his own; but the regulations, under which they were placed, were often minute, and in minor matters they were often failing, even when, in other respects, they most faithfully and laboriously fulfilled their ministry. Stewards, leaders, and trustees, came in also occasionally for their share of remonstrance and rebuke on account of inattention; while the societies, as being exposed to the various errors of the day, and to the ordinary influences of the temptations of an earthly state, sometimes declined, and then again revived; in some places were negligent, and in others were almost every thing he could wish them to be, so that he could say, with an apostle, respecting them, "Great is my glorying." To Mr. Wesley's frequent trials of patience were to be added the controversies, often very illiberal, in which he was engaged, and the constant misrepresentations and persecutions, to which he and the societies were for many years exposed. When all these things are considered, and when it is also recollected how much every man who himself works by a strict method is apt to be affected by the irregularities and carelessness of others, the full and tranquil flow of his zeal and energy, and the temper, at once so strict and so mild, which breathes in the minutes of the conferences, place him in a very admirable point of light. Vexation and disappointment passed over his serene mind like the light clouds over the bright summer field. The principle of an entire devotedness to serve God, and "his generation according to the will of God," in him never relaxed; and the words of one of his own beautiful hymns, to which, in advanced life, in a conversation with a friend, he once alluded, as expressing his own past and habitual experience, were in him finely realized:

"Jesus, confirm my heart's desire,
To work, and speak, and think for thee;
Still let me guard the holy fire,
And still stir up thy gift in me.

Ready for all thy perfect will,
My acts of faith, and love repeat,
Till death thy endless mercies seal,
And make the sacrifice complete."

CHAPTER X.

The doctrines and principal branches of the discipline of the body being generally settled, Mr. Wesley desisted from publishing extracts from the minutes of the annual conferences from 1749 to 1765. In the minutes of the latter year we find for the first time a published list of the circuits, and of the preachers.* The circuits were then *twenty-five* in England, extending from Cornwall to Newcastle upon Tyne; in Scotland *four;* in Wales *two;* in Ireland *eight;* in all *thirty-nine.* The total number of the preachers, given up entirely to the work, and acting under Mr. Wesley's direction, had then risen to *ninety-two.* But it will be necessary to look back upon the labors of the two brothers during this interval. Instead, however, of tracing Mr. Wesley's journeys into various parts of the

* In the manuscript copy of the first minutes before mentioned, lists of circuits occasionally appear, as in 1746: "How many circuits are there? *Answer.*—Seven. 1. London, including Surrey and Kent. 2. Bristol, including Somersetshire, Portland, Wiltshire, Oxfordshire, and Gloucestershire. 3. Cornwall. 4. Evesham, including Shrewsbury, Leominster, Hereford, Stroud, and Wednesbury. 5. York, including Yorkshire, Cheshire, Lancashire, Derbyshire, Nottinghamshire, and Lincolnshire. 6. Newcastle. 7. Wales."

kingdom in detail from his journals, which present one uniform and unwearied activity in his high calling, it will be sufficient to notice the principal incidents.

Mr. Charles Wesley married in 1749, yet still continued his labors with but little abatement. He was in London at the time of the earthquake, and was preaching at the Foundery early in the morning when the second shock occurred. The entry in his journal presents him in a sublime attitude, and may be given as an instance of what may be truly called the majesty of faith: "March 8, 1750. This morning, a quarter after five, we had another shock of an earthquake, far more violent than that of February 8th. I was just repeating my text, when it shook the Foundery so violently, that we all expected it to fall on our heads. A great cry followed from the women and children. I immediately called out, 'Therefore, we will not fear, though the earth be moved, and the hills be carried into the midst of the sea; for the Lord of hosts is with us; the God of Jacob is our refuge.' He filled my heart with faith, and my mouth with words, shaking their souls as well as their bodies. The earth moved westward, then eastward, then westward again, through all London and Westminster. It was a strong and jarring motion, attended with a rumbling noise like that of thunder. Many houses were much shaken, and some chimneys thrown down, but without any farther hurt." (Journal.)

The impression produced in London by this visitation is thus recorded in a letter from Mr. Briggs to Mr. John Wesley: "This great city has been, for some days past, under terrible apprehensions of another earthquake. Yesterday, thousands fled out of town, it having been confidently asserted by a dragoon, that he had a revelation that great part of London, and Westminster especially, would be destroyed by an earthquake on the 4th instant between twelve and one at night. The whole city was under direful apprehensions. Places of worship were crowded with frightened sinners, especially our two chapels, and the Tabernacle, where Mr. Whitefield preached. Several of the classes came to their leaders, and desired that they would spend the night with them in prayer; which was done, and God gave them a blessing. Indeed, all around was awful. Being not at all convinced of the prophet's mission, and having no call from any of my brethren, I went to bed at my usual time, believing I was safe in the hands of Christ; and likewise that, by doing so, I should be the more ready to rise to the preaching in the morning; which I did, praised be my kind Protector." In a postscript he adds, "Though crowds left the town on Wednesday night, yet crowds were left behind; multitudes of whom, for fear of being suddenly overwhelmed, left their houses, and repaired to the fields, and open places in the city. Tower Hill, Moorfields, but, above all, Hyde Park, were filled, the best part of the night, with men, women, and children, lamenting. Some, with stronger imaginations than others, mostly women, ran crying in the streets, 'An earthquake! an earthquake!' Such distress, perhaps, is not recorded to have happened before in this careless city. Mr. Whitefield preached at midnight in Hyde Park. Surely God will visit this city; it will be a time of mercy to some. O may I be found watching!" (Whitehead's Life.)

So ready were these great preachers of the time to take advantage of every event by which they might lead men to God. One knows not which most to admire, Mr. Whitefield preaching at midnight in Hyde Park to a crowd of affrighted people, expecting the earth to swallow them up, or Mr. Charles Wesley, with the very ground reeling under him, calling out to the congregation, "Therefore, we will not fear, though the earth be moved, and the hills be carried into the midst of the sea; for the Lord of hosts is with us; the God of Jacob is our refuge," and using this as his text.

The detected immorality and expulsion of one of the preachers, James Wheatley,* led the brothers to determine upon instituting a more strict inquiry into the life and behavior of every preacher in connection with them. Mr. Charles Wesley undertook that office, as being, perhaps, more confident in his own discernment of character, and less influenced by affection to the preachers. The result was, however, highly creditable to them, for no irregularity of conduct was detected; but as the visitation was not conducted, to say the least of it, in the bland manner in which it would have been executed by Mr. John Wesley, who was indeed alone regarded as the father of the connection, it led, as might be expected, to bickerings. Many of the preachers did not come up to Mr. Charles Wesley's notions of attachment to the Church; some began to wish a little larger share in the government; and a few did not rise to his standard of ministerial abilities, although of this he judged only by report. From this time a stronger feeling of disunion between the preachers and him grew up, which ultimately led to his taking a much less active part in the affairs of the body, except to interfere occasionally with his advice, and, in still later years, now and then to censure the increasing irregularity of his brother's proceedings. The fact was, Mr. John Wesley was only carried forward

* Mr. Wesley has been censured by some persons for sanctioning the publication of a pamphlet on the "Duties of Husbands and Wives," written, as they supposed, by this wretched man, and especially for doing this after the misconduct of the author had been brought to light. But the charge is without foundation. The pamphlet in question was not written by James Wheatley, the preacher, but by William Whateley, the Puritan minister of Banbury; a man of the most exemplary piety, and one of the best practical writers of his age, who died in 1639. The work from which the pamphlet was extracted is entitled, "A Bride-Bush," and bears the date of 1619, which was at least a hundred years before Wheatley was born.

by the same stream which had impelled both the brothers irretrievably far beyond the line prescribed to regular Churchmen; and Charles was chafing himself with the vain attempt to buffet back the tide, or at least to render it stationary. He saw, no doubt, during the visitation which he had lately undertaken, a growing tendency to separation from the Church both among many of the preachers and the people, which, although it was the natural, nay, almost necessary, result of the circumstances in which they were placed, he somewhat uncandidly attributed to the ambition of the former; and, laying it down as a necessary qualification, that no preacher ought to be employed without giving some explicit pledge as to his purpose of adherence to the Church, he attempted to associate himself with his brother in the management, with equal power to call preachers into the work, and then to govern them. He appears laudably to have wished to improve their talents; but he proposed also greatly to restrict their number, and to subject them to stricter tests as to their attachment to the Establishment. Here began an important difference between the two brothers. Some impression was made upon the mind of Mr. John Wesley by his brother's letters written to him during his tour of inquisition, principally as they exaggerated the growing danger of separation from the Church; and upon Charles' return to London, John was persuaded, although "with difficulty," to sign an agreement, engaging that no preacher should be called into the work except by both of them conjointly, nor any readmitted but with mutual consent. The intention of Charles was evidently to obtain a controlling power over his brother's proceedings; but there was one great rule to which Mr. John Wesley was more steadily faithful. This was to carry on and extend that which he knew to be the work of God, without regarding probable future consequences of separation from the

Church after his death;* which was in fact the principle on which they had agreed at the first conference of 1774, (see pages 136, 137,) and to which Charles stood pledged as fully as himself. It seems, therefore, that when Mr. John Wesley more fully discovered his brother's intention to restrict the number of preachers, under the plea of employing only men of superior abilities, and more especially after all that had passed between Charles and them during the inquisitorial visitation just named had been reported to him, he felt little disposed to assent to his having co-authority with himself in the management of the connection; and Charles withdrawing more from public life, the government remained with John still more exclusively than before. This *acquisition* of entire authority, as it has been called, has been referred to by one of Mr. Wesley's biographers as a proof of his ambition, and his inability to bear a rival. The affection of the brothers itself affords a strong presumption against the existence of any such jealousy between them: and beside we find no previous instance of a single struggle for authority. But the fact was, that John always led the way, as sole director, with Charles as a confidential adviser; and they long acted together in this relation as with one soul. In the present case it was Charles only who grasped at a power which he had not previously possessed; and this was for a moment yielded, though hesitatingly, upon an *ex parte* statement, and under views not fully manifested. When, however, those were disclosed, John recoiled; and his brother, by a partial secession from the work, left the whole care of it upon his hands. Mr. Charles Wesley had, indeed, some time before this, rather hastily interposed to prevent the marriage of his brother with a very pious and respectable woman,

* "Church or no Church," he observes in one of his letters to Charles, "we must attend to the work of saving souls." And in another, "I neither set it up, nor pull it down: but let you and I build the city of God."

Mrs. Grace Murray, to whom he was attached, and that probably under the influence of a little family pride, as she was not in an elevated rank of life;* and this affair, in which there appears to have been somewhat of treachery, although no doubt well intended, had for the first time interrupted their harmony. But it is not all likely that any feeling of resentment remained in the mind of John; and indeed the commission of visitation, with which Charles had been invested, was a sufficient proof that confidence had been restored. The true reason of the difference was, that the one wished to contract the work, from fear of the probable consequence of separation from the Church; the other pursued his course of enlarging and extending it, resolving to prevent separation to the best of his power, but leaving that issue in higher hands. Still, however, the affection of the brothers remained unimpaired.

In the year 1751, as Mr. Wesley was still resolved to marry, believing that his usefulness would be thereby pro-

* Mr. Charles Wesley and Mr. Whitefield got the lady hastily married to Mr. Bennett, one of the preachers, while his brother was at a distance, probably not being himself aware, any more than she, of the strength of his attachment. The following extract from one of Mr. Wesley's unpublished letters shows, however, that he deeply felt it: "The sons of Zeruiah were too strong for me. The whole world fought against me, but, above all, *my own familiar friend*. Then was the word fulfilled, 'Son of man, behold, I take from thee the desire of thine eyes at a stroke, yet shalt thou not lament, neither shall thy tears run down.' The fatal, irrecoverable stroke was struck on Thursday last. Yesterday I saw my friend—that was—and him to whom she is sacrificed. 'But why should a living man complain, a man for the punishment of his sins?'" The following passages, from a letter of the venerable vicar of Shoreham to Mr. Charles, intimate how much he sympathized with Mr. John Wesley on the occasion, and how anxious he was to prevent a breach between the brothers, which this, certainly unbrotherly, act, the only one into which Charles seems to have been betrayed, was near producing. The letter is dated Shoreham, 1749: "Yours came this day to hand. I leave you to guess how such news must affect a person whose very soul is one with yours, and our friend. Let me conjure you to soothe his sorrows. Pour nothing but oil and wine into his wounds. Indulge no views, no designs, but what tend to the honor of God, the promoting the kingdom of his dear Son, and the healing of our wounded friend. How would the Philistines rejoice

moted, he took to wife Mrs. Vizelle, a widow lady of independent fortune. She was a woman of a cultivated understanding, as her remaining letters testify; and that she appeared to Mr. Wesley to possess every other qualification, which promised to increase both his usefulness and happiness, we may conclude from his having made choice of her as his companion. We must suppose, also, that as he never intended to relax his labors, and adopt a more settled mode of life, this matter also was fully understood, and agreed to before marriage. But whatever good qualities Mrs. Wesley might appear to have, they were at length wholly swallowed up in the fierce passion of jealousy. For some time she traveled with him; but becoming weary of this, and not being able to bind him down to a more domestic life, this passion increased. The violence of her temper broke out, also, against Mr. Charles Wesley and his wife. This arose from very trifling circumstances, magnified into personal slights; and various unpleasant

could they hear that Saul and Jonathan were in danger from their own swords!"

I have seen an explanation of Mr. Charles Wesley's conduct in this affair by the late Miss Wesley; but as the matter occurred before her birth, I have much doubt as to her perfect knowledge of the circumstances, so that I shall not fully state it. She lays the fault chiefly on the lady's want of explicitness; states that she formed a previous, but concealed, attachment to Mr. Bennett; and that Mr. Charles having discovered this, he hastened the marriage.

Whatever the ostensible reason might be, it was no doubt eagerly seized by Mr. Charles Wesley as an occasion of breaking off a match, which he appears some time before to have interfered with, influenced, it is most probable, by the consideration of Mrs. Murray's inferior rank. From this feeling Mr. John Wesley was much more exempt, as the following anecdote, found in one of Miss Wesley's letters, indicates in a way very creditable to his amiable temper: "My brother Charles had an attachment in early youth to an amiable girl of inferior birth; this was much opposed by my mother and her family, who mentioned it with concern to my uncle. Finding from my father that this was the chief objection, my uncle only replied, 'Then there is no family blood? I hear the girl is good; but of no family?' 'Nor fortune either,' said my mother. He made no reply but sent my brother a sum of money as a wedding present; and I believe sincerely regretted that he was ultimately crossed in his inclination."

scenes are mentioned in Mr. Charles Wesley's unpublished letters, and described with a sprightliness which, while it shows that he was unconscious of having given her any just cause of offense, equally indicates the absence of sympathy. Perhaps this had been worn out by the long continuance of her caustic attacks upon him and his family, both by word and by letter. Certainly Mr. Charles Wesley must have felt her to be an annoying correspondent, if we may judge from some of her letters still preserved, and in which, singular as it may appear, she zealously contends for her husband's superiority, and is indignant that he should be wearing himself out with excessive labor, while Charles was remaining at home in ease. Dr. Southey has candidly and justly stated the matter between her and her persecuted husband:

"Had Mrs. Wesley been capable of understanding her husband's character, she could not possibly have been jealous; but the spirit of jealousy possessed her, and drove her to the most unwarrantable actions. It is said that she frequently traveled a hundred miles for the purpose of watching, from a window, who was in the carriage with him when he entered a town. She searched his pockets, opened his letters, put his letters and papers into the hands of his enemies, in hopes that they might be made use of to blast his character, and sometimes laid violent hands upon him and tore his hair. She frequently left his house, and, upon his earnest entreaties, returned again; till, after having thus disquieted twenty years of his life, as far as it was possible for any domestic vexations to disquiet a man whose life was passed in locomotion, she seized on part of his journals, and many other papers, which were never restored, and departed, leaving word that she never intended to return. He simply states the fact in his journal, saying that he knew not what the cause had been; and he briefly adds, *Non eam reliqui, non dimisi, non revocabo:* 'I did not forsake her, I did not dismiss her, I will not recall her.' " (Southey's Life.)

The worst part of Mrs. Wesley's conduct, and which only the supposition of a degree of insanity, excited by jealousy, can palliate, was that she interpolated several letters, which she had intercepted, so as to make them bear a bad construction; and as Mr. Wesley had always maintained a large correspondence with all classes of persons, and among others with pious females, in some of whose letters there were strong expressions of Christian affection, she availed herself of this means of defaming him. Some of these she read to different persons in private, and especially to Mr. Wesley's opponents and enemies, adding extempore passages in the same tone of voice, but taking care not to allow the letters themselves to be read by the auditors; and in one or two instances she published interpolated or forged letters in the public prints. How he conducted himself amidst these vexations, the following passages in a letter from Miss Wesley to a friend, written a little before her death, will show. They are at once important, as explanatory of the kind of annoyance to which this unhappy marriage subjected her uncle, and as containing an anecdote strongly illustrative of his character:

"I think it was in the year 1775 my uncle promised to take me with him to Canterbury and Dover. About this time Mrs. Wesley had obtained some letters which she used to the most injurious purposes, misinterpreting spiritual expressions, and interpolating words. These she read to some Calvinists, and they were to be sent to the Morning Post. A Calvinist gentleman, who esteemed my father and uncle, came to the former, and told him that, for the sake of religion, the publication should be stopped, and Mr. John Wesley be allowed to answer for himself. As Mrs. Wesley had read, but did not show the letters to him, he had some doubts of their authenticity; and, though they were addressed to Mr. John Wesley, they might be forgeries; at any rate he ought not to leave town at such a juncture, but clear the matter satisfactorily.

"My dear father, to whom the reputation of my uncle was far dearer than his own, immediately saw the importance of refutation, and set off to the Foundery to induce him to postpone his journey, while I, in my own mind, was lamenting such a disappointment, having anticipated it with all the impatience natural to my years. Never shall I forget the manner in which my father accosted my mother on his return home. 'My brother,' says he, 'is indeed an extraordinary man. I placed before him the importance of the character of a minister; the evil consequences which might result from his indifference to it; the cause of religion; stumbling-blocks cast in the way of the weak; and urged him by every relative and public motive to answer for himself, and stop the publication. His reply was, Brother, when I devoted to God my ease, my time, my life, did I except my reputation? No. Tell Sally I will take her to Canterbury to-morrow.'

"I ought to add, that the letters in question were satisfactorily proved to be mutilated, and no scandal resulted from his trust in God."

Some of these letters, mutilated, interpolated, or forged by this unhappy woman, have got into different hands, and are still preserved. In the papers of the Wesley family, recently collected, there are, however, sufficient materials for a full explanation of the whole case in detail; but as Mr. Wesley himself spared it, no one will, I presume, ever farther disturb this unpleasant affair, unless some publication on the part of an enemy, for the sake of gain, or to gratify a party feeling, should render it necessary to defend the character of this holy and unsuspecting man.*

* The following passage, in a letter from Mr. Perronet to Mr. Charles

A school at Kingswood, near Bristol, for the children of the poor, had been long built; but that neighborhood was also fixed upon by Mr. Wesley for an institution, in which the sons of the preachers, and those of the richer Methodists, should receive at once the best education, and the most efficient religious training. It was opened in June, 1748, and he published soon after a "Short Account" of the institution, with the plan of education adopted, particularly for those who were to remain so long in it as to go through a course of academical learning; and adds, "Whoever carefully goes through this course will be a better scholar than nine in ten of the graduates at Oxford and Cambridge." In this great and good design he

Wesley, dated Shoreham, November 3, 1752, shows that Mr. Wesley's matrimonial afflictions must have commenced a very short time after marriage: "I am truly concerned that matters are in so melancholy a situation. I think the unhappy lady is most to be pitied, though the gentleman's case is mournful enough. Their sufferings proceed from widely different causes. His are the visible chastisements of a loving Father. Hers the immediate effects of an angry, bitter spirit; and, indeed, it is a sad consideration, that, after so many months have elapsed, the same warmth and bitterness should remain." This truly venerable and holy man died in 1785, in the ninety-second year of his age. Two days before his death, his granddaughter, Miss Briggs, who attended him day and night, read to him the three last chapters of Isaiah. He then desired her to go into the garden, to take a little fresh air. Upon her return, she found him in an ecstasy, with the tears running down his cheeks, from a deep and lively sense of the glorious things which she had just been reading to him; and which he believed would shortly be fulfilled in a still more glorious sense than heretofore. He continued unspeakably happy all that day. On Sunday, his happiness seemed even to increase, till he retired to rest. Miss Briggs then went into the room to see if any thing was wanting; and as she stood at the foot of the bed, he smiled and said, "God bless thee, my dear child, and all that belongs to thee! Yea, he will bless thee!" This he earnestly repeated till she left the room. When she went in the next morning, his happy spirit had returned to God!

Mr. Perronet, like those great and good men, Messrs. Grimshaw and Fletcher, continued steadily attached to Mr. Wesley and to the Methodists. He received the preachers joyfully, fitted up a room in the parsonage house for their use, and attended their ministry himself at every opportunity. His house was one of the regular places of the Kent circuit, and so continued to the day of his death. All his family were members of the society, and two of his sons preachers.

grasped at too much; and the school came in time to be confined to the sons of the preachers, and ceased, as at first, to receive boarders. Indeed, from the increase of the preachers' families, the school was rapidly filled, and required enlargement at different times; and finally it was necessary to establish a second school at Woodhouse Grove, in Yorkshire. The circumstance of the preachers being so much from home, and removing every one or two years from their circuits, rendered an institution of this kind imperative; and, as it necessarily grew out of the system of itinerancy, it was cheerfully and liberally, though often inadequately, supported by private subscriptions, and a public annual collection throughout all the congregations. The most gratifying moral results have followed; and a useful and religious education has been secured to the sons of the preachers, many of whom, especially of late years, having afforded undeniable proofs of genuine conversion, and of a Divine call to public labors in the Church of Christ, have been admitted into the ministry, and are among its highest ornaments, or its brightest hopes. It is, however, to be regretted that the original plan of Mr. Wesley, to found an institution for the connection at large, which should unite the advantages of a school and a college, has not been resumed in later and more favorable times. Various circumstances, at that early period, militated against the success of this excellent project, which have gradually disappeared; and if in that infant state of the cause, Mr. Wesley wisely thought that Methodism should provide for all its wants, religious and educational, within itself, much more incumbent is it to do so now. Many of the sons of our friends, for want of such a provision, have been placed in schools where their religious principles have been neglected or perverted, and too often have been taught to ridicule, or to be ashamed of, the religious profession of their fathers.*

In 1753 Mr. Wesley visited Scotland a second time, and preached at Glasgow to large congregations. He had gone there on the invitation of that excellent man, Dr. Gillies, minister of the College kirk, who, a few days after he left, wrote to him as follows: "The singing of hymns here meets with greater opposition than I expected. Serious people are much divided. Those of better understanding and education are silent; but many others are so prejudiced, especially at the singing publicly, that they speak openly against it, and look upon me as led to do a very wrong or sinful thing. I beg your advice, whether to answer them only by continuing in the practice of the thing, with such as have freedom to join, looking to the Lord for a blessing upon his own ordinance; or, if I should publish a sheet of arguments from reason, and Scripture, and the example of the godly. Your experience of the most effectual way of dealing with people's prejudices, makes your advice on this head of the greater importance.

"I bless the Lord for the benefit and comfort of your acquantaince, for your important assistance in my Historical Collections, and for your edifying conversation and sermons in this place. May our gracious God prosper you wherever you are! O my dear sir, pray for your brother, that I may be employed in doing something for

[* The striking application of the above remarks to the state of things in relation to Methodism in this country, can not escape the observation of intelligent readers; and it is no little gratification to perceive that the testimony of both Mr. Wesley's and Mr. Watson's approbation stands thus recorded in support of the views which, with many others of our brethren in America, we have steadily entertained and frequently expressed, on this important subject. The public developments recently made of the fatal consequences of sending Protestant youth to seminaries under the direction of Papists especially, are worthy of the deepest and most serious consideration.—AMER. EDIT.]

the advancement of his glory, who has done so much for me, and who is my only hope."

This prejudice in favor of their own doggerel version of the Psalms of David generally remains among the Scotch to this day; and even in the Wesleyan societies raised up there, great opposition was at first made to the use of hymns. The Historical Collections of Dr. Gillies, mentioned in his letter, do justice to that revival of religion in this country of which Methodism was the instrument, and gives many valuable accounts of similar revivals, and special effusions of the Holy Spirit upon the Churches of Christ in different ages.

The following extracts from two of Mr. Wesley's letters written about this time, show how meekly this admirable man could take reproof, and with how patient a temper he could deal with peevish and complaining men.

"You give," says he, "five reasons why the Rev. Mr. P—— will come no more among us: 1. 'Because we despise the ministers of the Church of England.' This I flatly deny. I am answering letters this very post, which bitterly blame me for just the contrary. 2. 'Because so much backbiting and evil speaking is suffered among our people.' It is not suffered; all possible means are used, both to prevent and remove it. 3. 'Because I, who have written so much against hoarding up money, have put out seven hundred pounds to interest.' I never put a sixpence out to interest since I was born; nor had I ever one hun-hundred pounds together, my own, since I came into the world. 4. 'Because our lay preachers have told many stories of my brother and me.' If they did, I am sorry for them: when I hear the particulars I can answer, and perhaps make those ashamed who believed them. 5. 'Because we did not help a friend in distress.' We did help him as far as we were able. 'But we might have made his case known to Mr. G——, Lady H——, etc.'

So we did, more than once; but we could not pull money from them, whether they would or no. Therefore, these reasons are of no weight. You conclude with praying, that God would remove pride and malice from among us. Of pride I have too much; of malice I have none: however, the prayer is good, and I thank you for it."

The other letter from which I shall give an extract was written apparently to a gentleman of some rank and influence: "I do not recollect, for I kept no copy of my last, that I charged you with want of humility, or meekness. Doubtless these may be found in the most splendid palaces. But did they ever move a man to build a splendid palace? Upon what motive you did this, I know not; but you are to answer it to God, not to me.

"If your soul is as much alive to God, if your thirst after pardon and holiness is as strong, if you are as dead to the desire of the eye and the pride of life, as you were six or seven years ago, I rejoice; if not, I pray God you may; and then you will know how to value a real friend.

"With regard to myself, you do well to warn me against 'popularity, a thirst of power and of applause; against envy, producing a seeming contempt for the conveniences or grandeur of this life; against an affected humility; against sparing from myself to give to others, from no other motive than ostentation.' I am not conscious to myself, that this is my case. However, the warning is always friendly, and it is always seasonable, considering how deceitful my heart is, and how many the enemies that surround me. What follows I do not understand: 'You behold me in the ditch, wherein you helped, though innocently, to cast me, and with a Levitical pity pass by on the other side. He and you, sir, have not any merit, though Providence should permit all these sufferings to work together for my good.' I do not comprehend one line of this, and, therefore, can not plead either guilty or not guilty. I presume they are some that are dependent on me, who, you say, 'keep not the commandments of God; who show a repugnance to serve and obey; who are as full of pride and arrogance, as of filth and nastiness; who do not pay lawful debts, nor comply with civil obligations; who make the waiting on the offices of religion a plea for sloth and idleness; who, after I had strongly recommended them, did not perform their moral duty, but increased the number of those incumbrances which they forced on you, against your will.' To this I can only say, 1. I know not whom you mean; I am not certain that I can so much as guess at one of them. 2. Whoever they are, had they followed my instructions, they would have acted in a quite different manner. 3. If you will tell me them by name, I will renounce all fellowship with them.

In the autumn of 1753 Mr. Wesley was threatened with consumption, brought on by repeated attacks of cold. By the advice of Dr. Fothergill he retired to Lewisham; and here, not knowing how it might please God to dispose of him, and wishing "to prevent vile panegyric" in case of death, he wrote his epitaph as follows:

HERE LIETH

THE BODY OF JOHN WESLEY,

A BRAND PLUCKED OUT OF THE BURNING;

WHO DIED OF A CONSUMPTION IN THE FIFTY-FIRST
YEAR OF HIS AGE.

NOT LEAVING, AFTER HIS DEBTS ARE PAID,
TEN POUNDS BEHIND HIM:

PRAYING,
God be merciful to me an unprofitable servant!

He ordered that this, if any, inscription should be placed on his tombstone.

During Mr. Wesley's illness, Mr. Whitefield wrote to him in a strain which shows the fullness of affection which existed between those great and good men, notwithstand ing their differences of opinion:

"*Bristol, December* 3, 1753.

"REV. AND VERY DEAR SIR,—If seeing you so weak when leaving London distressed me, the news and prospects of your approaching dissolution hath quite weighed me down. I pity myself and the Church, but not you. A radiant throne awaits you, and erelong you will enter into your Master's joy. Yonder he stands with a massy crown, ready to put it on your head, amidst an admiring throng of saints and angels. But I, poor I, that have been waiting for my dissolution these nineteen years, must be left behind to grovel here below! Well! this is my comfort: it can not be long ere the chariots will be sent even for worthless me. If prayers can detain them, even you, reverend and very dear sir, shall not leave us yet: but if the decree has gone forth, that you must now fall asleep in Jesus, may he kiss your soul away, and give you to die in the embraces of triumphant love! If in the land of the dying, I hope to pay my last respects to you next week. If not, reverend and very dear sir, F—a—r—e—w—e—ll. *Ego sequar, etsi non passibus œquis.** My heart is too big, tears trickle down too fast, and you are, I fear, too weak for me to enlarge. Underneath you may there be Christ's everlasting arms!

"I commend you to his never-failing mercy, and am, reverend and very dear sir, your most affectionate, sympathizing, and afflicted younger brother in the Gospel of our common Lord, G. WHITEFIELD."

From Lewisham he removed to the Hot Wells, near Bristol; and, ever intent upon improving time, began his Notes on the New Testament. For some time after this, he appears to have remained in an invalid state. During his retirement at Paddington he read a work which made

* "I shall follow, though not with equal steps."

a forcible attack upon his prejudices as a Churchman; and soon afterward, another, which still farther shook the deference he had once been disposed to pay to ecclesiastical antiquity.

"In my hours of walking, I read Dr. Calamy's Abridgment of Mr. Baxter's Life. What a scene is opened there! In spite of all my prejudices of education, I could not but see, that the poor Non-Conformists had been used without either justice or mercy; and that many of the Protestant bishops of King Charles had neither more religion nor humanity than the Popish bishops of Queen Mary."

"I read Mr. Baxter's History of the Councils. It is utterly astonishing, and would be wholly incredible, but that his vouchers are beyond all exception. What a company of execrable wretches have they been—one can not justly give them a milder title—who have, almost in every age since St. Cyprian, taken upon them to govern the Church! How has one council been perpetually cursing another, and delivering all over to Satan, whether predecessors or cotemporaries, who did not implicitly receive their determinations, though generally trifling, sometimes false, and frequently unintelligible, or self-contradictory! Surely Mohammedanism was let loose to reform the Christians! I know not but Constantinople has gained by the change."

During Mr. Wesley's illness, Mr. Charles Wesley went forth to visit the societies, and to supply his brother's place.

In 1755, at the conference held in Leeds, a subject which had been frequently stirring itself, was formally discussed:

"The point on which we desired all the preachers to speak their minds at large, was, whether we ought to separate from the Church. Whatever was advanced on one side or the other was seriously and calmly considered: and on the third day we were all fully agreed in that general conclusion, that, whether it was *lawful* or not, it was no ways *expedient*."

Part of the preachers were, without restraint, permitted to speak in favor of a measure, which, in former conferences, would not have been listened to in the shape of discussion; and the conclusion was, that the question of the lawfulness of separation was evaded, and the whole matter was reduced to "expediency." Of this conference we have no minutes; but where was Mr. Charles Wesley?* Mr. Charles Perronet and some others, for whom Mr. Wesley had great respect, were at this time urging him to make full provision for the spiritual wants of his people, as being in fact in a state of real and hopeless separation from the Church; and he did some years afterward so far relax, as to allow of preaching in Church hours under certain circumstances, as 1. When the minister was wicked, or held pernicious doctrine; 2. When the churches would not contain the population of a town, or where the church was distant. In that case he prescribed reading the psalms and lessons and part of the liturgy. And for this purpose, as well as for the use of the American societies, he published his Abridgment of the Common Prayer, under the title of the "Sunday Service of the Methodists."

In 1756 he printed an Address to the Clergy, plain, affectionate, and powerful; breathing at once the spirit of an apostle, and the feeling of a brother. Happy if that call had been heard! He might perhaps be influenced in this by a still lingering hope of a revival of the spirit of zeal and piety among the ministers of the Established

* Three years after, Mr. Wesley published twelve reasons against separation, all, however, of a prudential kind. To these Mr. Charles Wesley added his separate testimony; but as to *himself*, he adds that he thought it not *lawful*. Here, then, was another difference in the views of the brothers.

Church; in which case that separation of his people from the Church, which he began to foresee as otherwise inevitable, he thought might be prevented; and this he had undoubtedly much at heart. Under the same view it probably was, that in 1764 he addressed a circular to all the serious clergy whom he knew, inviting them to a closer co-operation in promoting the influence of religion in the land, without any sacrifice of opinion, and being still at liberty, as to outward order, to remain "quite regular, or quite irregular, or partly regular and partly irregular." Of the thirty-four clergymen addressed, only three returned any answer. This seems to have surprised both him and some of his biographers. The reason is, however, very obvious: Mr. Wesley did not propose to abandon his plan and his preachers, or to get the latter ordained and settled in curacies, as proposed a few years before by Mr. Walker of Truro; and the matter had now obviously gone too far for the clergy to attach themselves to Methodism. They saw, with perhaps clearer eyes than Mr. Wesley's, that the Methodists could not now be embodied in the Church; and that for them to co-operate directly with him, would only be to partake of his reproach, and to put difficulties in their own way, to which they had not the same call. A few clergymen, and but a few, still continued to give him, with fullness of heart, the right hand of fellowship, and to co-operate in some degree with him. Backward he could not go; but the forward career of still more extended usefulness was before him. From this time he gave up all hope of a formal connection with even the pious clergy. "They are," he observes, "a rope of sand, and such they will continue;" and he therefore set himself with deep seriousness to perpetuate the union of his preachers. At the conference of 1769 he read a paper, the object of which was to bind the preachers together by a closer tie, and to provide for the continuance of their union after his death. They were to engage solemnly to devote themselves to God, to preach the old Methodist doctrines, and to maintain the whole Methodist discipline: after Mr. Wesley's death they were to repair to London, and those who chose to act in concert were to draw up articles of agreement; while such as did not so agree were to be dismissed "in the most friendly way possible." They were then to choose a committee by vote, each of the members of which was to be moderator in his turn, and this committee was to enjoy Mr. Wesley's power of proposing preachers to be admitted or excluded, of appointing their stations for the ensuing year, and of fixing the time of the next conference. This appears to have been the first sketch of an ecclesiastical constitution for the body, and it mainly consisted in the entire delegation of the power which Mr. Wesley had always, to a committee of preachers to be chosen by the rest when assembled in conference. The form of government he thus proposed was, therefore, a species of episcopacy, to be exercised by a committee of three, five, or seven, as the case might be. Another and a more eligible provision was subsequently made; but this sufficiently shows that Mr. Wesley had given up all hope of union with the Church; and his efforts were henceforth directed merely to prevent any thing like formal separation, and the open renunciation of her communion, during his own life, by allowing his preachers to administer the sacraments.

About this time much prejudice was excited against Mr. Wesley in Scotland by the republication of Hervey's Eleven Letters. He had three times visited this country; and, preaching only upon the fundamental truths of Christianity, had been received with great affection. The societies had increased, and several of his preachers were stationed in different towns. Lady Frances Gardiner, the widow of Colonel Gardiner, and other persons eminent for piety and rank, attended the Methodist ministry; but the publication of this wretched work caused a temporary odium. Hervey, who had been one of the little band at Oxford, became a Calvinist; and, as his notions grew more rigid with age, so his former feelings of gratitude and friendship to Mr. Wesley were blunted. He had also fallen into the hands of Cudworth, a decided Antinomian, who "put in and out" of the Letters "what he pleased." They were not, however, published till Hervey's death, and against his dying injunction. It is just to so excellent a man to record this fact; but the work was published in England, and republished, with a violent preface by Dr. Erskine, in Scotland; and among the Calvinists it produced the effect of inspiring great horror of Mr. Wesley as a most pestilent heretic, whom it was doing God service to abuse without measure or modesty. The feelings of Mr. Charles Wesley, at this treatment of his brother, may be gathered from the answer he returned upon being requested to write Hervey's epitaph:

ON BEING DESIRED TO WRITE AN EPITAPH FOR MR. JAMES HERVEY.

"O'erreached, impell'd by a sly Gnostic's art,
To stab his father, guide, and faithful friend,
Would pious Hervey act the accuser's part?
And *could* a life like his in malice end?

No: by redeeming love the snare is broke;
In death his rash ingratitude he blames;
Desires and *wills* the evil to revoke,
And dooms the unfinish'd libel to the flames.

Who then for filthy gain betray'd his trust,
And show'd a kinsman's fault in open light?
Let *him* adorn the monumental bust—
Th' encomium fair in brass or marble write:

Or if they need a nobler trophy raise,
As long as Theron and Aspasio live,
Let Madan or Romaine record his praise;
Enough that Wesley's brother can *forgive!*"*

The unfavorable impression made by Hervey's Letters,

* Mr. Charles Wesley, however, afterward wrote and published some verses upon Mr. Hervey's death in which the kind recollections of old

surcharged by Cudworth's Antinomian venom, was, however, quickly effaced from all but the bigots; and with them, judging from Moncrief's Life of Erskine, it remains to this day. In his future visits to Scotland Mr. Wesley was received with marks of the highest respect, and at Perth he had the freedom of the city handsomely conferred upon him.

CHAPTER XI.

METHODISM having begun to make some progress in America, in consequence of the emigration of some of the members of the society from England and Ireland,* Mr. Wesley inquired of the preachers of the conference of

friendship are embodied, and the anticipations of a happy meeting in heaven are sweetly expressed. The following are the concluding stanzas·

"Father, to us vouchsafe the grace,
Which brought our friend victorious through;
Let us his shining footsteps trace,
Let us his steadfast faith pursue;
Follow this follower of the Lamb,
And conquer all through Jesus' name.

Free from the law of sin and death,
Free from the Antinomian leaven,
He led his Master's life beneath;
And, laboring for the rest of heaven,
By active love and watchful prayer,
He show'd his heart already there.

O might we all, like him, believe,
And keep the faith, and win the prize'
Father, prepare and then receive
Our hallow'd spirits to the skies,
To chant with all our friends above,
Thy glorious, everlasting love."

[* Ireland seems to have had the special honor of furnishing the chief instruments of forming the first Methodist societies in America. *Mr. Philip Embury*, who formed the first permanent society in the city of New York, in 1766, and *Mr. Robert Strawbridge*, in Frederick county Maryland, in the same year, were both from Ireland.—AMERICAN EDIT.]

1769, whether any of them would embark in that service. Messrs. Boardman and Pilmoor, two excellent men, of good gifts, volunteered their services, and were sent to take the charge of the societies. From this time the work spread with great rapidity; more than twenty preachers had devoted themselves to it previously to the war of independence; and societies were raised up in Maryland, Virginia, New York, and Pennsylvania.* During the war they still prosecuted their labors; though as several of them took the side of the mother country, they were exposed to danger.† Others, with more discretion, held on their way in silence, speaking only of the things of God. The warm loyalty of Mr. Wesley led him to publish a pamphlet on the subject of the quarrel, entitled, "A Calm address to the American Colonies;" but the copies which were shipped for America were laid hold of by a friend, who suppressed

[* New Jersey, and we think Delaware, ought to be added here; and in 1776 a circuit was formed in North Carolina also. Delaware especially ought ever to be honored by us for her generous and early protection to Methodism in the time of its greatest trial. It was within that small state, where the laws—to quote the words of Mr. Cooper—were more favorable, and the rulers and influential men more friendly, that Mr. Asbury, when the storm of the Revolutionary war was at its hight, and persecution raged furiously, found an asylum in the house of his never-to-be-forgotten friend, *Judge White.*—AMERICAN EDIT.]

[† Some of the English preachers did act imprudently in this respect, and were under the necessity, in consequence, of leaving America. Mr. Asbury's course was marked "with more discretion;" which we are happy to perceive is also Mr. Watson's view of the subject. Of the American preachers, there is no evidence within our knowledge that any of them "took the side of the mother country;" although some of them, as well as of the members, were subjected to suspicion and persecution in consequence of their connection with Mr. Wesley, a known loyalist, and of the imprudence of some of the English preachers above mentioned; and also on account of their own conscientious scruples in relation to the spirit and practice of war in general, and particularly in regard to the nature of the oaths required of them in some of the states, and which they refused to take. For a fuller account of those times and scenes, the reader may consult the *Life of Garrettson* by Dr. Bangs, and a small volume entitled *Cooper on Asbury*, by Rev. Ezekiel Cooper.—AMERICAN EDIT.]

them; so that the work remained unknown in the colonies till a considerable time afterward. This was probably a fortunate incident for the infant cause. After the war had terminated, political views were of course laid aside, and Mr. Wesley made a provision for the government of his American societies, which will be subsequently adverted to. They became, of course, independent of British Methodism, but have most honorably preserved the doctrines, the general discipline, and, above all, the spirit of the body. Great, and even astonishing, has been their success in that new and rising country, to the wide-spread settlements of which their plan of itinerancy was admirably adapted. The Methodists are become, as to numbers, the leading religious body of the Union; and their annual increase is very great. In the last year it was thirty-six thousand, making a total in their communion of one thousand, nine hundred ministers, and four hundred and seventy-six thousand members, having, as stated in a recent statistical account published in the United States, upward of two millions, five hundred thousand of the population under their immediate influence. In the number of their ministers, members, and congregations, the Baptists nearly equal the Methodists; and these two bodies, both itinerant in their labors,* have left all the other religious denominations far behind. It is also satisfactory to remark, that the leading preachers and

[* As regards the Baptists, this is a mistake. In their numbers, too, both of ministers and members, however respectable, they are, we think, much less nearly equal to those of the Methodist community than our excellent author seems to suppose. In making a correct statistical comparison of the number of ministers particularly, in the two communions, on the principle of enumeration which we believe our Baptist brethren adopt, all the local as well as the itinerant ministers of the Methodist Episcopal Church ought to be included; and then there is almost no comparison. We make not this note with any view or disposition to disparage, in any respect, the numerous and respectable denomination to which it relates, but simply for the sake of what we believe to be due in a faithful record of historical facts.—AMERICAN EDIT.]

members of the Methodist Church in the United States appear to be looking forward with enlarged views, and with prudent regard, to the future, and to aim at the cultivation of learning in conjunction with piety. Several colleges have been from time to time established; and recently a university, for the education of the youth of the American connection has been founded.* The work in the United States has been distinguished by frequent and extraordinary revivals of religion, in which a signal effect has been produced upon the moral condition of large districts of country, and great numbers of people have been rapidly brought under a concern for their salvation. In the contemplation of results so vast, and in so few years, we may devoutly exclaim, "What hath God wrought!"

The mention of what are called revivals of religion in the United States may properly here lead us to notice, that, in Great Britain also, almost every Methodist society has at different times experienced some sudden and extraordinary increase of members, the result of what has been believed to be, and that not without good reason, a special effusion of Divine influence upon the minds of men. Sometimes these effects have attended the preaching of eminently-energetic preachers, but have often appeared where those stationed in the circuits have not been remarkably distinguished for energy or pathos. Sometimes they have followed the continued and earnest prayers of the people; at others they have come suddenly and unlooked for. The effects, however, have been, that the

[* The Wesleyan University, recently established at Middletown, in the state of Connecticut, is by no means designed for the education of the youth of the Methodist connection exclusively. It is founded on the general principles of other American colleges and universities, and for the education of youth generally. All classes, without subjection to any religious test, or any question in regard to their religious tenets, provided only their moral conduct be good, are admitted on the same terms, and to the enjoyment of equal privileges.—AMERICAN EDIT.]

piety of the societies has been greatly quickened, and rendered more deep and active, and that their number has increased; and of the real conversion of many, who have thus been wrought upon, often very suddenly, the best evidence has been afforded. To sudden conversions, as such, great objections have been indeed taken. For these, however, there is but little reason; for if we believe the testimony of Scripture, that the Spirit is not only given to the disciples of Christ, *after* they assume that character, but *in order to* their becoming such, that, according to the words of our Lord, this Spirit is sent "to convince the world of sin," to the end that they may believe in Christ, and that the Gospel, faithfully and fully proclaimed by the ministers of Christ, is "the power of God unto salvation to every one that believeth," and is made so by the accompanying influence of the Holy Ghost, who shall prescribe a mode to Divine operation? Who, if he believes in such an influence accompanying the truth, shall presume to say that when that truth is proposed, the attention of the careless shall be roused only by a gradual and slow process?—that the heart shall not be brought into a state of right feeling as to eternal concerns, but by a reiteration of means which we think most adapted to produce that effect?—that no influence on the mind is genuine and Divine, if it operates not in a prescribed manner?—that the Holy Spirit shall not avail himself of the variety which exists in the mental constitutions of men, to effect his purposes of mercy by different methods?—and that the operations of grace shall not present, as well as those of nature, that beauteous variety which so much illustrates the glory of Him "who worketh all in all?" And, farther, who shall say, that even the peculiarities of men's natures shall not, in some instances, be set aside in the course of a Divine and secret operation, which, touching the springs of action, and opening the sources of feeling, gives an intensity of energy to the one, and a flow to the other, more eminently indicative of the finger of God in a work which his own glory, and the humility proper to man, require should be known and acknowledged as his work alone? Assuredly there is nothing in the reason of the case to fix the manner of producing such effects to one rule, and nothing in Scripture. Instances of sudden conversion occur in the New Testament in sufficient number to warrant us to conclude, that this may be often the mode adopted by divine Wisdom, and especially in a slumbering age, to arouse attention to long-despised and neglected truths. The conversions at the day of pentecost were sudden, and, for any thing that appears to the contrary, they were real; for the persons so influenced were thought worthy to be "added to the Church." Nor was it by the miracle of tongues that the effect was produced. If miracles could have converted them, they had witnessed greater than even that glorious day exhibited. The dead had been raised up in their sight, the earth had quaked beneath their feet, the sun had hid himself and made an untimely night, and Christ himself had arisen from a tomb sealed and watched. It was not by the impression of the miracle of tongues alone, but by that supervenient gracious influence which operated with the demonstrative sermon of Peter, after the miracle had excited the attention of his hearers, that they were "pricked in their hearts, and cried, Men and brethren, what shall we do?"

The only true rule of judging of professed conversion is its fruits. The modes of it may vary from circumstances of which we are not the fit judges, and never shall be, till we know more of the mystic powers of mind, and of that intercourse which almighty God, in his goodness, condescends to hold with it.

It is granted, however, that in such cases a spurious

feeling has been often mixed up with these genuine visitations; that some ardent minds, when even sincere, have not sufficiently respected the rules of propriety in their acts of worship; that some religious deception has taken place; that some persons have confounded susceptibility of feeling with depth of grace; that censoriousness and spiritual pride have displaced that humility and charity which must exist wherever the influence of the Spirit of God is really present; and that, in some cases, a real fanaticism has sprung up, as in the case of George Bell and his followers in London, at an early period of Methodism. But these are accidents—tares sown in the field among the good seed, which were never spared by Mr. Wesley or his most judicious successors. In the early stages of their growth, indeed, and before they assumed a decided character, they were careful lest, by plucking them up, they should root out the good seed also; but both in Great Britain and in America, no extravagance has ever been encouraged by the authorities of either society, and no importance is attached to any thing but the genuine fruits of conversion.

In the early part of 1770 we find Mr. Wesley, as usual, prosecuting his indefatigable labors in different parts of the kingdom, and every-where diffusing the influence of spirituality and zeal, and the light of a "sound doctrine." His journals present a picture of unwearied exertion, such as was, perhaps, never before exhibited, and in themselves they form ample volumes of great interest, not only as a record of his astonishing and successful labors, but from their miscellaneous and almost uniformly instructive character. Now he is seen braving the storms and tempests in his journeys, fearless of the snows of winter, and the heats of summer; then, with a deep susceptibility of all that is beautiful and grand in nature, recording the pleasures produced by a smiling landscape or by mountain scenery: here, turning aside to view some curious object of nature;

there, some splendid mansion of the great; showing at the same time in his pious and often elegant, though brief reflections, with what skill he made all things contribute to devotion and cheerfulness. Again, we trace him into his proper work, preaching in crowded chapels, or to multitudes collected in the most public resorts in towns, or in the most picturesque places of their vicinity. Now he is seen by the side of the sick and dying, and then, surrounded with his societies, uttering his pastoral advices. An interesting and instructive letter frequently occurs; then a jet of playful and good-humored wit upon his persecutors or the stupidity of his casual hearers; occasionally, in spite of the philosophers, an apparition story is given as he heard it, and of which his readers are left to judge; and often we meet with a grateful record of providential escapes, from the falls of his horses, or from the violence of mobs. Notices of books also appear, which are often exceedingly just and striking; always short and characteristic; and, as he read much on his journeys, they are very frequent. A few of these notices, in his journal of this year, taken without selection, may be given as a specimen:

"I read with all the attention I was master of, Mr. Hutchinson's Life, and Mr. Spearman's Index to his Works. And I was more convinced than ever, 1. That he had not the least conception, much less experience, of inward religion; 2. That an ingenious man may prove just what he pleases, by well-devised Scriptural etymologies, especially if he be in the fashion—if he affect to read the Hebrew without vowels; and, 3. That his whole hypothesis, philosophical and theological, is unsupported by any solid proof.

"I sat down to read and seriously consider some of the writings of Baron Swedenborg. I began with huge prejudice in his favor, knowing him to be a pious man, one of a strong understanding, of much learning, and one who thoroughly believed himself. But I could not hold out long. Any one of his visions puts his real character out of doubt. He is one of the most ingenious, lively, entertaining madmen, that ever set pen to paper. But his waking dreams are so wild, so far remote both from Scripture and common sense, that one might as easily swallow the stories of Tom Thumb, or Jack the Giant-killer.

"I met with an ingenious book, the late Lord Lyttleton's 'Dialogues of the Dead.' A great part of it I could heartily subscribe to, though not to every word. I believe Madam Guion was in several mistakes, speculative and practical too; yet I would no more dare to call her, than her friend Archbishop Fenelon, 'a distracted enthusiast.' She was undoubtedly a woman of very uncommon understanding, and of excellent piety. Nor was she any more 'a lunatic' than she was a 'heretic.'

"Another of this lively writer's assertions is, 'Martin has spawned a strange brood of fellows, called Methodists, Moravians, Hutchinsonians, who are madder than Jack was in his worst days.' I would ask any one who knows what good breeding means, Is this language for a nobleman or for a porter? But let the language be as it may, is the sentiment just? To say nothing of the Methodists—although some of them, too, are not quite out of their senses—could his lordship show me in England many more sensible men than Mr. Gambold and Mr. Okeley? And yet both of these were called Moravians. Or could he point out many men of stronger and deeper understanding than Dr. Horne and Mr. William Jones?—if he could pardon them for believing the Trinity—and yet both of these are Hutchinsonians. What pity is it that so ingenious a man, like many others gone before him, should pass so peremptory a sentence, in a cause which he does not understand! Indeed, how could he understand it? How much has he read upon the question? What sensible Methodist, Moravian, or Hutchinsonian, did he ever calmly converse with?

What does he know of them, but from the caricatures drawn by Bishop Lavington, or Bishop Warburton? And did he ever give himself the trouble of reading the answers to those warm, lively men? Why should a good-natured and a thinking man thus condemn whole bodies of men by the lump? In this I can neither read the gentleman, the scholar, nor the Christian."

"I set out for London; and read over in the way that celebrated book, 'Martin Luther's Comment on the Epistle to the Galatians.' I was utterly ashamed. How have I esteemed this book, only because I heard it so commended by others! or, at best, because I had read some excellent sentences, occasionally quoted from it! But what shall I say, now I judge for myself? now I see with my own eyes? Why, not only that the author makes nothing out, clears up not one considerable difficulty; that he is quite shallow in his remarks on many passages, and muddy and confused almost on all; but that he is deeply tinctured with mysticism throughout, and hence often dangerously wrong. To instance only in one or two points. How does he—almost in the words of Tauler—decry reason, right or wrong, as an irreconcilable enemy to the Gospel of Christ! Whereas, what is reason—the faculty so called—but the power of apprehending, judging, and discoursing? which power is no more to be condemned in the gross, than seeing, hearing, or feeling. Again, how blasphemously does he speak of good works and of the law of God; constantly coupling the law with sin, death, hell, or the devil; and teaching, that Christ delivers us from them all alike! Whereas, it can no more be proved by Scripture, that Christ delivers us from the law of God, than that he delivers us from holiness or from heaven. Here—I apprehend—is the real spring of the grand error of the Moravians. They follow Luther, for better for worse. Hence their 'No works, no law, no commandment.' But who art thou that 'speakest evil of the law, and judgest the law?'

"I read over, and partly transcribed, Bishop Bull's 'Harmonia Apostolica.' The position with which he sets out is this, 'that all good works, and not faith alone, are the necessarily previous condition of justification,' or the forgiveness of our sins. But in the middle of the treatise he asserts, 'that faith alone is the condition of justification;' 'for faith,' says he, 'referred to justification, means all inward and outward good works.' In the latter end he affirms, 'that there are two justifications: and that only inward good works necessarily precede the former, but both inward and outward the latter."

Mr. Wesley meant this brief but just analysis to be Bishop Bull's refutation, and it is sufficient.

"Looking for a book in our college library, I took down, by mistake, the Works of Episcopius; which opening on an account of the Synod of Dort, I believed it might be useful to read it through. But what a scene is here disclosed! I wonder not at the heavy curse of God, which so soon after fell on the Church and nation. What a pity it is, that the holy Synod of Trent, and that of Dort, did not sit at the same time! nearly allied as they were, not only as to the purity of doctrine, which each of them established, but also as to the spirit wherewith they acted; if the latter did not exceed.

"Being in the Bodleian library, I lit on Mr. Calvin's account of the case of Michael Servetus; several of whose letters he occasionally inserts: wherein Servetus often declares in terms, 'I believe the Father is God, the Son is God, and the Holy Ghost is God.' Mr. Calvin, however, paints him such a monster as never was, an Arian, a blasphemer, and what not; beside strewing over him his flowers of dog, devil, swine, and so on, which are the usual appellations he gives to his opponents. But still he utterly denies his being the cause of Servetus' death. 'No,' says he, 'I only advised our magistrates, as having a right to restrain heretics by the sword, to seize upon and try that archheretic. But after he was condemned, I said not one word about his execution!' "

The above may be taken as instances of his laconic reviews of books.

Mr. Wesley's defense of the power he exercised in the government of the Methodist societies may also here be given; observing that it is easier, considering the circumstances in which he was placed, to carp at it, than to find a solid answer. Few men, it is true, have had so much power; but, on the other hand, he could not have retained it in a perfectly-voluntary society, had he not used it mildly and wisely, and with a perfectly-disinterested and public spirit.

"What is that power? It is a power of admitting into and excluding from the societies under my care; of choosing and removing stewards; of receiving or not receiving helpers; of appointing them when, where, and how to help me, and of desiring any of them to confer with me when I see good. And as it was merely in obedience to the providence of God, and for the good of the people, that I at first accepted this power, which I never sought, so it is on the same consideration, not for profit, honor, or pleasure, that I use it at this day.

" 'But several gentlemen are offended at your having so much power.' I did not seek any part of it. But when it was come unawares, not daring to bury that talent, I used it to the best of my judgment. Yet I never was fond of it. I always did, and do now, bear it as my burden, the burden which God lays upon me; and therefore I dare not lay it down.

"But if you can tell me any one, or any five men, to whom I may transfer this burden, who can and will do just what I do now, I will heartily thank both them and you." (Wesley's Works.)

This year—1770—is memorable in the history of Methodism, for having given birth to a long and very ardent controversy on the doctrines of Calvinism. It took its rise from the publication of the Minutes of the Conference, in which it was determined, that, in some particulars then pointed out, the preachers had "leaned too much to Calvinism." This is easily explained. Mr. Whitefield, and Howell Harris, the early coadjutors of the Wesleys, became Calvinists; but the affection, which existed among this little band, was strong; and as they all agreed in preaching, what was at that time most needed, the doctrine of salvation by faith, "an agreement" was made at a very early period, between the Wesleys and Howell Harris, to forget all peculiarities of opinion as much as possible in their sermons, to use as far as they could, with a good conscience, the same phrases in expressing the points on which they substantially agreed, and to avoid controversy. Such an agreement shows the liberal feeling which existed among the parties; but it was not of a nature to be so rigidly kept as to give entire satisfaction. On these articles of peace, we find, therefore, indorsed, at a subsequent period, in the handwriting of Mr. Charles Wesley, "Vain agreement." Mr. Wesley's anxiety to maintain unity of effort as well as affection with Mr. Whitefield, led him also, in 1743, to concede to his Calvinistic views, as far as possible; and he appears not to have been disposed to deny, though he says he could not prove it, that some persons might be unconditionally elected to eternal glory; but not to the necessary exclusion of any other from salvation. And he was then "inclined to believe" that there is a state attainable in this life, "from which a man can not finally fall." But he was subsequently convinced by the arguments of Mr. Thomas Walsh, that this was an error.* These considerations will account for the existence of what Mr. Wesley called "a leaning to Calvinism," both in himself, and among some of the preachers, and rendered a review of the case necessary.† Though the leaders had approached so near "the very edge of Calvinism" on one side, and "of Antinomianism" also, with safety, it was not to be wondered at that others should overstep the line. Beside, circumstances had greatly changed. A strong tide of Antinomianism had set in, and threatened great injury to practical godliness throughout the land. Dr. Southey attributes this to the natural tendency of Methodism; but here he shows himself only partially acquainted with the subject. The decline of religion among many of the Dissenting Churches, had scattered the seeds of this heresy all around them, though not without calling forth a noble testimony against it from some of their ablest ministers; and when they began to feel the influence of the revival of piety in the last century, the tares sprung up with the plants of better quality. The Calvinism taught by Mr. Howell Harris, and Mr. Whitefield, was also per-

* Mr. Walsh was received by Mr. Wesley as a preacher, in 1750, and died in 1759. The following is Mr. Wesley's character of him: "That blessed man sometimes preached in Irish, mostly in English; and wherever he preached, whether in English or Irish, the word was sharper than a two-edged sword. So that I do not remember ever to have known any preacher, who, in so few years as he remained upon earth, was an instrument of converting so many sinners from the error of their ways. By violent straining of his voice, he contracted a true pulmonary consumption, which carried him off. O what a man to be snatched away in the strength of his years! Surely thy 'judgments are a great deep!'

"He was so thoroughly acquainted with the Bible, that if he was questioned concerning any Hebrew word in the Old, or any Greek word in the New Testament, he would tell, after a little pause, not only how often one or the other occurred in the Bible, but also what is meant in every place. Such a master of Biblical knowledge I never knew before, and never expect to see again."

† Mr. Wesley's Sermon on Imputed Righteousness is an instance of his anxiety to approach his Calvinistic brethren, in his modes of expression, as far as possible; and in this attempt he sometimes laid himself open to be misunderstood on both sides.

verted by many of their hearers to sanction the same error. Several of the evangelical clergy, likewise, who had no immediate connection with Mr. Wesley, were Calvinists of the highest grade; and as their number increased, their incautious statements of the doctrines of grace and faith, carried beyond their own intentions, became more mischievous. To show, however, that Antinomianism can graft itself upon other stocks beside that of the Calvinistic decrees, it was found also among many of the Moravians; and the Methodists did not escape. Wherever, indeed, the doctrine of justification by faith is preached, there is a danger, as St. Paul himself anticipated in his Epistle to the Romans, lest perverse, vain, and evil minds should pervert it to licentiousness; heavenly as it is in authority, and pure in its influence, when rightly understood. In fact, there is no such exclusive connection between the more sober Calvinistic theories of predestination, and this great error, as some have supposed. It is too often met with, also, among those who hold the doctrine of general redemption; though it must be acknowledged that, for the most part, such persons, at length, go over to predestinarian notions, as affording, at least, some collateral confirmation of the solifidian theory. That Calvinistic opinions, in their various forms, were at this time greatly revived and diffused, is certain. The religious excitement produced gave activity to theological inquiries; and speculative minds, especially those who had some taste for metaphysical discussions, were soon entangled in questions of predestination, prescience, necessity, and human freedom. The views of Calvin on these subjects were also held by many, who, connecting them with vital and saving truths, were honored with great usefulness; and, as the Wesleyan societies were often involved in these discussions, and in danger of having their faith unsettled, and their practical piety injured by those in whom Calvinism had begun to luxuriate into the ease and carelessness of Antinomian license, no subject at that period more urgently required attention. For this reason, Mr. Wesley brought it before his conference of preachers. The withering effects of this delusion were also strongly pointed out in his sermons, and were afterward still more powerfully depicted by the master pencil of Mr. Fletcher, in those great works to which he now began to apply himself, in order to stem the torrent. Dr. Southey has fallen into the error of imagining that Mr. Fletcher's descriptions of the ravages of Antinomianism were drawn from its effects upon the Wesleyan societies; but that mistake arose from his not adverting to the circumstance, that neither Mr. Wesley nor Mr. Fletcher confined their cares to these societies, but kept an equally watchful eye upon the state of religion in the land at large, and consequently in the Church of which they were ministers. The societies under Mr. Wesley's charge were, indeed, at no time more than very partially affected by this form of error. Still, in some places they had suffered, and in all were exposed to danger; and as Mr. Wesley regarded them, not only as a people given to him by God to preserve from error, but to engage to bear a zealous and steadfast testimony "against the evils of the time," in every place he endeavored to prepare them for their warfare, by instructing them fully in the questions at issue.

The Minutes of 1770 contained, therefore, the following passages:

"We said, in 1744, 'We have leaned too much toward Calvinism.' Wherein?

"1. With regard to man's faithfulness. Our Lord himself taught us to use the expression. And we ought never to be ashamed of it. We ought steadily to assert, on his authority, that if a man is not 'faithful in the unrighteous mammon,' God will not give 'him the true riches.'

"2. With regard to 'working for life.' This also our Lord has expressly commanded us. 'Labor,' ἐργάζεσθε, literally, 'work for the meat that endureth to everlasting life.' And, in fact, every believer, till he comes to glory, works *for* as well as *from* life.

"3. We have received it as a maxim, that 'a man is to do nothing in order to justification.' Nothing can be more false. Whoever desires to find favor with God should 'cease from evil, and learn to do well.' Whoever repents should do 'works meet for repentance.' And if this is not in order to find favor, what does he do them for?

"Review the whole affair.

"1. Who of us is *now* accepted of God?

"He that now believes in Christ, with a loving and obedient heart.

"2. But who among those that never heard of Christ?

"He that feareth God and worketh righteousness according to the light he has.

"3. Is this the same with 'he that is sincere?'

"Nearly, if not quite.

"4. Is not this 'salvation by works?'

"Not by the *merit* of works, but by works as a *condition.*

"6. What have we then been disputing about for these thirty years?

"I am afraid, about words.

"7. The grand objection to one of the preceding propositions is drawn from matter of fact. God does in fact justify those who, by their own confession, neither feared God nor wrought righteousness. Is this an exception to the general rule?

"It is a doubt whether God makes any exception at all. But how are we sure that the person in question never did fear God and work righteousness? His own saying so is not proof: for we know how all that are convinced of sin undervalue themselves in every respect.

"8. Does not talking of a justified or a sanctified *state* tend to mislead men? almost naturally leading them to trust in what was done in one moment? Whereas we are every hour and every moment pleasing or displeasing to God, 'according to our works'—according to the whole of our inward tempers and our outward behavior."

"That these were passages calculated to awaken suspicion, and that they gave the appearance of inconsistency to Mr. Wesley's opinions, and indicated a tendency to run to one extreme, in order to avoid another—an error which Mr. Wesley more generally avoided than most men—can not be denied. They, however, when fairly examined, expressed nothing but what is found in substance in the doctrinal conversations at the conferences from 1744 to 1747; but the sentiments were put in a stronger form, and were made to bear directly against the Antinomian opinions of the day. To "man's faithfulness" nothing surely could be reasonably objected; it is enjoined upon believers in the whole Gospel, and might have been known by the objectors to have been always held by Mr. Wesley, but so as necessarily to imply a constant dependence upon the influence of the Holy Spirit. That the rewards of eternity are also to be distributed in higher or lower degrees according to the obedient works of believers, yet still on a principle of *grace*, is a doctrine held by divines of almost every class, and is confirmed by many passages of Scripture. To the Antinomian notion, that a man is to do nothing in order to justification, Mr. Wesley opposes the same sentiment which he held in 1744, that previously to justification men must repent, and, if there be opportunity, do works meet for repentance; and when he asks, "if they do them not *in order* to justification, what do they do them for?"—these words are far enough from intimating that such works are meritorious, although they are capable of being misunderstood. Repentance is indeed a condition of justification, as well as faith, but indirectly and remotely—"Repent ye and believe the Gospel;" and seeing that Mr. Wesley, so expressly in the same page, shuts out the *merit* of works, no one could be justly offended with this statement—except as far as the phrase is concerned—who did not embrace some obvious form of practical error.

The doctrine of the acceptance of such heathens as "fear God and work righteousness," might be offensive to those who shut out all heathens, *as such*, from the mercies of God—a tenet, however, which is not necessarily connected with Calvinism; and it ought not to have been objected to by others, unless Mr. Wesley had stated, as some of his opponents understood him to do, that "a heathen might be saved without a Savior." No such thought was ever entertained by him, as Mr. Fletcher observes in his defense; for he held that whenever a heathen is accepted, it is merely through the merits of Christ, although it is in connection with his "fearing God, and working righteousness." "'But how comes he to see that God is to be feared, and that righteousness is his delight?' Because a beam of our Sun of righteousness shines in his darkness. All is therefore of grace; the light, the works of righteousness done by that light, and acceptance in consequence of them." (Fletcher's Works.)

But when the Minutes went on to state that this shows that salvation is by works as a "*condition*, though not by the merit of works," the highest point of heresy was supposed to be reached. Yet from this charge, though it derived some color from a paradoxical mode of expression not to be commended, Mr. Fletcher brings off his friend unhurt:

"Our Church expresses herself more fully on this head in the Homily on Salvation, to which the article refers. 'St. Paul,' says he, 'declares nothing [necessary] on the behalf of man concerning his justification, but only a true and lively faith, and yet (N. B.) that faith does not shut out repentance, hope, love, [of desire when we are coming, love of delight when we are come,] dread, and the fear of God, to be joined with it in every man that is justified; but it shutteth them out from the office of justifying; so that they be all present together in him that is justified, yet they justify not altogether.' This is agreeable to St. Peter's doctrine, maintained by Mr. Wesley. Only *faith in Christ* for Christians, and *faith in the light* of their dispensation for heathens, is necessary in order to acceptance; but though faith only justifies, yet it is never alone; for repentance, hope, love of desire, and the fear of God, necessarily accompany this faith, if it be living. Our Church, therefore, is not at all against works proceeding from, or accompanying faith in all its stages. She grants, that whether faith seeks or finds its object, whether it longs for or embraces it, it is still a lively, active, and working grace. She is only against the vain conceit that works have any hand in *meriting* justification or *purchasing* salvation, which is what Mr. Wesley likewise strongly opposes.

"If any still urge, 'I do not love the word condition,' I reply, it is no wonder; since thousands so hate the thing, that they even choose to go to hell, rather than perform it. But let an old worthy divine, approved by all but Crisp's disciples, tell you what we mean by condition: 'An antecedent condition [says Mr. Flavel in his 'Discourse of Errors'] signifies no more than an act of ours, which, though it be neither perfect in any degree, nor in the least meritorious of the benefit conferred, nor performed in our own natural strength, is yet, according to the constitution of the covenant required of us, in order to the blessings consequent thereupon, by virtue of the promise; and, consequently, benefits and mercies granted in this order are and must be suspended by the donor, till it be performed.' Such a condition we affirm faith to be, with all that faith necessarily implies." (Fletcher's Works.)

The greatest stone of stumbling was, however, the remarks on *merit:*

"As to merit itself, of which we have been so dreadfully afraid: we are rewarded 'according to our works,' yea, 'because of our works.' How does this differ from 'for the sake of our works?' And how differs this from *secundum merita operum,* 'as our works deserve?' Can you split this hair? I doubt I can not."

The outcry of "dreadful heresy" raised against him, particularly on this article, was the more uncandid, because by explaining the phrase *secundum merita operum,* to mean, *as our works deserve,* it was clear, especially taking the passage in connection with what he had previously stated, that he understood merit in that loose, and not perhaps always correct, sense in which it had often been used by several of the ancient fathers; and also that he was not speaking of our present justification, but of our final reward. But here Mr. Fletcher shall again be heard:

"If Mr. Wesley meant, that we are saved by the *merit of works,* and not entirely by that of Christ, you might exclaim against his proposition as erroneous; and I would echo back your exclamation. But as he flatly denies it in those words, 'Not by the merit of works,' and has constantly asserted the contrary for above thirty years, we can not, without monstrous injustice, fix that sense upon the word merit in this paragraph.

"Divesting himself of bigotry and party spirit, he generously acknowledges truth even when it is held forth by his adversaries: an instance of candor worthy of our imitation! He sees that God offers and gives his children, here on earth, particular rewards for particular instances of obedience. He knows that when a man is saved meritoriously by Christ, and *conditionally by*—or if you please, *upon the terms of—the work of faith, the patience of hope, and the labor of love,* he shall particularly be rewarded in heaven for his works: and he observes, that the Scriptures steadily maintain, we are recompensed *according to our works*, yea, *because of our works.*

"The former of these assertions is plain from the parable of the talents, and from these words of our Lord, Matt. xvi, 27, 'The Son of man shall come in the glory of his Father, and reward every man according to his works;' unbelievers according to the various degrees of demerit belonging to their evil works—for some of them shall comparatively 'be beaten with few stripes;' and believers according to the various degrees of excellence found in their good works; 'for as one star differeth from another star in glory, so also is the resurrection of the' righteous 'dead.'

"If we detach from the word *merit* the idea of 'obligation on God's part to bestow any thing upon creatures, who have a thousand times forfeited their comforts and existence'—if we take it in the sense we fix to it in a hundred cases; for instance this: 'A master may reward his scholars according to the *merit* of their exercises, or he may not; for the *merit* of the best exercise can never bind him to bestow a premium for it, unless he has promised it of his own accord'—if we take, I say, the word *merit* in this simple sense, it may be joined to the words *good works*, and bear an evangelical meaning.

"To be convinced of it, candid reader, consider, with Mr. Wesley, that 'God accepts and rewards no work but so far as it proceeds from his own grace through the Beloved.' Forget not that Christ's Spirit is the savor of each believer's salt, and that he puts excellence into the *good* works of his people, or else they could not be *good.* Remember, he is as much concerned in the good tempers, words, and actions of his living members, as a tree is concerned in the sap, leaves, and fruit of the branches it bears, John xv, 5. Consider, I say, all this, and tell us whether it can reflect dishonor upon Christ and his grace to affirm, that as his personal merit—the merit of his holy life and painful death—'opens the kingdom of heaven to all believers,' so the merit of those works which he enables his members to do, will determine the peculiar degrees of glory graciously allotted to each of them." (Fletcher's Works.)

Mr. Fletcher came forward to defend his venerable friend, on account of the great uproar which the Calvinistic party had raised against him upon the publication of these minutes. The countess of Huntingdon had taken serious alarm and offense; and the Rev. Walter Shirley, her brother and chaplain, had written a circular letter to all the serious clergy, and several others, inviting them to go in a body to the ensuing conference, and "insist upon a formal recantation of the said minutes, and, in case of a refusal, to sign and publish their protest against them." Mr. Shirley and a few others accordingly attended the Bristol conference, where, says Mr. Wesley, "we had more preachers than usual in consequence of Mr. Shirley's circular letter. At ten on Thursday morning he came, with nine or ten of his friends; we conversed freely for about two hours; and, I believe, they were satisfied, that we were not such 'dreadful heretics' as they imagined, but were tolerably sound in the faith."

The meeting was creditable to each party. Mr. Wesley acknowledged that the minutes were "not sufficiently guarded." This must be felt by all; they were out of his usual manner of expressing himself, and he had said the same truths often in a clearer, and safer, and even stronger manner. He certainly did not mean to alter his previous opinions, or formally to adopt other terms in which to express them; and, therefore, to employ new modes of speaking, though for a temporary purpose, was not without danger, although they were capable of an innocent explanation. Even Mr. Fletcher confesses that the minutes wore "a new aspect," and that at first they appeared to him "unguarded, if not erroneous." Mr. Wesley showed his candor in admitting the former; and to prevent all future misconstruction, he and the conference issued the following "Declaration," to which was appended a note from Mr. Shirley, acknowledging his mistake as to the meaning of the minutes:

"*Bristol, August* 9, 1771.

"Whereas the doctrinal points in the minutes of a conference held in London, August 7, 1770, have been understood to favor 'justification by works:' now the Rev. John Wesley and others, assembled in conference, do declare that we had no such meaning; and that we abhor the doctrine of 'justification by works,' as a most perilous and abominable doctrine. And as the said minutes are not sufficiently guarded in the way they are expressed, we hereby solemnly declare, in the sight of God, that we have no trust or confidence but in the alone *merits* of our Lord and Savior Jesus Christ for justification or salvation, either in life, death, or the day of judgment. And though no one is a real Christian believer—and consequently can not be saved—who doeth not good works, where there is time and opportunity, yet our works have no part in meriting or purchasing our justification, from first to last, either in whole or in part.

"Signed by the Rev. Mr. Wesley and fifty-three preachers."

MR. SHIRLEY'S NOTE.

"Mr. Shirley's Christian respects wait on Mr. Wesley. The declaration agreed to in conference the 8th of August, 1771, has convinced Mr. Shirley he had mistaken the meaning of the doctrinal points in the minutes of the conference held in London, August 7, 1770; and he hereby wishes to testify the full satisfaction he has in the said declaration, and his hearty concurrence and agreement with the same.

"Mr. Wesley is at full liberty to make what use he pleases of this. August 10, 1771."*

Mr. Fletcher had entitled his Defense of Mr. Wesley "The First Check to Antinomianism;" but he did not content himself with *evangelizing* the apparently *legal* minutes, and defending the doctrinal consistency and

* This affair is capable of more illustration than it has received from Mr. Wesley's biographers hitherto. Mr. Shirley's circular letter was naturally resented by Mr. Wesley, as being published before any explanations respecting the minutes had been asked from him their author; and also from its assuming that Mr. S., and the clergy who might obey his summons, had the right to come into the conference, and to demand a recantation. Mr. Shirley, therefore, soon found, that he must approach in a more brotherly manner, or that Mr. Wesley and the conference would have no intercourse with him. This led Lady Huntingdon and Mr. Shirley to address explanatory letters to Mr. Wesley. "As the method of proceeding, as well as the terms in which we had delivered ourselves," says Mr. Shirley, "was objected to by many as by no means proper, and in submission to the precept, 'Give no offense to Jew or Gentile, or to the Church of God,' Lady Huntingdon and I wrote the following letters, which were delivered to Mr. Wesley the evening before the conference met." Lady Huntingdon says, "As you and your friends, and many others, have objected to the mode of the application to you in conference, as an arbitrary way of proceeding, we wish to retract what a more deliberate consideration might have prevented," etc. Mr. Shirley's letter acknowledges "that the circular was too hastily drawn up, and improperly expressed; and therefore, for the offensive expressions in it, we desire we may be hereby understood to make every suitable submission to you." On this explanation, Mr. Shirley and his friends were *invited* by Mr. Wesley to come to the conference on the third day of its sitting. Mr. Shirley's published narrative thus proceeds: "To say the truth, I was pleased that the invitation came from Mr. Wesley, without any application made on our parts, that there might not be left the least room for censuring our proceedings as violent. On that day, therefore, I went thither, accompanied with Rev. Mr. Glascot, Rev. Mr. Owen—two ministers officiating in Lady Huntingdon's chapels—John Lloyd, Esq., of Bath; Mr. James Ireland, merchant, of Bristol; Mr. Winter, and two students belonging to Lady Huntingdon's college.

"I shall only give you a brief detail of what passed, and rather the

orthodoxy of Mr. Wesley. He incidentally discussed various other points of the quinquarticular controversy; and he, as well as Mr. Wesley, was quickly assailed by a number of replies not couched in the most courteous style.

substance of what was spoken, than the exact words; omitting, likewise, many things of no great weight or consequence.

"After Mr. Wesley had prayed, I desired to know whether Lady Huntingdon's letter and mine to Mr. Wesley had been read to the conference. Being answered in the negative, I begged leave to read the copies of them; which was granted. I then said that I hoped the submission made was satisfactory to the gentlemen of the conference. This was admitted; but then it was urged, that as the offense given by the circular letter had been very public, so ought the letter of submission. I therefore readily consented to the publication of it, and have now fulfilled my promise. Mr. Wesley then stood up; the purport of his speech was a sketch of his ministry from his first setting out to the present time; with a view—as I understood—to prove that he had ever maintained justification by faith, and that there was nothing in the minutes contrary thereto. He complained of ill treatment from many persons, that he apprehended had been under obligations to him; and said that the present opposition was not to the minutes, but to himself personally. In answer I assured them, in the most solemn manner, that, with respect to myself, my opposition was not to Mr. Wesley, or any particular person, but to the doctrines themselves. And they were pleased thus far to give me credit. I then proceeded to speak to the point; informed them of the great and general offense the minutes had given; that I had numerous protests and testimonies against them sent me from Scotland, and from various parts of these kingdoms; that it must seem very extraordinary, indeed, if so many men of sense and learning should be mistaken, and that there was nothing really offensive in the plain, natural import of the minutes; that I believed they themselves—whatever meaning they might have intended—would allow that the more obvious meaning was reprehensible; and, therefore, I recommended to them, nay, I begged and entreated, for the Lord's sake, that they would go as far as they could with a good conscience, in giving the world satisfaction. I said I hoped they would not take offense—for I did not mean to give it—as my proposing to them a declaration which I had drawn up, wishing that something at least analogous to it might be agreed to. I then took the liberty to read it; and Mr. Wesley, after he had made some—not very material—alterations in it, readily consented to sign it; in which he was followed by fifty-three of the preachers in connection with him; there being only one or two that were against it.

"Thus was this important matter settled. But one of the preachers—namely, Mr. Thomas Olivers—kept us a long time in debate; strenuously opposed the declaration; and to the last would not consent to sign it. He maintained that our second justification—that is, at the day of judgment—is by works; and he saw very clearly that for one that holds that tenet solemnly 'to declare in the sight of God that he has no trust or confidence

Mr. Fletcher's skill and admirable temper so fully fitted him to conduct the dispute which had arisen, that Mr. Wesley left the contest chiefly to him, and calmly pursued his labors; and the whole issued in a series of

but in the alone merits of our Lord and Savior Jesus Christ, for justification or salvation, either in life, death, or the day of judgment,' would be acting neither a consistent nor an upright part; for all the subtilties of metaphysical distinction can never reconcile tenets so diametrically opposite as these. But, blessed be God, Mr. Wesley, and fifty-three of his preachers, do not agree with Mr. Olivers in this material article; for it appears, from their subscribing the declaration, that they do not maintain a second justification by works.

"After the declaration had been agreed to, it was required of me, on my part, that I would make some public acknowledgment that I had mistaken the meaning of the minutes. Here I hesitated a little; for though I was desirous to do every thing—consistently with truth and a good conscience—for the establishment of peace and Christian fellowship, yet I was very unwilling to give any thing under my hand that might seem to countenance the minutes in their obvious sense. But then, when I was asked by one of the preachers whether I did not believe Mr. Wesley to be an honest man, I was distressed on the other hand, lest, by refusing what was desired, I should seem to infer a doubt to Mr. Wesley's disadvantage. Having confidence, therefore, in Mr. Wesley's integrity, who had declared he had no such meaning in the minutes as was favorable to justification by works, and considering that every man is the best judge of his own meaning, and has a right, so far, to our credit, and that, though nothing else could, yet the declaration did convince me, they had some other meaning than what appeared, I say—these things considered—I promised them satisfaction in this particular, and, a few days afterward, sent Mr. Wesley the following message, with which he was very well pleased:

[Then follows Mr. Shirley's note as given above.]

"Thus far all was well. The foundation was secured. And, with respect to lesser matters of difference, we might well bear with one another; and if either party should see occasion to oppose the other's peculiar opinion, it might be done without vehemence, and without using any reproachful terms. The whole was conducted with great decency on all sides. We concluded with prayer, and with the warmest indications of mutual peace and love. For my own part, believe me, I was perfectly sincere, and thought this one of the happiest, and most honorable days of my life."

The whole conduct of Mr. Shirley, in this affair, affords a pleasing contrast to that of the Hills, Toplady, and others, who soon rushed hot and reckless into the controversy. Mr. Shirley, it is true, complains, that after this adjustment Mr. Fletcher should have so severely attacked him in his five letters; but he appears never to have departed from the meekness of a Christian and the manners of a gentleman.

publications, from the pen of the vicar of Madeley, which, as a whole, can scarcely be too highly praised or valued.* While the language endures, they will operate as checks to Antinomianism in every subtile form which it may assume, and present the pure and beautiful system of evangelical truth, as well guarded on the other hand against Pelagian self-sufficiency. The Rev. Augustus Toplady, Mr.—afterward Sir Richard—Hill, and his brother, the Rev. Rowland Hill, with the Rev. John Berridge, were his principal antagonists; but his learning, his acuteness, his brilliant talent at illustrating an argument, and, above all, the hallowed spirit in which he conducted the controversy, gave him a mighty superiority over his opponents; and although there will be a difference of opinion, according to the systems which different readers have adopted, as to the side on which the victory of *argument* remains, there can be none as to which bore away the prize of *temper*. Amidst the scurrilities and vulgar abuse of Mr. Toplady, otherwise an able writer, and a man of learning, and the coarse virulence or buffoonery of the Hills and Berridge,†

* It ought to be observed, that Mr. Fletcher's writings are not to be considered, in every particular, as expressing the views of Mr. Wesley, and the body of Methodists, and that, though greatly admired among us, they are not reckoned among the *standards* of our doctrines.

† The titles of several of the pieces, written by Toplady and others, such as "An old Fox tarred and feathered," "The Serpent and the Fox," "Pope John," etc., are sufficient evidences of the temper and manners of this band of controversialists. In what Rev. Rowland Hill calls "*Some Gentle Strictures*" on a sermon by Mr. Wesley, preached on laying the foundation stone of the City Road Chapel, Mr. Wesley is subjected to certain not very *gentle* objurgations, which it would be too sickening a task to copy or to read. The Gospel Magazine, so called, was equally unmeasured in its abuse, and as vulgar; but, to do justice to all parties, the Calvinists even of that day disapproved of this publication, and it was given up. Even Mr. Rowland Hill appears to have incurred the displeasure of some of his brethren; for in a second edition of his "Gentle Strictures," he explains himself—awkwardly enough, certainly—that when he called Mr. Wesley "wretch," and "miscreant," they must remember that "wretch" means "an unhappy person;" and "miscreant," "one whose belief is wrong!" We have, happily, no recent instances of

it is refreshing to remark, in the writings of "the saintly Fletcher," so fine a union of strength and meekness; an edge so keen, and yet so smooth; and a heart kept in such perfect charity with his assailants, and so intent upon establishing truth, not for victory, but for salvation.

In this dispute Mr. Wesley wrote but little, and that chiefly in defense of his own consistency, in reply to Mr. Hill. His pamphlets also are models of temper, logical and calm, but occasionally powerfully reproving; not so much as feeling that he had received abuse and insult, as holding it his duty to bring the aggressor to a due sense of his own misdoings. The conclusion of his first reply to Mr. Hill is a strong illustration:

"Having now answered the queries you proposed, suffer me, sir, to propose one to you; the same which a gentleman of your own opinion proposed to me some years since: 'Sir, how is it that as soon as a man comes to the knowledge of THE TRUTH, it spoils his temper?' That it does so I had observed over and over, as well as Mr. J. had. But how can we account for it? Has the truth—so Mr. J. termed what many love to term the doctrine of free grace—a natural tendency to spoil the temper? To inspire pride, haughtiness, superciliousness? To make a man 'wiser in his own eyes than seven men that can render a reason?' Does it naturally turn a man into a cynic, a bear, a Toplady? Does it at once set him free from all the restraints of good-nature, decency, and good manners? Can-not a man hold distinguishing grace, as it is called, but he must distinguish himself for passion, sourness, bitterness? Must

equally unbrotherly and unchristian temper in connection with this controversy, except in the bitter and unsanctified spirit of Bogue and Bennett's History of the Dissenters. The two doctors, however, were in the habit of declining the merit of the passages on Methodism, in favor of each other; and to which of them the honor of their authorship is due, has never yet, I believe, been ascertained. "Where there is shame," says Dr. Johnson, "there may in time be virtue."

a man, as soon as he looks upon himself to be an absolute favorite of Heaven, look upon all that oppose him as Diabolonians—as predestinated dogs of hell? Truly, the melancholy instance now before us would almost induce us to think so. For who was of a more amiable temper than Mr. Hill, a few years ago? When I first conversed with him in London, I thought I had seldom seen a man of fortune who appeared to be of a more humble, modest, gentle, friendly disposition. And yet this same Mr. H., when he has once been grounded in the knowledge of THE TRUTH, is of a temper as totally different from this, as light is from darkness! He is now haughty, supercilious, disdaining his opponents, as unworthy to be set with the dogs of his flock! He is violent, impetuous, bitter of spirit! in a word, the author of the Review!

"O, sir, what a commendation is this of your doctrine? Look at Mr. Hill the Arminian! The loving, amiable, generous, friendly man. Look at Mr. Hill the Calvinist! Is it the same person? this spiteful, morose, touchy man? Alas, what has the knowledge of THE TRUTH done? What a deplorable change has it made? Sir, I love you still; though I can not esteem you, as I did once. Let me entreat you, if not for the honor of God, yet for the honor of your cause, avoid, for the time to come, all anger, all spite, all sourness and bitterness, all contemptuous usage of your opponents, not inferior to you, unless in fortune. O put on again bowels of mercies, kindness, gentleness, long-suffering; endeavoring to hold, even with them that differ from you in opinion, the unity of the Spirit in the bond of peace!"

This controversy, painful as it was in many respects, and the cause of much unhallowed joy to the profane wits of the day, who were not a little gratified at this exhibition of what they termed "spiritual gladiatorship," has been productive of important consequences in this country. It showed to the pious and moderate Calvinists how well the richest views of evangelical truth could be united with Arminianism; and it effected, by its bold and fearless exhibition of the logical consequences of the doctrines or the decrees, much greater moderation in those who still admitted them, and gave birth to some softened modifications of Calvinism in the age that followed—an effect which has remained to this day. The disputes on these subjects have, since that time, been less frequent, and more temperate; nor have good men so much labored to depart to the greatest distance from each other, as to find a ground on which they could make the nearest approaches. This has been especially the case between the Methodists and the evangelical Dissenters. Of late a Calvinism of a higher and sterner form has sprung up among a certain sect of the clergy of the Church of England; though some of them, whatever their private theory may be, feel that these points are not fit subjects for the edification of their congregations in public discourses. Of Calvinism since the period of this controversy the Methodist preachers and societies have been in no danger; so powerful and complete was its effect upon them. At no conference, since that of 1770, has it been necessary again to ask, "Wherein have we leaned too much to Calvinism?" There has been, indeed, not in the body, but in some of its ministers occasionally, a leaning to what is worse than Calvinism—to a sapless, legal, and philosophizing theology. The influence of the opinions of the majority of the preachers has always, however, counteracted this; and the true balance between the extremes of each system, as set up in the doctrinal writings of Mr. Wesley, has been of late years better preserved than formerly. Those writings are, indeed, more read and better appreciated in the connection, than at some former periods; and perhaps at the present time they exert a more powerful influence than they ever did over the theological views of both preachers and people. To this the admirably-complete, correct, and elegant edition of Mr. Wesley's Works, lately put forth by the labor and judgment of Rev. Thomas Jackson, will still farther contribute. Numerous valuable pieces on different subjects, which had been quite lost to the public, have been recovered; and others, but very partially known, have been collected.

In the midst of all these controversies and cares, the societies continued to spread and flourish under the influence of the zeal and piety of the preachers, animated by the ceaseless activity and regular visits of Mr. Wesley, who, though now upward of seventy years of age, seemed to possess his natural strength unabated.* His thoughts were, however, frequently turning with anxiety to some arrangement for the government of the connection after his death; and not being satisfied that the plan he had sketched out a few years before would provide for a case of so much consequence, he directed his attention to Mr. Fletcher, and warmly invited him to come forth into the work, and to allow himself to be introduced by him to the societies and preachers as their future head. Earnestly as this was pressed, Mr. Fletcher could not be induced to undertake a task to which, in his humility, he thought himself inadequate. This seems to have been his only objection; but had he accepted the offer, the plan would

* In his seventy-second year he thus speaks of himself, "This being my birthday, the first day of my seventy-second year, I was considering, How is this that I find just the same strength as I did thirty years ago? that my sight is considerably better now, and my nerves firmer, than they were then? that I have none of the infirmities of old age, and have lost several I had in my youth? The grand cause is the good pleasure of God, who doeth whatsoever pleaseth him. The chief means are, 1. My constantly rising at four for about fifty years; 2. My generally preaching at five in the morning, one of the most healthy exercises in the world; 3. My never traveling less, by sea or land, than four thousand, five hundred miles in a year."

have failed, as Mr. Fletcher was a few years afterward called into another world. From Mr. Charles Wesley, who had become a family man, and had nearly given up traveling, he had no hope as a successor; and even then a farther settlement would have been necessary, because he could not be expected long to survive his brother. Still, therefore, this important matter remained undetermined. At the time the overture was made to Mr. Fletcher, the preachers who were fully engaged in the work amounted to one hundred and fifty; and the societies, in Great Britain and Ireland, to upward of thirty-five thousand, exclusive of the regular hearers. This rapid and constant enlargement of the connection hightened the urgency of the question of its future settlement; and it is pleasing to remark, that Mr. Charles Wesley at length entered into this feeling, and offered his suggestions. In spite of the little misunderstandings which had arisen, he maintained a strong interest in a work of which he had been so eminent an instrument; and this grew upon him in his latter years. Thus we have seen him springing into activity upon the sickness of his brother, before mentioned, and performing for him the full "work of an evangelist," by traveling in his place; and, upon Mr. Wesley's recovery, his labors were afforded locally to the chapels in London and Bristol, to the great edification of the congregations. In one of his latest letters to his brother, entering into the question of a provision for the settlement of the future government of the connection, he says, "I served West-street Chapel on Friday and Sunday. Stand to your own proposal: 'Let us agree to differ.' I leave America and Scotland to your latest thoughts and recognitions; only observing now, that you are exactly right. Keep your authority while you live; and, after your death, *detur digniori*—let it be given to the worthiest individual—or rather, *dignioribus*—to the worthiest individuals. You can not settle the *succession*. You can not divine how God will settle it."

Thus Charles gave up as hopeless the return to the Church, and suggested the plan which his brother adopted, to devolve the government, not indeed upon one, but upon many whom he esteemed "the worthiest," for age, experience, talent, and moderation.

CHAPTER XII.

In 1775 Mr. Wesley, during a tour in the north of Ireland, had a dangerous sickness, occasioned by sleeping on the ground, in an orchard, in the hot weather, which he says he had been "accustomed to do for forty years without ever being injured by it." He was slow to admit that old age had arrived, or he trusted to triumph long over its infirmities. The consequence in this case, however, was that, after manfully struggling with the incipient symptoms of the complaint, and attempting to throw them off by reading, journeying, and preaching, he sunk into a severe fever, from which, after lying insensible, for some days, he recovered with extraordinary rapidity, and resumed a service which, extended as it had been through so many years, was not yet to be terminated. While in London the next year, the following incident occurred:

An order had been made by the house of lords, "That the commissioners of his Majesty's excise do write circular letters to all persons whom they have reason to suspect to have plate, as also to those who have not paid regularly the duty on the same," etc. In consequence of this order, the accountant-general for household plate sent Mr. Wesley a copy of the order, with the following letter:

"Reverend Sir,—As the commissioners can not doubt

but you have plate for which you have hitherto neglected to make an entry, they have directed me to send you the above copy of the lords' order, and to inform you they expect that you forthwith make due entry of all your plate, such entry to bear date from the commencement of the plate duty, or from such time as you have owned, used, had, or kept any quantity of silver plate, chargeable by the act of Parliament; as in default hereof, the board will be obliged to signify your refusal to their lordships.

"N. B. An immediate answer is desired."

Mr. Wesley replied as follows:

"Sir,—I have two silver tea-spoons at London, and two at Bristol. This is all the plate which I have at present; and I shall not buy any more while so many around me want bread. I am, sir, your most humble servant,

"John Wesley."

No doubt the commissioners of his Majesty's excise thought that the head of so numerous a people had not forgotten his own interests, and that the interior of his *episcopal* residence in London was not without superfluities and splendor.

The bishop of Sodor and Man having written a pastoral letter to all the clergy within his diocess, to warn their flocks against Methodism, and exhorting them to present all who attended its meetings in the spiritual courts, and to repel every Methodist preacher from the sacrament, Mr. Wesley hastened to the island, and in May, 1777, landed at Douglas. In every place he appears to have been cordially received by all ranks; and his prompt visit probably put a stop to this threatened ecclesiastical violence, for no farther mention is made of it. The societies in the island continued to flourish; and, on Mr. Wesley's second visit, he found a new bishop of a more liberal character.

The Foundery having become too small for the comfortable accommodation of the congregation in that part of

London, and being also gloomy and dilapidated, a new chapel had been erected. "November 1st," says Mr. Wesley, "was the day appointed for opening the new chapel in the City Road. It is perfectly neat, but not fine, and contains far more than the Foundery; I believe, together with the morning chapel, as many as the Tabernacle. Many were afraid that the multitudes, crowding from all parts, would have occasioned much disturbance; but they were happily disappointed—there was none at all—all was quietness, decency, and order. I preached on part of Solomon's prayer at the dedication of the temple; and both in the morning and afternoon God was eminently present in the midst of the congregation." (Journal.)

Here the brothers agreed to officiate as often as possible till the congregation should be settled. Two resident clergymen were also employed at this chapel as curates, for reading the full Church service, administering the sacraments, and burying the dead. But Mr. Charles Wesley took some little offense at the liberty given to the preachers to officiate in his brother's absence, and when he himself could not supply. His letter of complaint produced, however, no change in his brother's appointments, nor was it likely. Mr. Wesley knew well that his own preaching at the new chapel, and the ministrations of the other clergymen, during the hours of service in the parish church, without a license from the bishop, or the acknowledgment of his spiritual jurisdiction, was just as irregular an affair, considered ecclesiastically, as the other. The City Road Chapel, with its establishment of clergy, service in canonical hours, and sacraments, was, in the eye of the law, as much as any Dissenting place of worship in London, a conventicle; though, when tried by a better rule, it was eminently, in those days of power and simplicity, "none other than the house of God, and the gate of heaven," to devout worshipers. An influence of a very extraordinary kind often rested upon the vast congregations assembled there; thousands were trained up in it for the kingdom of God; and the society exhibited a greater number of members, perhaps, than any other, except that in Bristol, who, for intelligence, deep experience in the things of God, stability, meekness of spirit, and holiness of life, were at once the ornaments of Methodism, and an influential example to the other societies of the metropolis.

In 1778 Mr. Wesley began to publish a periodical work, which he entitled, "The Arminian Magazine; consisting of Extracts and Original Treatises on Universal Redemption." He needed a medium through which he could reply to the numerous attacks made upon him; and he made use of it farther to introduce into general circulation several choice treatises on Universal Redemption, and to publish selections from his valuable correspondence with pious persons. He conducted this work while he lived; and it is still continued by the conference, under the title of the "Wesleyan Methodist Magazine," on the same general principles as to its theology, though on a more enlarged plan.

A dispute of a somewhat serious aspect arose in the following year, out of the appointment of a clergyman by Mr. Wesley to preach every Sunday evening in the chapel at Bath. It was not probable that the preachers of the circuit should pay the same deference to a strange clergyman, recently introduced, as to Mr. Wesley; but when this exclusive occupation of the pulpit on Sunday evenings was objected to by them and part of the society, Mr. Wesley, supported by his brother, who had accompanied him to Bath, stood firmly upon his right to appoint *when* and *where* the preachers should officiate, as a fundamental part of the compact between them; and the assistant preacher, Mr. M'Nab, was suspended till "he came to another mind." As Mr. M'Nab, who had thus fallen under Mr. Wesley's displeasure, was supported by many of the other preachers, a stormy conference was anticipated. To this meeting Mr. Wesley, therefore, foreseeing that his authority would be put to the trial, strongly invited his brother, in order that he might assist him with his advice. At first Mr. Charles Wesley declined, on the ground that he could not trust to his brother's vigor and resolution. He, however, attended, but when he saw that Mr. Wesley was determined to heal the breach by concession, he kept entire silence. The offending preacher was received back without censure, and, from this time, Dr. Whitehead thinks that Mr. Wesley's authority in the conference declined. This is not correct; but that authority was exercised in a different manner. Many of the preachers had become old in the work, and were men of great talents, tried fidelity, and influence with the societies These qualities were duly appreciated by Mr. Wesley, who now regarded them more than formerly, when they were young, and inexperienced, as his counselors and coadjutors. It was an eminent proof of Mr. Wesley's practical wisdom, that he never attempted to contend with circumstances not to be controlled; and from this time he placed his supremacy no longer upon authority, but upon the influence of wisdom, character, and age, and thus confirmed rather than diminished it. Had Mr. Charles Wesley felt sure of being supported by his brother with what he called "vigor," it is plain, from his letter on the occasion, that he would have stood upon the alternative of the unconditional submission of all the preachers, or a separation. His brother chose a more excellent way, and no doubt foresaw, not only that if a separation had been driven on by violence, it would have been an extensive one, but that among the societies which remained the same process would naturally, and necessarily, at some future time take place, and so nothing be ultimately gained, to counterbalance the immediate mischief. The silence maintained by Mr. Charles Wesley in this conference did him also great honor. He suspected "the warmth of his temper;" he saw that, as his brother was bent upon conciliation, any thing he could say would only endanger the mutual confidence between him and his preachers, and he held his peace. He himself believed that a formal separation of the body of preachers and people from the Church would inevitably take place after his brother's death, and thought it best to bring on the crisis before that event. "You," says he to his brother, "think otherwise, and I submit." The fact has been, that no *such* separation as he feared, that is, separation on such principles, and under such feelings of hostility to the Established Church, has yet taken place.

The following letter written by Mr. Wesley in 1782, to a nobleman high in office, shows how much his mind was alive to every thing which concerned the morals and religion of the country, and is an instance of the happy manner in which he could unite courtesy with reproof without destroying its point. A report prevailed that the ministry designed to embody the militia, and exercise them on a Sunday:

"My Lord,—If I wrong your lordship I am sorry for it; but I really believe your lordship fears God; and I hope your lordship has no unfavorable opinion of the Christian revelation. This encourages me to trouble your lordship with a few lines, which otherwise I should not take upon me to do.

"Above thirty years ago, a motion was made in Parliament, for raising and embodying the militia, and for exercising them, to save time, on Sunday. When the motion was like to pass, an old gentleman stood up and said, 'Mr. Speaker, I have one objection to this: I believe an old book, called the Bible.' The members looked at one another, and the motion was dropped.

"Must not all others, who believe the Bible, have the very same objection? And from what I have seen, I can not but think, these are still three-fourths of the nation. Now, setting religion out of the question, is it expedient to give such a shock to so many millions of people at once? And certainly it would shock them extremely: it would wound them in a very tender part. For would not they, would not all England, would not all Europe, consider this as a virtual repeal of the Bible? And would not all serious persons say, 'We have little religion in the land now; but by this step we shall have less still. For wherever this pretty show is to be seen, the people will flock together, and will lounge away so much time before and after it, that the churches will be emptier than they are already!'

"My lord, I am concerned for this on a double account. First, because I have personal obligations to your lordship, and would fain, even for this reason, recommend your lordship to the love and esteem of all over whom I have any influence. Secondly, because I now reverence your lordship for your office's sake; and believe it to be my bounden duty to do all that is in my little power, to advance your lordship's influence and reputation.

"Will your lordship permit me to add a word in my old-fashioned way? I pray Him that has all power in heaven and earth, to prosper all your endeavors for the public good, and am, my lord, your lordship's willing servant,

"John Wesley."

In 1783 Mr. Wesley paid a visit to Holland, having been pressed to undertake this journey by a Mr. Ferguson, formerly a member of the London society, who had made acquaintance with some pious people, who, having read Mr. Wesley's Sermons, were desirous of seeing him.

The following are extracts from his journal; and they will be read with pleasure, both as exhibiting his activity at so advanced an age, and as they present an interesting picture of his intercourse with a pious remnant in several parts of that morally-deteriorated country:

"Wednesday, June 11.—I took coach with Mr. Brackenbury, Broadbent, and Whitefield, and in the evening we reached Harwich. I went immediately to Dr. Jones, who received me in the most affectionate manner. About nine in the morning we sailed, and at nine on Friday, 13th, landed at Helvoetsluys. Here we hired a coach for Briel; but were forced to hire a wagon also, to carry a box, which one of us could have carried on his shoulders. At Briel we took a boat to Rotterdam. We had not been long there when Mr. Bennet, a bookseller, who had invited me to his house, called for me. But as Mr. Loyal, the minister of the Scotch congregation, had invited me, he gave up his claim, and went with us to Mr. Loyal's. I found a friendly, sensible, hospitable, and, I am persuaded, a pious man.

"Saturday 14.—I had much conversation with the two English ministers, sensible, well-bred, serious men. These, as well as Mr. Loyal, were very willing I should preach in their churches; but they thought it would be best for me to preach in the episcopal church. By our conversing freely together many prejudices were removed, and all our hearts seemed to be united together.

"Sunday 15.—The episcopal church is not quite so large as the chapel in West-street: it is very elegant both without and within. The service began at half past nine. Such a congregation had not often been there before. I preached on, 'God created man in his own image.' The people 'seemed all, but their attention, dead.' In the afternoon the church was so filled, as—they informed me—it had not been for these fifty years. I preached on, 'God hath given us eternal life; and this life is in his Son.'

I believe God applied it to many hearts. Were it only for this hour, I am glad I came to Holland.

"Monday 16.—We set out in a track-skuit for the Hague: by the way, we saw a curiosity—the gallows near the canal surrounded with a knot of beautiful trees! so the dying man will have one pleasant prospect here, whatever befalls him hereafter.

"At eleven we came to Delft, a large, handsome town; where we spent an hour at a merchant's house; who, as well as his wife, a very agreeable woman, seemed both to fear and to love God. Afterward we saw the great church, I think nearly, if not quite, as long as York Minster. It is exceedingly light and elegant within, and every part is kept exquisitely clean.

"When we came to the Hague, though we had heard much of it, we were not disappointed. It is indeed beautiful beyond expression. Many of the houses are exceedingly grand, and are finely intermixed with water and wood; yet not too close, but so as to be sufficiently ventilated by the air.

"Being invited to tea by Madam de Vassenaar—one of the first quality in the Hague—I waited upon her in the afternoon. She received us with that easy openness and affability, which is almost peculiar to Christians and persons of quality. Soon after came ten or twelve ladies more who seemed to be of her own rank—though dressed quite plainly—and two most agreeable gentlemen: one of whom, I afterward understood, was a colonel in the prince's guards. After tea I expounded the three first verses of the thirteenth chapter of the First Epistle to the Corinthians: Captain M. interpreted, sentence by sentence. I then prayed, and Colonel V. after me. I believe this hour was well employed.

"Tuesday 17.—We dined at Mrs. L.'s, in such a family as I have seldom seen. Her mother, upward of seventy, seemed to be continually rejoicing in God her Savior. The daughter breathes the same spirit; and her grandchildren, three little girls and a boy, seem to be all love. I have not seen four such children together in England. A gentleman coming in after dinner, I found a particular desire to pray for him. In a little while he melted into tears, as indeed did most of the company.

"Wednesday 18.—In the afternoon Madam de Vassenaar invited us to a meeting at a neighboring lady's house. I expounded Gal. vi, 14, and Mr. M. interpreted as before.

"Thursday 19.—We took boat at seven. Mrs. L., and one of her relations, being unwilling to part so soon, bore us company to Leyden, a large and populous town, but not so pleasant as Rotterdam. In the afternoon we went on to Haerlem, where a plain good man and his wife received us in a most affectionate manner. At six we took boat again: as it was filled from end to end, I was afraid we should not have a very pleasant journey. After Mr. Ferguson had told the people who we were, we made a slight excuse, and sung a hymn: they were all attention. We then talked a little, by means of our interpreter, and desired that any of them who pleased would sing. Four persons did so, and sung well: after awhile we sung again. So did one or two of them: and all our hearts were strangely knit together, so that when we came to Amsterdam, they dismissed us with abundance of blessings.

"Friday 20.—At five in the evening we drank tea at a merchant's, Mr. G.'s, where I had a long conversation with Mr. de H., one of the most learned as well as popular ministers in the city; and I believe—what is far more important—he is truly alive to God. He spoke Latin well, and seemed to be one of a strong understanding, as well as of an excellent spirit. In returning to our inn, we called at a stationer's, and though we spent but a few minutes, it was enough to convince us of his strong affection, even to strangers. What a change does the grace of God make in the heart! Shyness and stiffness are now no more!

"Sunday 22.—I went to the New Church, so called still, though four or five hundred years old. It is larger, higher, and better illuminated than most of our cathedrals. The screen that divides the church from the choir is of polished brass, and shines like gold. I understood the psalms that were sung, and the text, well, and a little of the sermon, which Mr. de H. delivered with great earnestness. At two I began the service at the English church, an elegant building, about the size of West-street Chapel; only it has no galleries, nor have any of the churches in Holland. I preached on Isaiah lv, 6, 7, and I am persuaded many received the truth in the love thereof.

"After service I spent another hour at Mr. V.'s. Mrs. V. again asked me abundance of questions concerning deliverance from sin, and seemed a great deal better satisfied with regard to the great and precious promises. Thence we went to Mr. B., who had lately found peace with God. He was full of faith and love, and could hardly mention the goodness of God without tears. His wife appeared to be of the same spirit, so that our hearts were soon knit together. From thence we went to another family, where a large company were assembled; but all seemed open to receive instruction, and desirous to be altogether Christians.

"Wednesday 25.—We took boat for Haerlem. The great church here is a noble structure, equaled by few cathedrals in England, either in length, breadth, or hight: the organ is the largest I ever saw, and is said to be the finest in Europe. Hence we went to Mr. Van K.'s, whose wife was convinced of sin, and brought to God, by reading Mr. Whitefield's Sermons.

"Here we were at home. Before dinner we took a walk in Haerlem wood. It adjoins to the town, and is cut out in many shady walks, with lovely vistas shooting out every way. The walk from Hague to Scheveling is pleasant; those near Amsterdam more so; but these exceed them all.

"We returned in the afternoon to Amsterdam, and in the evening took leave of as many of our friends as we could. How entirely were we mistaken in the Hollanders, supposing them to be of a cold, phlegmatic, unfriendly temper! I have not met with a more warmly-affectionate people in all Europe! No, not in Ireland!

"Thursday 26.—Our friends having largely provided us with wine and fruits for our little journey, we took boat in a lovely morning for Utrecht, with Mr. Van K.'s sister, who in the way gave us a striking account. 'In that house,' said she, pointing to it as we went by, 'my husband and I lived; and that church adjoining it, was his church. Five years ago, we were sitting together, being in perfect health, when he dropped down, and in a quarter of an hour died. I lifted up my heart and said, *Lord, thou art my husband now;* and found no will but his.' This was a trial worthy of a Christian: and she has ever since made her word good. We were scarcely got to our inn at Utrecht when Miss L. came; I found her just such as I expected. She came on purpose from her father's country house, where all the family were. I observe of all the pious people in Holland, that, without any rule but the word of God, they dress as plainly as Miss March did formerly, and Miss Johnson does now! And considering the vast disadvantage they are under, having no connection with each other, and being under no such discipline at all as we are, I wonder at the grace of God that is in them.

"Saturday 28.—I have this day lived fourscore years;

and by the mercy of God, my eyes are not waxed dim, and what little strength of body or mind I had thirty years since, is just the same as I have now. God grant I may never live to be useless. Rather may I

> 'My body with my charge lay down,
> And cease at once to work and live.'

"Sunday 29.—At ten I began the service in the English church in Utrecht. I believe all the English in the city were present, and forty or fifty Hollanders. I preached on the 13th of the First of Corinthians, I think as searchingly as ever in my life. Afterward a merchant invited me to dinner; for six years he had been at death's door by an asthma, and was extremely ill last night; but this morning, without any visible cause, he was well, and across the city to the church. He seemed to be deeply acquainted with religion, and made me promise, if I came to Utrecht again, to make his house my home.

"In the evening, a large company of us met at Miss L.'s, where I was desired to repeat the substance of my morning sermon. I did so, Mr. Toydemea—the professor of law in the university—interpreting it sentence by sentence. They then sung a Dutch hymn, and we an English one. Afterward Mr. Regulet, a venerable old man, spent some time in prayer for the establishment of peace and love between the two nations.

"Tuesday, July 1.—I called on as many as I could of my friends, and we parted with much affection. We then hired a yacht, which brought us to Helvoetsluys, about eleven the next day. At two we went on board; but the wind turning against us, we did not reach Harwich till about nine on Friday morning. After a little rest, we procured a carriage, and reached London about eleven at night.

"I can by no means regret either the trouble or expense which attended this little journey. It opened me a way into, as it were, a new world, where the land, the buildings, the people, the customs, were all such as I had never seen before; but as those with whom I conversed were of the same spirit with my friends in England, I was as much at home in Utrecht and Amsterdam, as in Bristol and London."

That provision for the stability and the government of the connection, after his death, which had been to Mr. Wesley a matter of serious concern for several years, was accomplished in 1784, and gave him, whenever he subsequently adverted to the subject, the greatest satisfaction. From this time he felt that he had nothing more to do, than to spend his remaining life in the same spiritual labors in which he had so long been engaged; and that he had done all that a true prudence required, to provide for the continuance and extension of a work which had so strangely enlarged under his superintendence.

This settlement was effected by a legal instrument, enrolled in chancery, called "A Deed of Declaration," in which one hundred preachers, mentioned by name, were declared to be "the conference of the people called Methodists." By means of this deed, a legal description was given to the term conference, and the settlement of the chapels upon trustees was provided for; so that the appointment of preachers to officiate in them should be vested in the conference, as it had heretofore been in Mr. Wesley. The deed also declares how the succession and identity of the yearly conference is to be continued, and contains various regulations as to the choice of a president and secretary, the filling up of vacancies, expulsions, etc. Thus "the succession," as it was called in Mr. Charles Wesley's letter, above quoted, was provided for; and the conference, with its president, chosen annually, came into the place of the founder of the connection, and has so continued to the present day. As the whole of the preachers were not included in the deed, and a few who thought themselves equally entitled to be of the hundred preachers who thus formed the legal conference, were excepted, some dissatisfaction arose; but as all the preachers were eligible to be introduced into that body, as vacancies occurred, this feeling was but partial, and soon subsided.* All the preachers in full connection were also allowed to vote in the conference; and subsequently, those who were not of the hundred, but had been in connection a certain number of years, were permitted, by their votes, to put the president into nomination for the confirmation of the legal conference. Thus all reasonable ground for mistrust and jealousy was removed from the body of the preachers at large; and with respect to the hundred preachers themselves, the president being chosen annually, and each being eligible to that honor, efficiency of administration was wisely connected with equality. The consequence has been, that the preachers have generally remained most firmly united by affection and mutual confidence, and that few serious disputes have ever arisen among them, or have extended beyond a very few individuals. Ecclesiastical history does not, perhaps, present an instance of an equal number of ministers brought into contact so close, and called so frequently together, for the discussion of various subjects, among whom so much general unanimity, both as to doc-

* "Messrs. John Hampson, sen., and John Hampson, jr., his son, William Eells, and Joseph Pilmoor, with a few other traveling preachers, were greatly offended that their names were not inserted in the deed. By Mr. Fletcher's friendly efforts, a partial reconciliation was effected between them and Mr. Wesley; but it was of short continuance. Soon after the conference, 1784, Mr. Hampson, senior, became an independent minister; but being old and infirm, and the people poor among whom he labored, he was assisted out of the preachers' fund while he lived. He died in the year 1795. Mr. Hampson, jr., procured ordination in the Established Church, and got a living in Sunderland, in the north of England. Mr. Eells also left the connection, and, some time after, joined Mr. Atlay at Dewsbury; and Mr. Pilmoor went to America." (Myles.)

trines and points of discipline, has prevailed, joined with so much real good-will and friendship toward each other, for so great a number of years. This is the more remarkable, as, by their frequent changes from station to station, opposite interests and feelings are very often brought into conflict. The final decisions of the conference on their appointment to these stations, generally the most perplexing part of its annual business, are, however, cheerfully or patiently submitted to, from the knowledge that each has of the public spirit with which that body is actuated, and the frank and brotherly manner in which all its proceedings are conducted. The order of proceeding in the business of the conference is the same as in the days of Mr. Wesley. It admits candidates for the ministry, on proper recommendation from the superintendents and district meetings; examines those who have completed their probation of four years, and receives the approved into full connection, which is its ordination; investigates, without any exception, the character and talents of those who are already in connection year by year; appoints the stations of the year ensuing; sends additional preachers to new places; receives the reports of the committees appointed to manage and distribute various funds; reviews the state of the societies; and issues an annual pastoral address. At the time of the meeting of the conferences, beside the Sunday services, public worship is held early in the morning, and in the evening of every day except Saturday, which is usually attended by great multitudes. The business of each conference, exclusive of that done in committees, which meet previously, occupies, on the average, about a fortnight in every year. Were it not for the district meetings, composed of the preachers and the stewards of a number of circuits, or stations, in different parts of the kingdom—an arrangement which was adopted after Mr.

Wesley's death—the business of the conference would require a much longer time to transact; but in these meetings much is prepared for its final decision.

In this important and wise settlement of the government of the connection by its founder, there appears but one regulation which seems to controvert that leading maxim to which he had always respect; namely, to be guided by circumstances in matters not determined by some great principle. I allude to the proviso which obliges the conference not to appoint any preacher to the same chapel for more than three years successively, thus binding an itinerant ministry upon the societies for ever. Whether this system of changing ministers be essential to the spiritual interests of the body or not, or whether it might not be usefully modified, will be matters of opinion; but the point ought, perhaps, to have been left more at liberty.*

CHAPTER XIII.

The state in which the separation of the United States from the mother country left the Methodist American societies, had become a matter of serious concern to Mr. Wesley, and presented to him a new case, for which it was

* [With the most respectful deference for the judgment of our beloved author, whose Methodistical orthodoxy can so rarely even be questioned, we must beg leave to say that in our humble opinion this very proviso in Mr. Wesley's Deed of Declaration, for the permanent establishment of the fundamental principles by which the conference should ever thereafter be governed, was one of the wisest measures in the whole instrument; and in this opinion, we greatly mistake if ninety-nine hundredths, at least, of the whole American Methodist Episcopal body do not accord. The great in convenience of this system to itinerant ministers themselves, and the consequent temptation to modify or to depart from it, we well know; and so did Mr. Wesley. His own inclination from youth, he often declared, was to saunter among academic shades, and be a philosophical sluggard, rather than an itinerant preacher. He knew that similar temptations, with the

imperative to make some provision. This, however, could not be done but by a proceeding which he foresaw would lay him open to much remark, and some censure from the rigid English Episcopalians. But with him, the principle of making every thing indifferent give place to the necessity of doing good or preventing evil, was paramount; and when that necessity was clearly made out, he was not a man to hesitate. The mission of Messrs. Boardman and Pilmoor to America has been already mentioned. Two years afterward, in 1771, Mr. Wesley sent out Messrs. Asbury and Wright; and in 1773, Messrs. Rankin and Shadford. In 1777 the preachers in the different circuits in America had amounted to forty, and the societies had also greatly increased. These were scattered in towns and settlements so distant that it required constant and extensive traveling from the preachers to supply them with the word

enjoyments of domestic life, etc., would increase in their enticing power, as Methodism itself should increase, and the circumstances both of the people and of the preachers become improved. And believing, as he firmly did, that an itinerant ministry was *essential* to the most rapid and extensive spread of the Gospel, and to the salvation of the greatest number of souls, till time shall end, he hence, in conformity with this conviction, made this unalterable principle in the economy of which he was the founder. And has not all our experience attested his wisdom? Mr. Watson, we know, says no more than that "perhaps" the point ought to have been left more at liberty; and is by no means to be understood, we are persuaded, as being in favor of a change, even if the liberty were possessed. Indeed, other denominations are now beginning both to see the incomparable efficiency of the itinerant system, and to act upon it—not only by the establishment of itinerant *missions*, but of regular *circuits*, very much on our plan. We wish them God speed. But let us not retrograde while others advance. Rather, let us give the more earnest heed that none take our crown—that we lose not the things we have already wrought, but receive a full reward. It is the glory of reviving this apostolical system that sheds its brightest luster on the name and the memory of Wesley. May it be that of his successors to perpetuate it, and, in order thereto, to keep themselves beyond the reach of even temptation to do otherwise! If in this note we seem to dissent in any measure from an incidental suggestion of our excellent author, we have the satisfaction, on the other hand, to be sustained by the judgment and wisdom of Mr. Wesley.—AMERICAN EDIT.]

of God.* The two last-mentioned preachers returned, after employing themselves on the mission for about five years; and Mr. Asbury, a true itinerant, who in this respect followed in America the unwearied example of Mr. Wesley, gradually acquired a great and deserved influence, which, supported as it was by his excellent sense, moderating temper, and entire devotedness to the service of God, increased rather than diminished to the end of a protracted life. The American preachers, like those in England, were at first restrained by Mr. Wesley from administering either of the sacraments; but when, through the war, and the acquisition of independence by the states, most of the clergy of the Church of England had left the country, neither the children of the members of the Methodist societies could be baptized, nor the Lord's supper administered among them, without a change of the original plan. Mr. Asbury's predilections for the former order of things prevented him from listening to the request of the American societies to be formed into a regular Church, and furnished with all its spiritual privileges; and a division had already taken place among them. This breach, however, Mr. Asbury had the address to heal; and at the peace he laid the whole case before Mr. Wesley. The result will be seen in the following letter:

"TO DR. COKE, MR. ASBURY, AND OUR BRETHREN IN NORTH AMERICA.

"*Bristol, September* 10, 1784.

"By a very uncommon train of providences, many of the provinces of North America are totally disjoined from their mother country, and erected into independent states. The

* [Messrs. Boardman and Pilmoor returned to England in 1774; Messrs. Rankin and Rodda in 1777; and Mr. Shadford in 1778. Mr. Pilmoor came to America again after the Revolutionary war, took orders in the Protestant Episcopal Church, and died, at an advanced age, in Philadelphia. Mr. Watson states, in a preceding note, that Mr. Pilmoor was one of those few itinerant preachers who were much offended because his

English government has no authority over them, either civil or ecclesiastical, any more than over the states of Holland. A civil authority is exercised over them, partly by the Congress, partly by the provincial assemblies. But no one either exercises or claims any ecclesiastical authority at all. In this peculiar situation, some thousands of the inhabitants of these states desire my advice; and, in compliance with their desire, I have drawn up a little sketch.

"Lord King's account of the primitive Church convinced me, many years ago, that bishops and presbyters are the same order, and, consequently, have the same right to ordain. For many years I have been importuned, from time to time, to exercise this right, by ordaining part of our traveling preachers; but I have still refused, not only for peace' sake, but because I was determined, as little as possible, to violate the established order of the National Church to which I belonged.

"But the case is widely different between England and North America. Here there are bishops who have a legal jurisdiction. In America there are none, neither any parish ministers, so that, for some hundred miles together, there is none either to baptize or to administer the Lord's supper. Here, therefore, my scruples are at an end; and I conceive myself at full liberty, as I violate no order, and invade no man's right, by appointing and sending laborers into the harvest.

"I have accordingly appointed Dr. Coke and Mr. Francis Asbury to be joint superintendents over our brethren in North America, as also Richard Whatcoat and Thomas Vasey to act as elders among them, by baptizing and

name was not inserted in Mr. Wesley's Deed of Declaration, constituting the legal conference. This, in all probability, had a principal influence in his coming to America again, and taking orders in the Protestant Episcopal Church. We believe, however, that he always continued friendly with our body, and lived and died an evangelical and highly-respected minister.—AMERICAN EDIT.]

administering the Lord's supper. And I have prepared a liturgy, little differing from that of the Church of England—I think the best constituted national Church in the world—which I advise all the traveling preachers to use on the Lord's day, in all the congregations, reading the litany only on Wednesdays and Fridays, and praying extempore on all other days. I also advise the elders to administer the supper of the Lord on every Lord's day.

"If any one will point out a more rational and Scriptural way of feeding and guiding those poor sheep in the wilderness, I will gladly embrace it. At present I can not see any better method than that I have taken.

"It has, indeed, been proposed to desire the English bishops to ordain part of our preachers for America. But to this I object, 1. I desired the bishop of London to ordain only one, but could not prevail; 2. If they consented, we know the slowness of their proceedings; but the matter admits of no delay; 3. If they would ordain them now, they would likewise expect to govern them. And how grievously would this entangle us! 4. As our American brethren are now totally disentangled both from the state and from the English hierarchy, we dare not entangle them again either with the one or the other. They are now at full liberty simply to follow the Scriptures and the primitive Church. And we judge it best that they should stand fast in that liberty wherewith God has so strangely made them free. JOHN WESLEY."

Two persons were thus appointed as superintendents or bishops, and two as elders, with power to administer the sacraments, and the American Methodists were formed into a Church, because they could no longer remain a society attached to a colonial establishment which then had ceased to exist. The propriety and even necessity of this step is sufficiently apparent; but the mode adopted exposed Mr. Wesley to the sarcasms of his brother, who was not a convert to his opinion as to the identity of the order of bishops and presbyters; and to all High Churchmen the proceeding has had the appearance of great irregularity. The only real irregularity, however, has been generally overlooked, while a merely-apparent one has been made the chief subject of animadversion. The true anomaly was, that a clergyman of the Church of England should ordain, in any form, without separating from that Church, and formally disavowing its authority; and yet, if its spiritual governors did not choose to censure and disown him for denying the figment of the uninterrupted succession, which he openly said "he knew to be a fable;" for maintaining that bishops and priests were originally one order only—points, let it be observed, which perhaps but few Churchmen will now, and certainly but few at that time, would very seriously maintain, so decisive is the evidence of Scripture and antiquity against them, and so completely was the doctrine of the *three* orders given up by the founders of the English Church itself;* nor, finally, for

* "I am not ashamed of the room and office which I have given to me by Christ to preach his Gospel; for it is the power of God, that is to say, the elect organ or instrument ordained by God, and endued with such virtue and efficacy, that it is able to give, and administer effectually, everlasting life to all those that will believe and obey to the same.

"Item. That this office, this power and authority, was committed and given by Christ and his apostles to certain persons only, that is to say, to priests and bishops whom they did elect, call and admit thereto, by their prayers, and imposition of their hands.

"*The truth is, there is no mention made of any degrees or distinctions in orders, but only of deacons or ministers, and of priests or bishops.*" A DECLARATION MADE OF THE FUNCTIONS AND DIVINE INSTITUTION OF BISHOPS AND PRIESTS, *Regno Hen.* [in the reign of Henry] VIII, *circiter* [about] *A. D.* 1537–40.

This declaration was signed by Cromwell, the vicar-general, Cranmer and Holgate, the archbishops, with many of their suffragans, together with other persons intituled,

"*Sacræ Theologiæ, Juris Ecclesiastici et Civilis, Professores,*" [Professors of Divinity and of Ecclesiastical and Civil Law.]

Archbishop Usher's plan for comprehending the Presbyterians and Episcopalians in the time of Charles I, was also founded upon the principle of bishops and presbyters being *one order.*

proceeding to act upon that principle by giving orders; it would be hard to prove that he was under any moral obligation to withdraw from the Church. The bishops did not institute proceedings against him, and why should he formally renounce them altogether? It was doubtless such a view of his liberty, in this respect, that made him say on this occasion, in answer to his brother, "I firmly believe that I am a Scriptural ἐπίσκοπος as much as any man in England, or in Europe; for the uninterrupted succession I know to be a fable, which no man ever did or can prove. But this does, in no wise, interfere with my remaining in the Church of England; from which I have no more desire to separate than I had fifty years ago."

The point which has been most insisted upon is the absurdity of a priest ordaining bishops. But this absurdity could not arise from the principle which Mr. Wesley had adopted, namely, that the orders were identical; and the censure, therefore, rests only upon the assumption, that bishops and priests were of different orders, which he denied. He never did pretend to ordain bishops in the modern sense, but only according to his view of primitive episcopacy. Little importance, therefore, is to be attached to Mr. Moore's statement, (Life of Wesley,) that Mr. Wesley having named Dr. Coke and Mr. Asbury simply superintendents, he was displeased when, in America, they took the title of bishops. The only objection he could have to the name was, that from long association it was likely to convey a meaning beyond his own intention. But this was a matter of mere prudential feeling, confined to himself: so that neither are Dr. Coke and Mr. Asbury to be blamed for using that appellation in Mr. Wesley's sense, which was the same as presbyter as far as order was concerned, nor the American societies—as they have sometimes inconsiderately been—for calling themselves, in the same view, "The American Methodist Episcopal Church;' since their episcopacy is founded upon the principle of bishops and presbyters being of the same *degree*—a more extended *office* only being assigned to the former, as in the primitive Church. For though nothing can be more obvious than that the primitive pastors are called bishops, or presbyters indiscriminately in the New Testament, yet at an early period those presbyters were, by way of distinction, denominated bishops, who presided in the meetings of the presbyters, and were finally invested with the government of several Churches, with their respective presbyteries; so that two *offices* were then, as in this case, grafted upon the same *order*. Such an arrangement was highly proper for America, where many of the preachers were young, and had also to labor in distant and extensive circuits, and were, therefore, incapable of assisting, advising, or controlling each other. A traveling episcopacy, or superintendency, was there an extension of the office of elder or presbyter, but it of course created no other distinction; and the bishops of the Methodist Episcopal Church have in practice as well exemplified the primitive spirit, as in principle they were conformed to the primitive discipline. Dr. Coke was only an occasional visitant in America, and though in the sense of *office* he was a bishop there, when he returned home, as here he had no such office, so he used no such title, and made no such pretension. Of this excellent man, it ought here to be said, that occasional visits to America could not satisfy his ardent mind; he became the founder and soul of the Methodist missions in various parts of the world, first under the direction of Mr. Wesley, and then in conjunction with the conference; and by his voyages, travels, and labors, he erected a monument of noble, disinterested zeal and charity, which will never be obliterated.* But Mr. Asbury remained

* Dr. Coke connected himself with Mr. Wesley in 1776, as stated by the latter in his journal: "Being at Kingston, near Taunton, I found a

the preaching, traveling, self-denying bishop of the American societies, till afterward others were associated with him, plain and simple in their manners as the rest of their brethren, and distinguished from them only by "labors more abundant."

It was thus by absurdly confounding episcopacy in the modern acceptation, and in Mr. Wesley's view, that a good deal of misplaced wit was played off on this occasion; and not a little bitterness was expressed by many. He, however, performed a great and a good work, and not only provided for the spiritual wants of a people who indirectly had sprung from his labors, but gave to the American Church a form of administration admirably suited to a new and extensive empire, and under which the societies have, by the Divine blessing, prospered beyond all precedent. Some letters passed between him and Mr. Charles Wesley on the subject of the American ordinations. The first, written by Charles, was warm and remonstrative; the second, upon receiving his brother's calm answer, was more mild, and shows, that he was less afraid of what his brother had done for America, than that Dr. Coke, on his return, should form the Methodists of England into a regular and separate Church also! The concluding paragraph of this letter is, however, so affecting, so illustrative of that oneness of heart which no difference of opinion between the brothers could destroy, that it would be unjust to the memory of both, not to insert it:

"I thank you for your intention to remain my friend. Herein my heart is as your heart. Whom God hath joined, let no man put asunder. We have taken each

clergyman, Dr. Coke, late gentleman commoner of Jesus College, in Oxford, who came twenty miles on purpose. I had much conversation with him, and a union then began, which, I trust, shall never end." His name did not appear on the minutes till the year 1778. In that year he was appointed to labor in London.

other for better for worse, till death do us—part? no: but eternally unite. Therefore, in the love which never faileth, I am,

"Your affectionate friend and brother,

"C. WESLEY."

Some time after this, Mr. Wesley appointed several of the English preachers, by imposition of hands, to administer the sacraments to the societies in Scotland. There the English establishment did not extend, and a necessity of a somewhat similar kind existed, though not of so pressing a nature as in America. He, however, steadily objected to give this liberty, generally, to his preachers in England: and those who administered the sacraments in Scotland were not permitted to perform the same office in England upon their return. The reason why he refused to appoint in the same manner, and for the same purpose, for England is stated in the letter above given. He was satisfied of his power, as a presbyter, to ordain for such an administration; but he says, "I have still refused, not only for peace' sake, but because I was determined as little as possible to violate the established order of the National Church to which I belonged." This was a prudent principle most sincerely held by him; and it explains his conduct in those particulars for which he has been censured by opposite parties. When it could not be avoided, without sacrificing some real good, he did violate "the established order," thinking that this order was in itself merely prudential. When that necessity did not exist, his own predilections, and the prejudices of many members of his societies, enforced upon him this abstinence from innovation. It may, however, be asked, in what light Mr. Wesley's appointments to the ministry, in the case of his own preachers, ought to be viewed. That they were ordinations to the work and office of the ministry, can not be reasonably and Scripturally doubted;

and that they were so in his own *intention,* we have before shown from his own minutes. It was required of them, as early as 1746, to profess to be "moved by the Holy Ghost, and to be called of God to preach." This professed call was to be tested by their piety, their gifts, and their usefulness; all which points were investigated; and after probation they were solemnly received by prayer "to labor with him in the Gospel;" and from that time were devoted wholly to their spiritual work,* including the *pastoral* care of societies. Here was ordination, though without imposition of hands, which, although an impressive ceremony, enters not, as both the Scriptures and the nature of the thing itself point out, into the essence of ordination; which is a separation of men, by ministers, to the work of the ministry by solemn prayer. This was done at every conference, by Mr. Wesley, who, as he had, as early as 1747, given up the uninterrupted succession, and the distinct order of bishops as a fable, left himself, therefore, at liberty to appoint to the ministry in his own way. He made, it is true, a distinction at one time between the primitive offices of evangelists or teachers, and pastors, as to the right of giving the sacraments, which he thought belonged to the latter only; but as this implied that the primitive pastors had powers which the primitive evangelists, who ordained them, had not, it was too unsupported a notion for him long to maintain. (See Moore's Life of Wesley, book viii, chap. ii.) Yet, had this view of the case been allowed, the preachers were not mere teachers, but pastors in the fullest sense. They not only taught, but guided, and managed the societies; receiving members, excluding members, and administering private, as well as public, admonitions; and if they were constituted teachers

* It is observable, that in the conference of 1768 he enjoined abstinence from all secular things upon them, both on the Scriptural principle, 1 Tim iv, 13, and on the ground that the Church, "in her office of ordination required this of ministers.

and pastors by his ordination, without the circumstance of the imposition of hands, it is utterly impossible to conceive that that ceremony conveyed any larger right, *as such*, to administer the sacraments, in the case of the few he did ordain in that manner for Scotland and America. As to them it was a form of *permission* and *appointment* to exercise the right. His appointments to the ministry every conference necessarily conveyed all the rights of a pastor, because they conveyed the pastoral office; but still it did not follow that all the abstract rights of the ministry thus conveyed to the body of the preachers, should be actually used. It was not imperative upon them to exercise all their functions; and he assumed no improper authority, as the father and founder of the connection, to determine to what extent it was prudent to exercise them, provided he was satisfied that the sacraments were not put out of the power of the societies to observe. He exercised this suspending authority even over those preachers whom he appointed to give the sacraments in Scotland, by prohibiting them from administering in the English societies, over which they became pastors. So little difference did his ordination by imposition of hands make in their case, even in his own estimation.* It was, when it followed the usual mode of introducing candidates into the ministry, a mere form of permission to exercise a previous right in a particular place, and a solemn designation to this service according to a liturgical form which he greatly admired; but the true ordination of those who were so set apart to administer the sacraments to the ministry itself, was the same as that of the rest of their brethren, and took place at the same time. Thus, in Mr. Wesley's strongest language to Mr. Charles Perronet and the other preachers who thought it their duty

* When a few of the preachers received ordination from a Greek bishop, then in England, and from whom he was falsely reported himself to have sought consecration, he would not suffer them to administer, although he did not doubt that the Greek was a true bishop.

to administer, he places his objection upon the decisive ground of his thinking it "a sin;" but not from their want of true ordination, to which he makes no allusion;* but he thought it sinful, because it would be injurious to the work of God, and so contrary to his word and will. That it was not in his view "a sin," for want of mere imposition of hands, is clear from the facts, that, in one case, he gave to one of the preachers leave to baptize and give the sacrament in particular circumstances, although he had no other ordination than his being "received into full connection" at the conference like the rest, and allowed two others, Mr. Highfield, in England, and Mr. Myles, in Dublin, to assist him in giving the sacrament, to the great offense of the Church people there.† That the original designation of the preachers to the ministry was considered by the conferences after his death—when they were obliged, in order to meet the spiritual wants and Scriptural demands of the people, to administer the Lord's supper to the societies in England—as a true and full ordination to the whole office of the Christian ministry, is clear from their authorizing the preachers to give the sacraments, when requested by the societies, without reordination for this purpose, although they had Mr. Wesley's Presbyterian ordination by

* As early as 1756, he says to some of the preachers, "You think it is a duty to administer. Do so, and therein follow your own conscience." That is, they were at liberty to leave him; but not a word about the invalidity of their appointment to the whole work of the ministry.

† Mr. Wesley's innovations on Church order in Dublin appear, from several of his letters, to have produced somewhat outrageous attacks upon him from several quarters in that city. In one of them he says, "Every week I am bespattered in the public papers. Many are in tears on the occasion; many terribly frightened, and crying out, 'O, what will the end be?' What will it be? Why, glory to God in the highest, and peace and good-will among men." Such was his rejoinder to these High Church alarms. At the same time it must be conceded, that, however faithful Mr. Wesley was in abiding by his leading principle of making mere adherence to what was called "*regular*" give place to the higher obligation of doing good, he was sometimes apt, in defending himself, to be too tenacious of appearing perfectly consistent.

imposition of hands among themselves, and at their command, if they had judged it necessary to employ it. Their whole proceeding in this respect was merely to grant permission to exercise powers which they believed to have been previously conveyed by Mr. Wesley, in doing which they differed from him only in not marking that permission with any new form. Perhaps it might have been an improvement, had they accompanied all their future ordinations by the laying on of the hands of the president for the time being, assisted by a few of the senior preachers, and by using the fine ordination service of the Church of England: not, indeed, that this would have given a tittle more of validity to the act; but the imposition of hands would have been in conformity to the usage of the majority of Churches, and an instance of deference to an ancient Scriptural form of solemn designation and blessing, used on various occasions. The whole of Mr. Wesley's proceedings, both as to America and Scotland, would have been as valid on Scriptural grounds, had there been no other form used than simple prayer for men, already in the ministry, going forth on an important mission; but as the New Testament exhibited a profitable example of imposition of hands in the case of Paul and Barnabas, who had been long before ordained to the highest order of the ministry, when sent forth into a new field of labor, this example was followed.*

But we return to the continued and unabated labors of this venerable servant of God. In 1786, at the Bristol

* From the preceding observations, it will appear that Mr. Wesley's ordinations, both for America and Scotland, stood upon much the same ground. The full powers of the ministry had before been conveyed to the parties; but now they had a special designation to exercise them in every respect, in a new and peculiar sphere. Still their ordination, by imposition of hands, did not imply that their former ordination was deficient, as to the *right* of administering the sacraments which it conveyed; for then, how came Dr. Coke, who was already a presbyter of the Church of England, to be ordained again, when, according to Mr. Wesley's own

conference, the old subject of separating from the Church was again discussed, and, "without one dissenting voice," it was determined to continue therein; "which determination," he remarks, "will, I doubt not, stand, at least till I am removed into a better world." After the conference was concluded, he paid a second visit to Holland, in company with Mr. Brackenbury and Mr. Broadbent, preached in various places, expounded to private companies, and engaged in conversation with many learned and pious individuals. On his return to England, his journal presents the usual record of constant preaching and traveling, inter-

view, he could not be higher *in order* than a presbyter, although his powers might be *enlarged* as to their application? The conference, after Mr. Wesley's death, took, therefore, the true ground, in considering the act of admission into the ministry, so as to be devoted wholly to it, and to exercise the pastoral charge, to be a true and Scriptural ordination both to preach the word and to administer the sacraments; making wholly light of the absurd pretensions of a few among the preachers, who thought that they had received something more than their brethren from the mere ceremony of the imposition of Mr. Wesley's hands, subsequent to their ordinary appointment by him when received into the body. Some of these, at the first conference after Mr. Wesley's death, stood upon this point; but Mr. Benson refuted their notion, that imposition of hands was essential to ordination. He proved from the New Testament that this was but a circumstance, and showed that the body had always possessed a ministry Scripturally and therefore validly ordained, although not in the most customary or perhaps in the most influential form. With Mr. Benson the conference coincided, so that ordination, without imposition of hands, has continued to be the general practice to the present time. It is remarkable, that the few preachers who insisted upon imposition of hands being essential to ordination, and plumed themselves upon being distinguished from their brethren because Mr. Wesley's hands had been laid upon them, did not remember a passage in a published letter of Mr. Wesley to Mr. Walker, of Truro, dated as long before as 1756, which sufficiently shows how totally disconnected the two things were in his mind; or that, if they adverted to it, its bearing in his controversy with Mr. Walker should not have been perceived: "That the seven deacons were outwardly ordained even to that low office, can not be denied. But Paul and Barnabas were separated for the work to which they were called. This was not ordaining them; it was only inducting them to the province for which our Lord had appointed them. For this end the prophets and teachers fasted, prayed, and 'laid their hands upon them,' a rite which was used, not *in ordination only, but in blessing, and on many other occasions.*"

spersed with useful remark and incident. A few gleanings from it will be read with interest:

"December 23, 1786.—By great importunity I was induced—having little hope of doing good—to visit two of the felons in Newgate, who lay under sentence of death. They appeared serious; but I can lay little stress on appearances of this kind. However, I wrote in their behalf to a great man; and perhaps it was in consequence of this that they had a reprieve.

"Sunday 24.—I was desired to preach at the Old Jewry; but the church was cold, and so was the congregation. We had congregations of another kind the next day—Christmas day—at four in the morning, as well as five in the evening, at the New Chapel, and at West-street Chapel about noon.

"Sunday 31.—From those words of Isaiah to Hezekiah, 'Set thy house in order,' I strongly exhorted all who had not done it already, to settle their temporal affairs without delay. It is a strange madness which still possesses many who are in other respects men of understanding, that they put this off from day to day, till death comes in an hour when they look not for it.

"Friday, January 5, 1787, and in the vacant hours of the following days, I read Dr. Hunter's Lectures. They are very lively and ingenious. The language is good, and the thoughts generally just. But they do not suit my taste. I do not admire that florid way of writing. Good sense does not need to be so studiously adorned. I love St. John's style, as well as matter.

"Sunday, February 25.—After taking a solemn leave of our friends, both at West-street and the New Chapel, I took the mail-coach, and the next evening reached Exeter a little after ten o'clock. Tuesday 27.—We went on to Plymouth Dock. The large, new house, far the best in the west of England, was well filled, though on so short a warning; and they seemed cordially to receive the exhortation, 'Rejoice in the Lord, O ye righteous.' I had the satisfaction to find the society here in a more flourishing state than ever. Notwithstanding all the pains that have been taken, and all the art that has been used to tear them asunder, they cleave close together, and consequently increase in number as well as in strength.

"Wednesday, March 7.—It rained much while we were at Plymouth and at the Dock, and most of the way from the Dock to Exeter. But we had lovely weather to-day, and came into Bath early in the evening. So crowded a house I had not seen here for many years. I fully delivered my own soul, by strongly enforcing those awful words, 'Many are called, but few are chosen.' I believe the word sunk deep into many hearts. The next evening we had another large congregation equally serious. Thursday 8.—I went on to Bristol, and the same afternoon Mrs. Fletcher came thither from Madeley. The congregation in the evening was exceedingly large. I took knowledge what spirit they were of. Indeed the work of God has much increased in Bristol since I was here last, especially among the young men, many of whom are a pattern to all the society.

"Monday, April 2.—About noon I preached at Stockport, and in the evening at Manchester, where I fully delivered my own soul, both then and the next day. Wednesday 4.—I went to Chester, and preached in the evening on Heb. iii, 12. Finding there was no packet at Parkgate, I immediately took places in the mail-coach for Holyhead. The porter called us at two in the morning on Thursday, but came again in half an hour to inform us the coach was full: so they returned my money, and at four I took a post-chaise. We overtook the coach at Conway, and, crossing the ferry with the passengers, went forward without delay; so we came to Holyhead an hour before them, and went on board between eleven and twelve o'clock. At one we left the harbor, and at two the next day came into Dublin bay.

"On the road, and in the ship, I read Mr. Blackwell's 'Sacred Classics Illustrated and Defended.' I think he fully proves his point, that there are no expressions in the New Testament which are not found in the best and purest Greek authors. In the evening we had a Sunday's congregation, and a blessing from on high.

"Sunday 8. (Easter day.)—I preached in Bethesda, Mr. Smyth's new chapel: it is very neat, but not gay, and I believe will hold about as many people as West-street Chapel. Mr. Smyth read prayers, and gave out the hymns, which were sung by fifteen or twenty fine singers: the rest of the congregation listening with much attention, and as much devotion as they would have done to an opera. But is this Christian worship? Or ought it ever to be suffered in a Christian church? It was thought we had between seven and eight hundred communicants; and, indeed, the power of God was in the midst of them. Our own room in the evening was well filled with people, and with the presence of God.

"On Monday and Tuesday I preached again at Bethesda, and God touched several hearts, even of the rich and great; so that, for the time at least, they were 'almost persuaded to be Christians.' It seems as if the good providence of God had prepared this place for those rich and honorable sinners who will not deign to receive any message from God, but in a *genteel* way.

"Friday 27.—We went to Kilkenny, nine and twenty Irish miles from Mount Mellick. Religion was here at a low ebb, and scarcely any society left, when God sent three troops of horse. Several of the men are full of faith and love; since they came, the work of God has revived.

I never saw the house so filled since it was built. And the power of God seemed to rest upon the congregation, as if he would still have a people in this place.

"Wednesday, April 9.—We went to Bandon: here, also, there has been a remarkable work of God, and yet not without many backsliders. It was, therefore, my chief business to strengthen the weak, and recall the wanderers. So in the evening I preached in the assembly room—which was offered me by the provost—on, 'How shall I give thee up, Ephraim?' and God applied his word. At noon we took a walk to Castle Barnard. Mr. Barnard has given it a beautiful front, nearly resembling that of Lord Mansfield's house at Caen Wood, and opened part of his lovely park to the house, which I think has now as beautiful a situation as Rockingham-house in Yorkshire. Mr. Barnard much resembles, in person and air, the late Sir George Saville. Though he is far the richest person in these parts, he keeps no race-horses or hounds, but loves his wife and home, and spends his time and fortune in improving his estate, and employing the poor. Gentlemen of this spirit are a blessing to their neighborhood. May God increase their number!

"In the evening, finding no building would contain the congregation, I stood in the main street, and testified to a listening multitude, 'This is not your rest.' I then administered the Lord's supper to the society, and God gave us a remarkable blessing.

"Friday, May 25.—I had a day of rest in this lovely family—Mr. Slack's—only preaching morning and evening.

"Saturday 26.—I preached at Ballyconnel about eleven. In the afternoon I took a walk in the bishop of Kilmore's garden. The house is finely situated; has two fronts, and is fit for a nobleman. We then went into the church-yard, and saw the venerable tomb, a plain flat stone inscribed, '*Depositum Gulielmi Bedel, quondam Episcopi Kilmoren-*

sis,' ['The body of William Bedel, formerly bishop of Kilmore;'] over whom even the rebel army sung, '*Requiescat in pace ultimus Anglorum*'—'Let the last of the Englishmen rest in peace.' At seven I preached to a large congregation: it blew a storm, but most of the congregation were covered by a kind of shed raised for the purpose; and not a few were greatly comforted.

"Tuesday 29.—One of my horses I was obliged to leave in Dublin, and afterward another, having bought two to supply their places. The third soon got a swelling in his shoulder, so that we doubted whether we could go on. And a boy at Clones, riding—I suppose galloping—the fourth over stones, the horse fell and nearly lamed himself; however, we went on softly to Aughalun, and found such a congregation as I had not seen before in the kingdom. The tent—that is, a covered pulpit—was placed at the foot of a green, sloping mountain, on the side of which the huge multitude sat—as their manner is—row above row. While I was explaining, 'God hath given unto us his Holy Spirit,' he was indeed poured out in a wonderful manner. Tears of joy, and cries were heard on every side, only so far suppressed as not to drown my voice. I can not but hope that many will have cause to bless God for that hour to all eternity.

"Thursday 31.—We went over mountains and dales to Kerlish Lodge, where we met with a hearty welcome, both from Alexander Boyle and his amiable wife, who are patterns to all the country. Mr. Boyle had spoken to Dr. Wilson, the rector of a neighboring town, concerning my preaching in the church, who wrote to the bishop, and received a letter in answer, giving a full and free consent. The Doctor desired me to breakfast with him. Meantime one of his parishioners, a warm seceder, took away the key of the church, so I preached in a neighboring orchard: I believe not in vain. The rector and his wife were in the front of the congregation. Afterward we took a view of Lord Abercorn's place. The house has a lovely situation: and the front of it is as elegant as any I have seen either in Great Britain or Ireland. The grounds are delightful indeed, perhaps equal to any in the kingdom.

"About five in the evening I preached at Killrail. No house would contain the congregation, so I preached in the open air. The wind was piercingly cold, but the people regarded it not. Afterward I administered the Lord's supper to about a hundred of them, and then slept in peace.

"Wednesday, June 6.—I took leave of my dear friends in Londonderry, and drove to Newton Limavady. I had no design to preach there. But while we were at breakfast, the people were gathered so fast that I could not deny them. The house was soon filled from end to end. I explained to them the fellowship believers have with God. Thence I went on to Colerain, and preached at six—as I did two years ago—in the barrack yard. The wind was high and sharp enough; but the people here are good old soldiers. Many attended at five in the morning, and a large congregation about six in the evening; most of whom, I believe, tasted the good word; for God was with us of a truth.

"Tuesday 12.—We came through a most beautiful country to Downpatrick, a much larger town than I imagined; I think not much inferior to Sligo. The evening was uncommonly mild and bright, there not being a cloud in the sky. The tall firs shaded us on every side, and the fruitful fields were spread all around. The people were, I think, half as many more as were at Lisburn even on Sunday evening. On them I enforced those important words, 'Acquaint thyself now with Him, and be at peace.'

"Wednesday 13.—Being informed we had only six and twenty miles to go, we did not set out till between six and seven. The country was uncommonly pleasant, running between two high ridges of mountains; but it was up hill and down all the way; so that we did not reach Rathfriland till nearly noon. Mr. Barber, the Presbyterian minister—a princely personage, I believe six feet and a half high—offering me his new, spacious preaching house, the congregation quickly gathered together. I began without delay to open and enforce, 'Now God commandeth all men, every-where, to repent.' I took chaise the instant I had done; but the road being still up hill and down, we were two hours going what they called six miles. I then quitted the chaise, and rode forward. But even then, four miles, so called, took an hour and a half riding; so that I did not reach Dr. Lesley's, at Tandaragee, till half an hour past four. About six I stood upon the steps at Mr. Godly's door, and preached on, 'This is not your rest,' to a larger congregation, by a third, than even that at Downpatrick. I scarcely remember to have seen a larger, unless in London, Yorkshire, or Cornwall.

"Tuesday 26.—Dublin. We were agreeably surprised with the arrival of Dr. Coke, who came from Philadelphia, in nine and twenty days, and gave us a pleasing account of the work of God in America. Thursday 28.—I had a conversation with Mr. Howard, I think one of the greatest men in Europe. Nothing but the mighty power of God can enable him to go through his difficult and dangerous employments. But what can hurt us, if God be on our side?

"Sunday, July 22.—Manchester. Our service began at ten. Notwithstanding the severe cold, which has continued many days, the house was well filled; but my work was easy, as Dr. Coke assisted me. As many as could crowded in, in the evening; but many were obliged to go away. Afterward I spent a comfortable hour with the society.

"Friday 27.—We went on to Bolton. Here are eight

hundred poor children taught in our Sunday schools by about eighty masters, who receive no pay but what they are to receive from their great Master. About a hundred of them, part boys, and part girls, are taught to sing. And they sung so true, that, all singing together, they seemed to be but one voice. The house was thoroughly filled, while I explained and applied the first and great commandment. What is all morality or religion without this? A mere castle in the air. In the evening, many of the children still hovering round the house, I desired forty or fifty to come in and sing,

'Vital spark of heavenly flame.'

Although some of them were silent, not being able to sing for tears, yet the harmony was such as I believe could not be equaled in the king's chapel.

"Monday, August 6.—Having taken the whole coach for Birmingham, we set out, expecting to be there, as usual, about five in the evening. But having six persons within, and eight without, the coach could not bear the burden, but broke down before three in the morning. Having patched it together as well as we could, we went on to Congleton, and got another. In an hour or two this broke also; and one of the horses was so thoroughly tired, that he could hardly set one foot before the other. After all these hinderances, we got to Birmingham just at seven. Finding a large congregation waiting, I stepped out of the coach into the house, and began preaching without delay. And such was the goodness of God, that I found no more weariness when I had done than if I had rested all the day.

"Here I took a tender leave of Mrs. Heath and her lovely daughters, about to embark with Mr. Heath for America, whom I hardly expect to see any more till we meet in Abraham's bosom.

"Friday 10.—Southampton. At six I preached on

Heb. iv, 14. In the afternoon I went with a gentleman—Mr. Taylor—to hear the famous musician that plays upon the glasses. By my appearing there—as I had foreseen—a heap of gentry attended in the evening. And I believe several of them, as well as Mr. T. himself, did not come in vain.

"Tuesday 14.—Sailing on with a fair wind, we fully expected to reach Guernsey in the afternoon; but the wind turning contrary, and blowing hard, we found that would be impossible. We then judged it best to put in at the isle of Alderney; but we were very near being shipwrecked in the bay. About eight I went down to a convenient spot on the beach, and began giving out a hymn; a woman and two little children joined us immediately. Before the hymn was ended, we had a tolerable congregation, all of whom behaved well: part indeed continued at forty or fifty yards' distance, but they were all quiet and attentive.

"It happened, to speak in the vulgar phrase, that three or four who sailed with us from England, a gentleman, with his wife and sister, were near relations of the governor. He came to us this morning; and when I went into the room behaved with the utmost courtesy. This little circumstance may remove prejudice, and make a more open way for the Gospel.

"Soon after we set sail; and after a very pleasant passage, through little islands on either hand, we came to the venerable castle, standing on a rock about a quarter of a mile from Guernsey. The isle itself makes a beautiful appearance, spreading as a crescent to the right and left; about seven miles long and five broad, part high land and part low. The town itself is boldly situated, rising higher and higher from the water. The first thing I observed in it was very narrow streets, and exceedingly-high houses. But we quickly went on to Mr. de Jersey's, hardly a mile from the town. Here I found a most cordial welcome, both from the master of the house and all his family. I preached at seven, in a large room, to as deeply-serious a congregation as I ever saw, on 'Jesus Christ, of God made unto us wisdom, righteousness, sanctification, and redemption.'

"Monday 20.—We took ship between three and four in the morning, in a very small, inconvenient sloop, and not a swift sailer, so that we were seven hours in sailing what is called seven leagues. About eleven we landed at St. Helier's, and went straight to Mr. Brackenbury's house. It stands very pleasantly near the end of the town, and has a large, convenient garden, with a lovely range of fruitful hills, which rise at a small distance from it. I preached in the evening to an exceedingly-serious congregation, on Matt. iii, ult. And almost as many were present at five in the morning, whom I exhorted to go on to perfection, which many of them, Mr. Clarke informs me, are earnestly endeavoring to do.

"Thursday 23.—I rode to St. Mary's, five or six miles from St. Helier's, through shady, pleasant lanes. None at the house could speak English, but I had interpreters enow. In the evening our large room was thoroughly filled. I preached on, 'By grace ye are saved, through faith.' Mr. Brackenbury interpreted sentence by sentence, and God owned his word, though delivered in so awkward a manner: but especially in prayer; I prayed in English, and Mr. B. in French.

"Saturday 25.—Having now leisure, I finished a sermon on 'Discerning the Signs of the Times.' This morning I had a particular conversation—as I had once or twice before—with Jeannie Bisson of this town, such a young woman as I have hardly seen elsewhere. She seems to be wholly devoted to God, and to have constant communion with him. She has a clear and strong understanding, and I can not perceive the least tincture of enthusiasm. I am afraid she will not live long. I am amazed at the grace of God which is in her. I think she is far beyond Madam Guion in deep communion with God; and I doubt whether I have found her fellow in England. Precious as my time is, it would have been worth my while to come to Jersey, had it been only to see this prodigy of grace.

"Monday 27.—I thought when I left Southampton to have been there again at this day; but God's thoughts were not as my thoughts. Here we are, shut up in Jersey, for how long we can not tell. But it is all well; for thou, Lord, hast done it. It is my part to improve the time, as it is not likely I should ever have another opportunity of visiting these islands.

"Tuesday 28.—Being still detained by contrary winds, I preached at six in the evening, to a larger congregation than ever, in the assembly room. It conveniently contains five or six hundred people.

"Wednesday 29.—I designed to have followed the blow in the morning, but I had quite lost my voice; however, it was restored in the evening, and I believe all in the assembly room—more than the last evening—heard distinctly, while I explained and applied, 'I saw the dead, small and great, stand before God.' In the morning, Thursday 30, I took a solemn leave of the society. We set out about nine, and reached St. Peter's in the afternoon. Good is the will of the Lord. I trust he has something more for us to do here also. After preaching to a larger congregation than was expected, on so short a notice, on, 'God was in Christ, reconciling the world unto himself,' I returned to Mont Plaisir, to stay just as long as it should please God. I preached there in the morning, Friday 31, to a congregation serious as death.

"Saturday, September 1.—This day twelvemonth I was detained in Holland by contrary winds. All is well, so we are doing and suffering the will of our Lord. In the evening the storm driving us into the house again, I strongly exhorted a very genteel audience—such as I have rarely seen in England—to 'ask for the old paths, and walk therein.'

"Sunday 2.—Being still pent up by the north-east wind, Dr. Coke preached at six in the morning to a deeply-affected congregation. I preached at eight, on Rom. viii, 33. At one, Mr. Vivian, a local preacher, preached in French, the language of the island. At five, as the house would not contain half the congregation, I preached in a tolerably-sheltered place, on the 'joy there is in heaven over one sinner that repenteth;' and both high and low seemed to hear it gladly. I then designed to meet the society, but could not. The people pressed so eagerly on every side, that the house was filled presently; so that I could only give a general exhortation, 'to walk worthy of their profession.'

"I was in hopes of sailing in the morning, Monday 3, but the storm so increased, that it was judged impracticable. The congregation, however, in the evening increased every day; and they appeared to be more and more affected; so that I believe we were not detained for nothing; but for the spiritual and eternal good of many.

"Tuesday 4.—The storm continued, so that we could not stir. I took a walk to-day, through what is called the New Ground, where the gentry are accustomed to walk in the evening: both the upper ground, which is as level as a bowling-green, and the lower, which is planted with rows of trees, is wonderfully beautiful. In the evening I fully delivered my own soul by showing what it is to 'build upon a rock.' But still we could not sail, the wind being quite contrary as well as exceedingly high. It was the same on Wednesday. In the afternoon we drank tea at a friend's who was mentioning a captain just come from France, that proposed to sail in the morning for Penzance, for which the wind would serve, though not for Southampton. In this we plainly saw the hand of God: so we agreed with him immediately.

"Penzance, Saturday 8.—Dr. Coke preached at six to as many as the preaching house would contain. At ten I was obliged to take the field, by the multitude of people that flocked together. I found a very uncommon liberty of speech among them, and can not doubt but the work of God will flourish in this place. In the evening I preached at St. Ives—but it being the market day, so that I could not stand, as usual, in the market-place—in a very convenient field at the end of the town, to a very numerous congregation, I need scarcely add, and very serious; for such are all the congregations in the county of Cornwall.

"Sunday 9.—About nine I preached at the copper works, three or four miles from St. Ives, to a large congregation, gathered from all parts, I believe 'with the demonstration of the Spirit.' I then met the society in the preaching house, which is unlike any other in England, both as to its form and materials. It is exactly round, and composed wholly of brazen slags, which I suppose will last as long as the earth. Between one and two I began in the market-place at Redruth to the largest congregation I ever saw there. They not only filled all the windows, but sat on the tops of the houses. About five I began in the amphitheater at Gwennap: I suppose we had a thousand more than ever were there before: but it was all one; my voice was strengthened accordingly, so that every one could hear distinctly.

"London, Sunday, November 4.—The congregation at the New Chapel was far larger than usual; and the number of communicants was so great, that I was obliged to consecrate thrice. Monday 5.—In my way to Dorking, I read Mr. Duff's Essay on Genius. It is beyond all comparison deeper and more judicious than Dr. G.'s essay on that subject. If the Doctor had seen it, which one can hardly doubt, it is a wonder he would publish his essay: yet I can not approve of his method. Why does he not first define his term, that we may know what he is talking about? I doubt, because his own idea of it was not clear; for genius is not imagination, any more than it is invention. If we mean by it a quality of the soul, it is, in its widest acceptation, an extraordinary capacity either for some particular art or science, or for all, for whatever may be undertaken. So Euclid had a genius for mathematics, Tully for oratory: Aristotle and Lord Bacon had a universal genius applicable to every thing.

"Friday 9.—A friend offering to bear my expenses, I set out in the evening, and on Saturday 10, dined at Nottingham. The preaching house, one of the most elegant in England, was pretty well filled in the evening.

"Sunday 11.—At ten, we had a lovely congregation; and a very numerous one in the afternoon: but I believe the house would hardly contain one-half of those that came to it. I preached a charity sermon for the infirmary, which was the design of my coming. This is not a county infirmary, but is open to all England, yea, to all the world. And every thing about it is so neat, so convenient, and so well ordered, that I have seen none like it in the three kingdoms. Monday 12.—In the afternoon we took coach again, and on Tuesday returned to London.

"Sunday 25.—I preached two charity sermons at West-street in behalf of our poor children; in which I endeavored to warn them, and all that have the care of them, against that English sin, ungodliness, that reproach of our nation, wherein we excel all the inhabitants of the earth.

"Tuesday, December 4.—I retired to Rainham to prepare another edition of the New Testament for the press.

"London, Sunday 9.—I went down at half an hour

past five, but found no preacher in the chapel, though we had three or four in the house: so I preached myself. Afterward, inquiring why none of my family attended the morning preaching, they said it was because they sat up too late. I resolved to put a stop to this, and, therefore, ordered, that, 1. Every one under my roof should go to bed at nine; that, 2. Every one might attend the morning preaching; and so they have done ever since.

"Monday 10.—I was desired to see the celebrated waxwork at the museum in Spring Gardens. It exhibits most of the crowned heads in Europe, and shows their characters in their countenances. Sense and majesty appear in the king of Spain; dullness and sottishness in the king of France; infernal subtilty in the late king of Prussia—as well as in the skeleton of Voltaire; calmness and humanity in the emperor and king of Portugal; exquisite stupidity in the prince of Orange; and amazing coarseness, with every thing that is unamiable, in the Czarina.

"Sunday 16.—After preaching at Spitalfields, I hastened to St. Johns, Clerkenwell, and preached a charity sermon for the Finsbury Dispensary, as I would gladly countenance every institution of the kind.

"Saturday 22.—I yielded to the importunity of a painter, and sat, an hour and a half in all, for my picture. I think it is the best that ever was taken. But what is the picture of a man above fourscore!"

These extracts are from the journal of 1787, when Mr. Wesley was in his eighty-fifth year. The labors and journeys of almost every day are similarly noticed, exhibiting at once a singular instance of natural strength, sustained, doubtless, by the special blessing of God, and of an entire consecration of time to the service of mankind, of which no similar example is probably on record, and which is rendered still more wonderful by the consideration that it had been continued for more than half a century, on the same scale of exertion, and almost without intermission. The vigor of his mind at this age is also as remarkable; the same power of acute observation as formerly is manifested; the same taste for reading and criticism; the same facility in literary composition. Nor is the buoyant cheerfulness of his spirit a less striking feature. Nothing of the old man of unrenewed nature appears; no forebodings of evil; no querulous comparisons of the present with the past; there is the same delight in the beautiful scenes of nature; the same enjoyment of conversation, provided it had the two qualities of usefulness and brevity; the same joy in hopeful appearances of good; and the same tact at turning the edge of little discomforts and disappointments by the power of an undisturbed equanimity. Above all we see the man of *one business*, living only to serve God and his generation, "instant in season and out of season," seriously intent, not upon doing so much duty, but upon saving souls; and preaching, conversing, and writing for this end alone. And yet this is the man whom we still sometimes see made the object of the sneers of infidel or semi-infidel philosophers; and whom book-makers, when they have turned the interesting points of his character and history into a *marketable* commodity, endeavor to dress up in the garb of a fanatic, or a dreamer, by way of rendering their works more acceptable to frivolous readers; the man to whose labors few even of the evangelical clergy of the National Church have the heart or the courage to do justice; forgetting how much that improved state of piety which exists in the Establishment is owing to the indirect influence of his long life of labor, and his successful ministry; and that even very many of themselves have sprung from families where Methodism first lighted the lamp of religious knowledge, and produced a religious influence. It will, indeed, provoke a smile, to observe what effort often discovers itself in writers of this party, when referring to the religious state of the nation in the last and present century, to keep this apostolic man wholly out of sight, as though he had never existed; feeling, we suppose, that because he did not conform to the order of their Church, in all particulars, it would be a sin against their own orthodoxy even to name him as one of those great instruments, in the hands of God, who, in mercy to these lands, were raised up to effect that vast moral and religious change, the benefits of which they themselves so richly enjoy. This may be attributed not only to that exclusive spirit which marks so many of the clergy of this class, even beyond others, notwithstanding their piety and general excellence, but to the Calvinism which many of them have imbibed. The evangelical Arminianism of Wesley has been forgiven by the orthodox Dissenters; but, by a curious anomaly, not by the Calvinistic party of the Church. It is probably better understood by the former.*

At the time to which the above extracts from his journal refer, Mr. Wesley had, however, no reason to complain of want of respect, or of a due appreciation of his labors by

* The following passage from a sermon lately preached in his diocese, by Bishop Coplestone, may be quoted, both as a better specimen of the spirit of a Churchman than that referred to, and as, perhaps, the only instance in which any thing approaching to a due estimate of Mr. Wesley's character, and the value of his labors, has been suffered publicly to escape the lips of a prelate. It was dictated, evidently, by a candid and liberal feeling, though not without being influenced by some of those mistaken views which will be corrected at the close of this account of Mr. Wesley's life:

"And here, not only candor and equity, but a just sense of the constitution of Christ's Church, compels me to draw a marked line of distinction between those whose religious assemblies are supplementary, as it were, to our own Establishment, offering spiritual comfort and instruction to hundreds unable to find it elsewhere, and those organized communities which exclude from their society any that communicate in the blessed sacrament of the Lord's supper with the National Church.

"Of the former I would not only think and speak mildly, but in many cases I would commend the piety and zeal which animates them, full of danger as it is to depart from the apostolic ordinance, even in matters of outward discipline and order. The author and founder of those socie-

the serious of all parties, although he regarded it not with improper exultation, but passed through "honor" as he had passed through "dishonor" in the former years of his life, as "seeing Him who is invisible." This period of his life must have been to him, on a much higher account, one of rich reflection. In his journal of 1785, March 24, he observes: "I was now considering how strangely the grain of mustard seed, planted about fifty years ago, had grown up. It has spread through all Great Britain, and

ties—for he was careful himself to keep them from being formed into a sect—was a regularly-ordained minister, a man orthodox in his belief, simple and disinterested in his own views, and adorned with the most amiable and distinguishing virtues of a true Christian. He found thousands of his countrymen, though nominally Christians, yet as ignorant of true Christianity as infidels and heathens; and in too many instances—it is useless to conceal or disguise the fact—ignorant, either through the inattention of the government in not providing for increased numbers, or through the carelessness and neglect of those whom the National Church had appointed to be their pastors.

"But the beginning of schism, like that of strife, is as when one letteth out water. The gentle stream of piety and benevolence in which this practice originated, irrigating only and refreshing some parched or barren lands, soon became a swelling and rapid torrent, widening as it flowed on, and opening for itself a breach which it may yet require the care and prudence of ages to close. And even the pious author himself was not proof against that snare of Satan, which, through the vanity and weakness of human nature, led him in his latter years to assume the authority of an apostle, and to establish a fraternity within the Church, to be called after his own name, and to remain a lasting monument of his activity and zeal. But over errors such as these let us cast a vail; and rather rejoice in reflecting on the many whom he reclaimed from sin and wickedness, and taught to seek for salvation through the merits of their Savior.

"Of such, I repeat, wherever a like deficiency of religious means is found, we ought to speak, not only with tenderness, but with brotherly love and esteem."

It seems pretty obvious that Bishop Coplestone has taken his impressions from Southey's life of the founder of Methodism, although somewhat modified by better views of spiritual religion. The moral destitution of the country, and the negligence of the Church are acknowledged, as well as the important effects produced by Mr. Wesley's labors, at least in their early stages; and yet these results are spoken of as somewhat of a religious calamity! The beginning of "schism," as to Church order, is compared to the letting out of water; and a fearful "breach" out of the Established Church completes the picture. How little does this sensible and amiable bishop know of the facts of the case—as, for instance, 1,

Ireland, the Isle of Wight, and the Isle of Man; then to America, through the whole continent, into Canada, the Leeward Islands, and Newfoundland. And the societies, in all these parts, walk by one rule, knowing that religion is in holy tempers, and striving to worship God, not in form only, but likewise in spirit and in truth."

He must, indeed, have been insensible to the emotions of a generous nature, had he not felt an honest satisfaction, that he had lived down calumnies; and that where mobs formerly awaited him, he met with the kind and cheering

That the Methodist societies were in great part gathered, not out of Church-goers, but Church-neglecters; 2. That the effect was generally, for many years, to increase the attendance at Church, and to lay the foundation in a great number of places, especially in the more populous towns, of large Church congregations which have continued to this day; 3. That the still more extensive and ultimate result was, after persecution or silent contempt had been tried in vain, and when it was found that obstinate perseverance in neglect would not be any longer tolerated, that the Establishment was roused into an activity by which it has doubtless been greatly benefited, as far as respects its moral influence, the only influence of a Church which can be permanent or valuable; 4. That very few of the Methodists of the present day would, in all probability, have been, in any sense which Bishop Coplestone would value, Church people; and so this supposed loss of ecclesiastical members affords but an imaginary ground for the regrets with which he seems to surround it. The intimation of Mr. Wesley's ambition is imitated from Southey. But of this enough has been said in refutation. Bishop Coplestone, indeed, regards it mildly as an infirmity, which he would charitably cover with Mr. Wesley's numerous and eminent virtues. That is kind; but Mr. Wesley himself would have taken a severer view of this "weakness," had he been conscious of the passion of ambition, in the sense in which it is here used. One might ask this respectable prelate to review the case, and say where Mr. Wesley, allowing him his conscientious conviction that he was bound to incessant activity in doing good to the souls of men, could have stopped. How he could have disposed of his societies in the then existing state of the Church. And whether, if he had this "ambition" to be the head of a sect, his whole life did not lay restraints upon it, since, from nearly the very outset of his itinerancy and success, it has been shown in this work, by extracts from the minutes of his first conferences, that he took views of ecclesiastical polity which then set him quite at liberty, had he chosen it, to form his societies into a regular Church, to put himself at their head, and to kindle up a spirit of hostility to the Establishment, and of warm partisanship in his own favor, throughout the land. A vicious ambition would have preferred this course. But it is not necessary to anticipate the remarks which will follow on these subjects.

attentions of the most respectable persons of all religious persuasions, in every part of the country. But, more than this, he could compare the dearth and barrenness of one age with the living verdure and fertility of another. Long-forgotten truths had been made familiar; a neglected population had been brought within the range of Christian instruction, and the constant preaching of the word of life by faithful men; religious societies had been raised up through the land, generally distinguished by piety and zeal; by the blessing of God upon the labors of Mr. Whitefield, and others of his first associates, the old Dissenting Churches had been quickened into life, and new ones multiplied; the Established Church had been awakened from her lethargy; the number of faithful ministers in her parishes greatly multiplied; the influence of religion spread into the colonies, and the United States of America; and, above all, a vast multitude, the fruit of his own ministerial zeal and faithfulness, had, since the time in which he commenced his labors, departed into a better world. These thoughts must often have passed through his mind, and inspired his heart with devout thanksgivings, although no allusion is ever made to them in a boastful manner. For the past, he knew to whom the praise belonged; and the future he left to God, certain, at least, of meeting in heaven a greater number of glorified spirits of whose salvation he had been, under God, the instrument, than any minister of modern ages. That "joyful hope" may explain an incident, which occurred toward the close of life, at the City Road Chapel, London. After prayers had been read one Sunday forenoon, he ascended the pulpit, where, instead of announcing the hymn immediately, he, to the great surprise of the congregation, stood silent, with his eyes closed, for the space of at least ten minutes, wrapt in thought; and then, with a feeling which at once conveyed to all present the subject which had so absorbed his attention, gave out the hymn commencing with the lines:

"Come, let us join our friends above,
Who have obtained the prize," etc.

It was also his constant practice to preach on All-Saints-Day, which was with him a favorite festival, on communion with the saints in heaven; a practice probably arising out of the same delightful association of remembrances and hope.

On his attaining his eighty-fifth year, he makes the following reflections:

"I this day enter on my eighty-fifth year. And what cause have I to praise God, as for a thousand spiritual blessings, so for bodily blessings also! How little have I suffered yet, by 'the rush of numerous years!' It is true, I am not so agile as I was in times past: I do not run or walk so fast as I did. My sight is a little decayed. My left eye is grown dim, and hardly serves me to read. I have daily some pain in the ball of my right eye, as also in my right temple—occasioned by a blow received some time since—and in my right shoulder and arm, which I impute partly to a sprain, and partly to the rheumatism. I find, likewise, some decay in my memory, with regard to names and things lately past; but not at all with regard to what I have read or heard, twenty, forty, or sixty years ago. Neither do I find any decay in my hearing, smell, taste, or appetite—though I want but a third part of the food I once did—nor do I feel any such thing as weariness, either in traveling or preaching. And I am not conscious of any decay in writing sermons, which I do as readily, and I believe as correctly, as ever.

"To what cause can I impute this, that I am as I am? First, doubtless, to the power of God, fitting me for the work to which I am called, as long as he pleases to continue me therein; and next, subordinately to this, to the prayers of his children. May we not impute it, as inferior means, 1. To my constant exercise and change of air?

2. To my never having lost a night's sleep, sick or well, at land or sea, since I was born? 3. To my having sleep at command, so that whenever I feel myself almost worn out, I call it, and it comes, day or night? 4. To my having constantly, for above sixty years, risen at four in the morning? 5. To my constant preaching at five in the morning, for above fifty years? 6. To my having had so little pain in my life, and so little sorrow or anxious care? Even now, though I find pain daily in my eye, temple, or arm, yet it is never violent, and seldom lasts many minutes at a time.

"Whether or not this is sent to give me warning that I am shortly to quit this tabernacle, I do not know; but, be it one way or the other, I have only to say:

'My remnant of days
I spend to His praise,
Who died the whole world to redeem:
Be they many or few,
My days are his due,
And they are all devoted to Him!'"

And, referring to some persons in the nation who thought themselves endowed with the gift of prophecy, he adds, "If this is to be the last year of my life, according to some of these prophets, I hope it will be the best. I am not careful about it, but heartily receive the advice of the angel in Milton:

'How well is thine, how long permit to heaven.'"

CHAPTER XIV.

The brothers, whose affection no differences of opinion and no conflicts of party could diminish, were now to be separated by death. Of the last days of Mr. Charles Wesley, Dr. Whitehead gives the following account:

"Mr. Charles Wesley had a weak body, and a poor state of health, during the greatest part of his life. I believe he laid the foundation of both at Oxford by too close application to study, and abstinence from food. He rode much on horseback, which probably contributed to lengthen out life to a good old age. I visited him several times in his last sickness; and his body was indeed reduced to the most extreme state of weakness. He possessed that state of mind which he had been always pleased to see in others—unaffected humility, and holy resignation to the will of God. He had no transports of joy, but solid hope and unshaken confidence in Christ, which kept his mind in perfect peace. A few days before his death he composed the following lines. Having been silent and quiet for some time, he called Mrs. Wesley to him, and bid her write as he dictated:

'In age and feebleness extreme,
Who shall a sinful worm redeem?
Jesus, my only hope thou art,
Strength of my failing flesh and heart;
O could I catch a smile from thee,
And drop into eternity.'

"He died, March 29, 1788, aged seventy-nine years and three months; and was buried, April 5th, in Marybone church-yard at his own desire. The pall was supported by eight clergymen of the Church of England. On his tombstone are the following lines written by himself on the death of one of his friends: they could not be more aptly applied to any person than to Mr. Charles Wesley:

'With poverty of spirit bless'd,
Rest, happy saint, in Jesus rest;
A sinner saved, through grace forgiven,
Redeem'd from earth to reign in heaven!
Thy labors of unwearied love,
By thee forgot, are crown'd above;
Crown'd through the mercy of thy Lord,
With a free, full, immense reward!'

"Mr. Charles Wesley was of a warm and lively disposition, of great frankness and integrity, and generous and steady in his friendships. In conversation he was pleasing, instructive, and cheerful; and his observations were often seasoned with wit and humor. His religion was genuine and unaffected. As a minister, he was familiarly acquainted with every part of divinity; and his mind was furnished with an uncommon knowledge of the Scriptures. His discourses from the pulpit were not dry and systematic, but flowed from the present views and feelings of his own mind. He had a remarkable talent of expressing the most important truths with simplicity and energy; and his discourses were sometimes truly apostolic, forcing conviction on the hearers in spite of the most determined opposition. As a husband, a father, and a friend, his character was amiable. Mrs. Wesley brought him five children, of whom two sons and a daughter are still living.* The sons dis-

* Miss Wesley, a lady of eminent talents, and great excellence, died September 19, 1828.

It would be improper to withhold, as I have them before me, in the unpublished letters with which I have been favored, some incidental remarks of the late Miss Wesley, on the character of her father:

"Mr. Moore seems to think that my father preferred *rest to going about to do good.* He had a rising family, and considered it his duty to confine his labors to Bristol and London, where he labored most sedulously in ministerial offices; and judged that it was incumbent upon him to watch over the youth of his sons, especially in a profession which nature so strongly pointed out, but which was peculiarly dangerous. He always said his brother was formed to lead, and he to follow. No one ever more rejoiced in another's superiority, or was more willing to confess it. Mr. Moore's statement of his absence of mind in his younger days was probably correct, as he was born impetuous, and ardent, and sincere. But what a change must have taken place when we were born! For his exactness in his accounts, in his manuscripts, in his bureau, etc., equaled my uncle's. Not in his dress, indeed; for my mother said, if she did not watch over him, he might have put on an old for a new coat, and marched out. Such was his power of abstraction, that he could read and compose with his children in the room, and visitors talking around him. He was near forty when he married, and had eight children, of whom we were the youngest. So kind and amiable a character in domestic life can scarcely be imagined. The tenderness he showed in every weakness, and the sympathy in every pain, would fill sheets to describe. But I am not writing his eulogy; only I must add, with so warm a temper, he never was heard to speak an angry word to a servant, or known to strike a child in anger—and he knew no guile!"

covered so fine a taste for music, at an early period of life, that they excited general astonishment; and they are now justly admired by the best judges for their talents in that pleasing art. The Methodists are greatly indebted to Charles Wesley, for his unwearied labors and great usefulness at the first formation of the societies, when every step was attended with difficulty and danger. And being dead he yet speaketh by his numerous and excellent hymns, written for the use of the societies, which still continue to be the means of daily edification and comfort to thousands." (Whitehead's Life.)

For the spiritual advantages which the Methodists have derived from his inestimable hymns, which are in constant use in their congregations, as well as for his early labors, the memory of Mr. Charles Wesley indeed deserves to be had in their everlasting remembrance, and they are not insensible of the value of the gift. Their taste has been formed by this high standard; and, notwithstanding all the charges of illiteracy, and want of mental cultivation, which have been often brought against them, we may venture to say, there are few collections of psalms and hymns in use in any other congregations, that would, as *a whole*, be tolerated among them; so powerful has been the effect produced by his superior compositions. The clear and decisive character of the religious experience which they describe—their force, and life, and earnestness—commended them, at the first, to the piety of the societies, and, through that, insensibly elevated the judgment of thousands, who, otherwise, might have relished, as strongly as others, the rudeness of the old version of the Psalms, the tameness of the new, and the tinsel metaphors and vapid sentimentalisms which disfigure numerous compositions of different authors, in most collections of hymns in use. It would seem, indeed, from the very small number of really good psalms and hymns, which are adapted to public worship and the use of religious societies, that this branch of sacred poetry has not been very successfully cultivated; and that the combination of genius, judgment, and taste, requisite to produce them, is very rarely found. Germany is said to be more abundant in good hymns than England; and some of the most excellent of the Wesleyan hymns are imitations of German hymns admirably versified. But in our language the number is small. Hymns, indeed, abounding in sweet thoughts, though often feebly expressed, and such as may be used profitably in the closet or the family circle, are not so rare. But the true sacred lyric, suited for public worship, and the select assemblies of the devout, is as scarce as it is valuable. From the rustic rhyming of Sternhold and Hopkins, to the psalms and hymns of Dr. Watts, the advance was, indeed, unspeakably great. A few, however, only of the latter, in comparison of the whole number, are unexceptionable throughout. When they are so, they leave nothing to be desired; but many of Dr. Watts' compositions begin well, often nobly, and then fall off into dullness and puerility; and not a few are utterly worthless, as being poor in thought, and still more so in expression. The piety and sweetness of Doddridge's hymns must be felt; but they are often verbose and languid, and withal faulty and affected in their metaphors. The Olney Collection has many delightful hymns for private use; but they are far from being generally fit for the public services of religion, and are often in bad taste; not even excepting many of Cowper's. This may be spoken without irreverence, for the greatest poets have not proved the best hymn-makers. Milton made but one tolerable psalm; and still more modern poets of note have seldom fully redeemed the credit of their class. The fact seems to be, that when the mind is very rich in sentiment and imagery, those qualities are usually infused into sacred song in too large proportions.

Sentiment and genuine religious feeling are things quite distinct, and seldom harmonize; at least, though they may sometimes approach to the verge of each other, they will not amalgamate; and exuberance of metaphor is inconsistent with strong and absorbing devotion, and proves too artificial to express the natural language of the heart. The talent of correct and vigorous versification is, for these reasons, more likely to produce the true "spiritual song" than luxuriance of imagination and great creative genius, provided the requisite theological and devotional qualities be also present. A hymn suitable for social worship ought to be terse and vigorous; and it is improved when every verse closes with a sense so full and pointed as frequently to make some approach to the character of the ancient epigram; or, as Mr. Montgomery has happily expressed it, "each stanza should be a poetical tune, played down to the last note." The meaning ought also to be so obvious as to be comprehended at once, that men may speak to God directly, without being distracted by investigating the real meaning of the words put into their lips. And when metaphor is efficiently employed, it must be generally such as the Scriptures have already sanctioned; for with *their* imagery we are all familiar, and it stands consecrated to the service of the sanctuary by inspired authority. Yet even this ought not to be adopted in an extended form, approaching to allegory; and is always more successful when rather lightly touched and suggested, than when dwelt upon with particularity. Cowper's fine hymn on providence is greatly improved by omitting the stanza:

"His purposes will ripen fast,
Unfolding every hour;
The bud may have a bitter taste,
But sweet will be the flower."

This is a figure not only not found in sacred inspired poetry, but which has too much *prettiness* to be the vehicle of a sublime thought, and the verse has, moreover, the fault of an absurd antithesis, as well as a false rhyme, Many modern hymns are indeed as objectionable from the character of their imagery, as from the meagerness of their thoughts; and there are a few somewhat popular, which, leaving out or changing a few sacred terms, would chime agreeably enough to the most common sentimental subjects.

To Dr. Watts and to Mr. Charles Wesley the largest share of gratitude is due, in modern times, from the Churches of Christ, for that rich supply of "psalms, and hymns, and spiritual songs," in which the assemblies of the pious may make melody unto the Lord, in strains which "angels might often delight to hear." No others are to be named with these sweet singers of the spiritual Israel; and it is probable that, through the medium of their verse chiefly, will the devotions of our Churches be poured forth till time shall be no more. No other poets ever attained such elevation as this. They honored God in their gifts, and God has thus honored them to be the mouth of his people to him, in their solemn assemblies, in their private devotions, and in the struggles of death itself.

It would be an unpardonable task to compare the merits of these two great psalmists. Each had excellences not found in the other. Watts, however, excels Mr. Charles Wesley only in the sweeter flow of his numbers, and in the feeling and sympathy of those of his hymns which are designed to administer comfort to the afflicted. In composition, he was, in all respects, decidedly his inferior—in good taste, classic elegance, uniformity of excellence, correct rhyming, and vigor. As to the theology of their hymns respectively, leaving particular doctrines out of the question, the great truths of religious experience are also far more clearly and forcibly embodied by Mr. Charles Wesley than by Dr. Watts. Most justly does his brother say of them in his preface to "the Collection of Hymns for the use of the people called Methodists," of which only a few are his own, and almost all the rest from the pen of Mr. Charles Wesley: "In these hymns there is no doggerel, no botches, nothing put in to patch up the rhyme, no feeble expletives. Here is nothing turgid or bombastic, on the one hand, or low and creeping on the other. Here are no cant expressions, no words without meaning. Here are—allow me to say—both the purity, the strength, and the elegance of the English language; and, at the same time, the utmost simplicity and plainness, suited to every capacity."*

Few persons ever wrote so much poetry of the sacred and devotional kind, as Mr. Charles Wesley. It amounts

* In this collection, beside a few hymns by Mr. John Wesley, there are four or five from Dr. Watts. Several are translations by the Wesleys: one from the Spanish, "O God, my God, my all thou art," etc.; one from the French, "Come, Savior Jesus, from above;" and the others from the German hymns of the Lutheran and Moravian Churches. Several of these translated hymns Mr. Montgomery has inserted in his "Psalmist," and marked "Moravian." They appear, indeed, in the Moravian Hymn-Book, but in departments there, in which are also found the hymns of Dr. Watts and other English authors. The preface of the edition of 1754, the first authorized collection of the English Moravians, and which embodies their former unauthorized publications, acknowledges "the foregoing labors of Mr. Jacobi and the Rev. Mr. Wesley" in the translation of German hymns of the sixteenth and seventeenth centuries, beside extracts of English ones of the eighteenth, from "Watts, Stennett, Davis, Erskine, Wesley," etc.; which acknowledgment was no doubt overlooked by Mr. Montgomery. The hymns translated by the Wesleys, and said by Mr. Montgomery in his collection to be "Moravian," are, "Thou hidden love of God, whose hight;" "Thee will I love, my strength, my tower;" "Shall I for fear of feeble man;" "O thou who camest from above;" "Now I have found the ground wherein;" "My soul before thee prostrate lies;" and "Holy Lamb, who thee receive." Now, all these were published by the Wesleys before the Moravian Hymn-Book of 1754, in which the "foregoing labors of Mr. Wesley," in translating from the German, are acknowledged; and, indeed, most of them appear in the very first hymn-books published by John and Charles Wesley, two of which bear date so early as 1739, fifteen years previous to the publication of the authorized Moravian Collection. As translations, they are not therefore "Moravian;" and, when they are translated from "the German," it does not follow that they all have a Moravian original, though

to forty-eight distinct publications of different sizes, from the duodecimo volume to the pamphlet of one or two sheets. Beside what is published, several thick quarto volumes of poetry in MS. remain, chiefly consisting of brief illustrations or paraphrases of the leading texts in the Gospels and Acts of the Apostles, and not inferior to his "Short Hymns on the chief passages of the Old and New Testaments," which have passed through several

some of them may; for the Moravian German book, like the English, as we learn from the preface to their English hymn-book, "consists as well of hymns out of preceding Church collections of their neighbors as of others composed by themselves." The hymn, "High on his everlasting throne," marked "Moravian" by Mr. Montgomery, and mentioned also in his preface, is a Moravian German hymn; but the translation is by Mr. Charles Wesley; while "Give to the winds thy fears," also marked Moravian, is a German hymn of the Lutheran Church, and the translation is Mr. Charles Wesley's. Of this hymn there is a version in the Moravian English Hymn-Book; the last stanza of which, when placed beside Mr. C. Wesley's, will show with what strength of internal evidence his translations distinguish themselves:

WESLEY'S.	MORAVIAN.
Thou seest our weakness, Lord,	O Lord, thou seest our weakness,
Our hearts are known to thee:	Yet know'st what our hearts mean:
O lift thou up the sinking hand,	Against desponding slackness,
Confirm the feeble knee!	Our feeble knees sustain.
Let us in life and death,	Till, and beyond death's valley,
Thy steadfast truth declare;	Let us thy truth declare;
And publish with our latest breath	Yea, then emphatically,
Thy love and guardian care.	Boast of thy guardian care.

Some other comparisons might be made between Mr. C. Wesley's translations from German hymns and those from the same originals found in the Moravian Hymn-Book, which would sufficiently show that the Moravians, *then* at least, had no translator into English verse at all comparable to him; and, indeed, they had sufficient taste generally to adopt his translations in preference. But this is no reason why he should lose the credit of his own admirable performances in this department. Respect to literary justice has drawn out this note to so great a length; and it was the more necessary to state the matter correctly, because Mr. Montgomery's "Psalmist" might in future mislead. The first editions of the Hymns and Sacred Poems, by the Wesleys, namely, those of 1739, 1743 and 1745, in which most of the above hymns are found, with several others in the Moravian Hymn-Book, are now become scarce, and in a few years may not be forthcoming to correct the error. For this reason it may also be noticed that Mr. Montgomery has inserted in his collection several hymns by Charles Wesley as the composition of "authors unknown." These, too, are found in the early editions of the Wesley editions. A few of his poems are playful, a few others are keenly satirical. He satirized his brother's ordinations, and the preachers; but, High Churchman as he was, he is very unsparing in the use of his poetic whip upon the persecuting and irreligious clergy. Of this, some of his published, and several of his unpublished paraphrases, on passages of the Gospels, and the Acts of the Apostles, in which the persecuting deeds of the scribes and Pharisees are recorded, afford some caustic specimens;* and suffi-

Hymns and Poems, and in some later ones, as, "Come let us who in Christ believe;" "Come, O thou all-victorious Lord;" "Fountain of being, source of good;" "God of my life, whose gracious power;" "Jesus, my strength, my hope;" "Jesus, the name high over all;" "Leader of faithful souls, and guide;" "O that thou wouldst the heavens rent;" "Spirit of truth, come down;" "Thee, O my God and King;" "Thy ceaseless, unexhausted love;" and, "When quiet in my house I sit." There are two ways of accounting for Mr. Montgomery's want of information as to these hymns: that he was not in possession of the early editions of hymns published by John and Charles Wesley; and that some of the hymns in the hymn-book in use among us, which he has ascribed to authors unknown, are parts of longer hymns, and were selected by Mr. John Wesley from his brother's poetry, sometimes from the middle or end of a piece, so that the first lines would not be found in the old indexes when consulted. Mr. Charles Wesley's hymns have not been unfrequently claimed for others, without any design to be unjust. In the Christian Observer, a few years ago, that exquisite production of one of his happiest moments, "Jesus, lover of my soul," was assigned to Mr. Madan, although published by Mr. Charles Wesley, in the year 1743; and the translation from the French, "Come, Savior Jesus, from above," is found in the poetical works of Dr. John Byrom, published in 1773, although it appears in the Wesley "Hymns and Poems" of 1739. The probability is, that a copy of it was found among Byrom's papers, and so the editor of his poems concluded it to be his. A correct list of the different editions of the Hymns and Sacred Poems published by the Wesleys, will be found in the last volume of Wesley's Works, recently completed. The editions of 1739 are scarce, and it ought to be noticed that there are *two* distinct works published under the same title of "Hymns and Sacred Poems," each bearing that date. The hymn-book now in use was compiled by Mr. John Wesley out of the preceding hymn-books, of different sizes and editions, and from his brother's "Festival Hymns," "Scripture Hymns," etc. The whole underwent his severe criticism, and he abridged and corrected them with a taste and judgment which greatly increased their value.

* As almost all the family were poets, so they were all characterized by a vein of satire. This they appear to have inherited from their father,

ciently indicate that he did not bear the contumely and opposition of his High Church brethren with the equanimity and gentleness of his brother John. He also took a part in the Calvinistic controversy, by writing his Hymns or Poems on God's universal love. But by far the greater part of his poetry was consecrated to promote the work of God in the heart. Never were its different branches, from the first awakening of the soul out of the sleep of sin, to its state of perfected holiness, with all its intermediate conflicts and exercises, more justly or Scripturally expressed; and there is, perhaps, no uninspired book from which, as to "the deep things of God," so much is to be learned, as from his hymn-book in use in the Methodist congregations. The funeral hymns in this collection have but little of the softness of sorrow—perhaps too little; but they are written in that fullness of faith which exclaims over the open tomb, "Thanks be to God, who giveth us the victory through our Lord Jesus Christ." The hymns on the last day are characterized also by the same unflinching faith, which, rejoicing in the smile of the Judge, defies the wild uproar of elements, and the general conflagration itself.

whose wit was both ready and pungent. The following is an instance copied from the Gentleman's Magazine, for the year 1802:

"The authenticity of the following *extempore* grace by the Rev. Samuel Wesley—father of the Rev. John—formerly rector of Epworth, may be relied on. It is given on the authority of the late William Barnard, Esq., of Gainsboro, whose father, the preserver of John from the fire of 1707, was present at the time it was spoken, at Temple Belwood, after dinner. Mr. P., at whose house they dined, was a strange compound of avarice and oddity; many of his singularities are still remembered:

'Thanks for this feast, for 'tis no less
Than eating manna in the wilderness;
Here meager Famine bears controlless sway,
And ever drives each fainting wretch away.
Yet here—O how beyond a saint's belief!—
We've seen the glories of a chine of beef;
Here chimneys smoke, which never smoked before,
And we have dined, where we shall dine no more.'"

The design of this odd extemporaneous effusion we are bound to believe, was not to indulge in levity, but to convey a useful reproof.

In several of these, Mr. Charles Wesley has admirably Christianized the "just man" of Horace, deadless, amidst the ruins of a world:

"*Si fractus illabatur orbis,*
Impavidum ferient ruinæ;"
[If a dissolved world should fall upon him, its ruins would strike him fearless;]

placing the same fine thought in various aspects, and illustrating it by different circumstances. His hymns of invitation are sweet and persuasive; and those on justification by faith, admirably illustrative of that important doctrine. Of the value set upon this hymn-book by the Methodist congregations, this is a sufficient proof, that above sixty thousand copies are sold yearly in the United Kingdom alone.* The number in the United States of America must be considerably larger.

With reference to his brother's poetry a remark is incidentally and somewhat oddly introduced, by Mr. Wesley, in his journal of 1790, January 28:

"I retired to Peckham, and at leisure hours read part of a very pretty trifle—the life of Mrs. Bellamy. Surely never did any since John Dryden study more

'To make vice pleasing, and damnation shine,'

than this lively and elegant writer. She has a fine imagination, a strong understanding, an easy style, improved by much reading; a fine, benevolent temper, and every qualification that could consist with a total ignorance of God: but God was not in all her thoughts. Abundance of anecdotes she inserts, which may be true or false. One of them, concerning Mr. Garrick, is curious: she says, 'When he was taking ship for England, a lady presented

* As the number of hymns in this book, adapted for mixed congregations and festival occasions, was not thought sufficient, a supplement is now added; containing about an equal number of hymns, by Mr. Charles Wesley, and by other authors. Some of the best hymns he ever wrote are found in this smaller collection, chiefly on the festivals.

him with a parcel, which she desired him not to open till he was at sea. When he did, he found Wesley's Hymns, which he immediately threw overboard.' I can not believe it. I think Mr. G. had more sense. He knew my brother well. And he knew him to be not only far superior in learning, but in poetry, to Mr. Thomson, and all his theatrical writers put together: none of them can equal him, either in strong nervous sense, or purity and elegance of language. The musical compositions of his sons are not more excellent than the poetical ones of their father."

The last end of the truly-venerable John Wesley was now also approaching. He was on his regular pastoral visit to Ireland when he entered his eighty-seventh year, on which he remarks in his journal: "This day I enter on my eighty-seventh year. I now find I grow old. 1. My sight is decayed, so that I can not read a small print, unless in a strong light. 2. My strength is decayed, so that I walk much slower than I did some years since. 3. My memory of names, whether of persons or places, is decayed, till I stop a little to recollect them. What I should be afraid of is, if I took thought for the morrow, that my body should weigh down my mind, and create either stubbornness, by the decrease of my understanding, or peevishness, by the increase of bodily infirmities: but thou shalt answer for me, O Lord my God!"

Notwithstanding these infirmities, we find him still acting under the impression—"I must be about my Father's business." Although in comparison of his former rapidity of movement, he crept rather than ran, it was still in the same ceaseless course of service. After holding the Irish conference in Dublin, and the English conference at Leeds, in August, he returned to London; from thence he set out to Bristol, and proceeded on his usual tour through the west of England, and Cornwall. Notwithstanding his regular visits to Cornwall, he appears, from some reason, not to have turned aside to Falmouth, since the time of preaching there forty years before, when he met with so violent a reception. He now paid that place a visit, and remarks, "The last time I was here, about forty years ago, I was taken prisoner by an immense mob, gaping and roaring like lions; but how is the tide turned! High and low now lined the streets from one end of the town to the other, out of stark love and kindness, gaping and staring as if the king were going by. In the evening I preached on the smooth top of the hill, at a small distance from the sea, to the largest congregation I have ever seen in Cornwall, except in or near Redruth; and such a time I have not known before, since I returned from Ireland. God moved wonderfully on the hearts of the people, who all seemed to know the day of their visitation."

From Cornwall he returned by way of Bristol and Bath to London. In the early part of the next year, we find him again at Bristol; from whence he proceeded, preaching at several of the intermediate towns, to Birmingham; and from thence through Staffordshire to Madeley, where we find the following affecting entry in his journal:

"At nine I preached to a select congregation on the deep things of God; and in the evening on, 'He is able to save unto the uttermost all them that come unto God through him.' Friday 26th, I finished my sermon on the 'Wedding Garment;' perhaps the last that I shall write. My eyes are now waxed dim. My natural force is abated; however, while I can, I would fain do a little for God, before I drop into the dust."

The societies in Cheshire, Lancashire, and the north of England, once more, and for the last time, saw the man, to whom, under God, they owed their religious existence. On his return southward, he passed through the East Riding of Yorkshire, to Hull, preaching in every place as on the brink of eternity. He also visited Epworth, and various parts of Lincolnshire; and, upon attaining his eighty-eighth year, has the following reflections:

"This day I enter into my eighty-eighth year. For above eighty-six years I found none of the infirmities of old age; my eyes did not wax dim, neither was my natural strength abated; but last August I found almost a sudden change: my eyes were so dim that no glasses would help me; my strength likewise now quite forsook me, and probably will not return in this world: but I feel no pain from head to foot; only, it seems, nature is exhausted, and, humanly speaking, will sink more and more, till

'The weary springs of life stand still at last.'"

"This," says Dr. Whitehead, "at length was literally the case; the death of Mr. Wesley, like that of his brother Charles, being one of those rare instances in which nature, drooping under the load of years, sinks by a gentle decay. For several years preceding his death, this decay was, perhaps, more visible to others than to himself, particularly by a more frequent disposition to sleep during the day, by a growing defect in memory, a faculty he once possessed in a high degree of perfection, and by a general diminution of the vigor and agility he had so long enjoyed. His labors, however, suffered little interruption; and when the summons came, it found him, as he always wished it should, in the *harness*, still occupied in his Master's work!"

Still his journal records his regular visitation of the principal places where societies existed, and exhibits the same variety and raciness of remark on men and books, and other subjects, although writing must, at that time, have become exceedingly difficult to him from the failure of his sight. This most interesting record of unparalleled labors "in the Gospel" was, for this reason, it is presumed, discontinued, and closes on Sunday, October 24, 1790, when he states that he preached twice at Spitalfields church. He continued, however, during the autumn and winter, to visit various places till February, continually praying, "Lord, let me not live to be useless." The following account of his last days is taken from the memoir prefixed to the edition of his works by the Rev. Joseph Benson, and is there inserted as a proper close to his journal:

"He preached, as usual, in different places in London and its vicinity, generally meeting the society after preaching in each place, and exhorting them to *love as brethren, to fear God, and honor the king*, which he wished them to consider as his last advice. He then usually, if not invariably, concluded with giving out that verse,

'O that, without a lingering groan,
I may the welcome word receive;
My body with my charge lay down,
And cease at once to work and live!'

"He proceeded in this way till the usual time of his leaving London approached, when, with a view to take his accustomed journey through Ireland or Scotland, he sent his chaise and horses before him to Bristol, and took places for himself and his friend in the Bath coach. But his mind, with all its vigor, could no longer uphold his worn-out and sinking body. Its powers ceased, although by slow and almost imperceptible degrees, to perform their sundry offices, till, as he often expressed himself,

'The weary wheels of life stood still at last.'

"Thursday, February 17, 1791, he preached at Lambeth; but, on his return, seemed much indisposed, and said he had taken cold. The next day, however, he read and wrote as usual, and in the evening preached at Chelsea, from, "The King's business requires haste," although with some difficulty, having a high degree of fever upon him. Indeed he was obliged to stop once or twice, informing the people that his cold so affected his voice as to prevent his speaking without those necessary pauses. On

Saturday he still persevered in his usual employments, though, to those about him, his complaints seemed evidently increasing. He dined at Islington, and at dinner desired a friend to read to him four chapters out of the book of Job; namely, from the fourth to the seventh inclusive. On Sunday he rose early, according to custom, but quite unfit for any of his usual Sabbath day's exercises. At seven o'clock he was obliged to lie down, and slept between three and four hours. When he awoke, he said, 'I have not had such a comfortable sleep this fortnight past.' In the afternoon he lay down again, and slept an hour or two. Afterward two of his own discourses on our Lord's sermon on the Mount were read to him, and in the evening he came down to supper.

"Monday the 21st, he seemed much better; and though his friends tried to dissuade him from it, he would keep an engagement, made some time before, to dine at Twickenham. In his way thither he called on Lady Mary Fitzgerald: the conversation was truly profitable, and well became a last visit. On Tuesday he went on with his usual work, preached in the evening at the chapel in the City road, and seemed much better than he had been for some days. On Wednesday he went to Leatherhead, and preached to a small company on, 'Seek ye the Lord while he may be found; call ye upon him while he is near.' This proved to be his last sermon: here ended the public labors of this great minister of Jesus Christ. On Thursday he paid a visit to Mr. Wolff's family at Balham, where he was cheerful, and seemed nearly as well as usual, till Friday, about breakfast time, when he grew very heavy. About eleven o'clock he returned home, extremely ill. His friends were struck with the manner of his getting out of the carriage, and still more with his apparent weakness when he went up stairs and sat down in his chair. He now desired to be left alone, and not to be interrupted by any one, for half an hour. When that time was expired, some mulled wine was brought him, of which he drank a little. In a few minutes he threw it up, and said, 'I must lie down.' His friends were now alarmed, and Dr. Whitehead was immediately sent for. On his entering the room, he said in a cheerful voice, 'Doctor, they are more afraid than hurt.' Most of this day he lay in bed, had a quick pulse, with a considerable degree of fever and stupor. And Saturday, the 26th, he continued in much the same state; taking very little either of medicine or nourishment.

"Sunday morning he seemed much better, got up, and took a cup of tea. Sitting in his chair, he looked quite cheerful, and repeated the latter part of the verse, in his brother Charles' Scripture Hymns, on '*Forsake me not when my strength faileth;*' namely,

> 'Till glad I lay this body down,
> Thy servant, Lord, attend;
> And, O! my life of mercy crown
> With a triumphant end.'

Soon after, in a most emphatical manner, he said, 'Our friend Lazarus sleepeth.' Exerting himself to converse with some friends, he was soon fatigued, and obliged to lie down. After lying quiet some time, he looked up, and said, 'Speak to me; I can not speak.' On which one of the company said, 'Shall we pray with you, sir?' He earnestly replied, 'Yes.' And while they prayed, his whole soul seemed engaged with God for an answer, and his hearty *amen* showed that he perfectly understood what was said. About half an hour after, he said, 'There is no need of more; when at Bristol my words were,

> "I the chief of sinners am,
> But Jesus died for me."'*

"One said, 'Is this the present language of your heart,

* At the Bristol conference, in 1783, Mr. Wesley was taken very ill; neither he nor his friends thought he could recover. From the nature of

and do you now feel as you did then?' He replied, 'Yes.' When the same person repeated,

'Bold I approach the eternal throne,
And claim the crown, through Christ my own,'

and added, ''Tis enough. He our precious Immanuel has purchased, has promised, all,' he earnestly replied, 'He is all! He is all!' After this the fever was very high, and, at times, affected his recollection; but even then, though his head was subject to a temporary derangement, his heart seemed wholly engaged in his Master's work. In the evening he got up again, and, while sitting in his chair, he said, 'How necessary it is for every one to be on the right foundation!

"I the chief of sinners am,
But Jesus died for me!"'

"Monday, the 28th, his weakness increased. He slept most of the day, and spoke but little; yet that little testified how much his whole heart was taken up in the care of the societies, the glory of God, and the promotion of the things pertaining to that kingdom to which he was hastening. Once he said, in a low but distinct manner, 'There is no way into the holiest, but by the blood of Jesus.' He afterward inquired what the words were from which he had preached a little before at Hampstead. Being told they were these, 'Ye know the grace of our Lord

his complaint, he supposed a spasm would seize his stomach, and, probably, occasion sudden death. Under these views of his situation, he said to Mr. Bradford, "I have been reflecting on my past life: I have been wandering up and down, between fifty and sixty years, endeavoring, in my poor way, to do a little good to my fellow-creatures; and now it is probable, that there are but a few steps between me and death; and what have I to trust to for salvation? I can see nothing which I have done or suffered, that will bear looking at. I have no other plea than this

'I the chief of sinners am,
But Jesus died for me.'"

The sentiment here expressed, and his reference to it in his last sickness, plainly show how steadily he had persevered in the same views of the Gospel.

Jesus Christ, that though he was rich, yet for your sakes he became poor, that ye through his poverty might be rich,' he replied, 'That is the foundation, the only foundation: there is no other.' This day Dr. Whitehead desired he might be asked, if he would have any other physician called in to attend him; but this he absolutely refused. It is remarkable that he suffered very little pain, never complaining of any during his illness, but once of a pain in his left breast. This was a restless night. Tuesday morning he sung two verses of a hymn: then lying still, as if to recover strength, he called for pen and ink; but when they were brought, he could not write. A person said, 'Let me write for you, sir: tell me what you would say.' He replied, 'Nothing, but that God is with us.' In the forenoon he said, 'I will get up.' While they were preparing his clothes, he broke out in a manner which, considering his extreme weakness, astonished all present, in singing,

'I'll praise my Maker while I've breath,
And when my voice is lost in death,
Praise shall employ my nobler powers:
My days of praise shall ne'er be past,
While life, and thought, and being last,
Or immortality endures!'

"Having got him into his chair, they observed him change for death. But he, regardless of his dying body, said, with a weak voice, 'Lord, thou givest strength to those that can speak, and to those who can not. Speak, Lord, to all our hearts, and let them know that thou loosest tongues.' He then sung,

'To Father, Son, and Holy Ghost,
Who sweetly all agree—'

Here his voice failed. After gasping for breath, he said, 'Now we have done all.' He was then laid in the bed, from which he rose no more. After resting a little he called to those that were with him to 'pray and praise.' They kneeled down, and the room seemed to be filled with the Divine presence. A little after, he said, 'Let me be buried in nothing but what is woolen, and let my corpse be carried into the chapel.' Then, as if he had done with all below, he again begged they would pray and praise. Several friends that were in the house being called up, they all kneeled down again to prayer, at which time his fervor of spirit was manifest to every one present. But in particular parts of the prayer, his whole soul seemed to be engaged in a manner which evidently showed how ardently he longed for the full accomplishment of their united desires. And when one of the preachers was praying in a very expressive manner, that if God were about to take away their father to his eternal rest, he would be pleased to continue and increase his blessing upon the doctrine and discipline which he had long made his servant the means of propagating and establishing in the world, such a degree of fervor accompanied his loud *amen,* as was every way expressive of his soul's being engaged in the answer of the petitions. On rising from their knees, he took hold of all their hands, and, with the utmost placidness, saluted them, and said, 'Farewell, farewell.'

"A little after, a person coming in, he strove to speak, but could not. Finding they could not understand him, he paused a little, and then, with all the remaining strength he had, cried out, '*The best of all is, God is with us;*' and, soon after, lifting up his dying arm in token of victory, and raising his feeble voice with a holy triumph not to be expressed, he again repeated the heart-reviving words, '*The best of all is, God is with us.*' Being told that his brother's widow was come, he said, 'He giveth his servants rest.' He thanked her, as she pressed his hand, and affectionately endeavored to kiss her. On his lips being wetted, he said, 'We thank thee, O Lord, for these and all thy mercies: bless the Church and king; and grant us truth and peace, through Jesus Christ our Lord, forever and ever!' At another time he said, 'He causeth his servants to lie down in peace.' Then pausing a little, he cried, 'The clouds drop fatness!' and soon after, 'The Lord is with us, the God of Jacob is our refuge!' He then called those present to prayer; and though he was greatly exhausted, he appeared still more fervent in spirit. These exertions were, however, too much for his feeble frame; and most of the night following, though he often attempted to repeat the psalm before mentioned, he could only utter,

'I'll praise—I'll praise!'

"On Wednesday morning the closing scene drew near. Mr. Bradford, his faithful friend, prayed with him, and the last words he was heard to articulate were, 'Farewell!' A few minutes before ten, while several of his friends were kneeling around his bed, without a lingering groan, this man of God, this beloved pastor of thousands, entered into the joy of his Lord.

"He was in the eighty-eighth year of his age, had been sixty-five years in the ministry; and the preceding pages will be a lasting memorial of his uncommon zeal, diligence, and usefulness, in his Master's work, for more than half a century. His death was an admirable close to so laborious and useful a life.

"At the desire of many of his friends his corpse was placed in the new chapel, and remained there the day before his interment. His face during that time had a heavenly smile upon it, and a beauty which was admired by all that saw it.

"March the 9th was the day appointed for his interment. The preachers then in London requested that Dr. Whitehead should deliver the funeral discourse; and the executors afterward approved of the appointment. The intention was to carry the corpse into the chapel, and place it in a raised situation before the pulpit during the service. But the crowds which came to see the body while it lay in the coffin, both in the private house, and especially in the chapel the day before his funeral, were so great, that his friends were apprehensive of a tumult, if they should adopt the plan first intended. It was, therefore, resolved, the evening before, to bury him between five and six in the morning. Though the time of notice to his friends was short, and the design itself was spoken of with great caution, yet a considerable number of persons attended at that early hour. The late Rev. Mr. Richardson, who now lies with him in the same vault, read the funeral service in a manner that made it peculiarly affecting. When he came to that part of it, 'Forasmuch as it hath pleased almighty God to take to himself the soul of our dear *brother*,' etc., he substituted, with the most tender emphasis, the epithet *father*, instead of *brother*, which had so powerful an effect on the congregation, that from silent tears they seemed universally to burst out into loud weeping.

INSCRIPTION ON HIS COFFIN.

JOHANNES WESLEY, A. M.
Olim Soc. Coll. Lin. Oxon.
Ob. 2do. die Martii, 1791.
An. Æt. 88.*

"The discourse by Dr. Whitehead was delivered in the chapel at the hour appointed in the forenoon, to an astonishing multitude of people; among whom were many ministers of the Gospel, both of the Establishment and Dissenters. The audience was still and solemn as night; and all seemed to carry away with them enlarged views of Mr. Wesley's character, and serious impressions of the importance of religion."

* "John Wesley, Master of Arts, formerly Fellow of Lincoln College, Oxford, died on the second day of March, 1791, in the eighty-eighth year of his age."

The following is the inscription on the marble tablet erected to his memory, in the chapel, City road:

SACRED TO THE MEMORY
OF THE REV. JOHN WESLEY, M. A.,
SOMETIME FELLOW OF LINCOLN COLLEGE, OXFORD:
A Man in Learning and sincere Piety
Scarcely inferior to any;
In Zeal, Ministerial Labors, and Extensive Usefulness,
Superior, perhaps, to all Men,
Since the days of ST. PAUL.
Regardless of Fatigue, personal Danger, and Disgrace,
He went out into the highways and hedges,
Calling Sinners to Repentance,
And Publishing the GOSPEL OF PEACE.
He was the Founder of the Methodist Societies,
And the chief Promoter and Patron
Of the Plan of Itinerant Preaching,
Which he extended through GREAT BRITAIN and IRELAND,
The WEST INDIES, and AMERICA,
With unexampled Success.
He was born the 17th of June, 1703;
And died the 2d of March, 1791,
In sure and certain hope of Eternal Life,
Through the Atonement and Mediation of a Crucified Savior
He was sixty-five Years in the Ministry,
And fifty-two an Itinerant Preacher:
He lived to see, in these KINGDOMS only,
About three hundred Itinerant,
And one thousand Local Preachers,
Raised up from the midst of his own People;
And eighty thousand Persons in the Societies under his care.
His name will be ever had in grateful Remembrance
By all who rejoice in the universal Spread
Of the Gospel of CHRIST.
Soli Deo Gloria.
[Glory to God alone.]

It would be superfluous in closing this account of a man at once so extraordinary and so truly great for me to attempt a delineation of his character, since this has been done so ably that nothing can easily be added, with good effect. I shall, therefore, insert Dr. Whitehead's own summary, with notices by others who were personally acquainted with him. Taken together they transmit an interesting and instructive picture of the founder of Methodism to future ages.

Dr. Whitehead observes:

"Some persons have affected to insinuate that Mr. Wesley was a man of slender capacity; but certainly with great injustice. His apprehension was clear, his penetration quick, and his judgment discriminative and sound; of which his controversial writings, and his celebrity in the stations he held at Oxford, when young, are sufficient proofs. In governing a large body of preachers and people, of various habits, interests, and principles, with astonishing calmness and regularity for many years, he showed a strong and capacious mind, that could comprehend and combine together a vast variety of circumstances, and direct their influence through the great body he governed. As a scholar, he certainly held a conspicuous rank. He was a critic in the Latin and Greek classics; and was well acquainted with the Hebrew, and with several modern tongues. But the Greek was his favorite language, in which his knowledge was extensive and accurate. At college, he had studied Euclid, Keil, Sir Isaac Newton's Optics, etc.; but he never entered far into the more abstruse parts, or the higher branches of the mathematics; finding they would fascinate his mind, absorb his attention, and divert him from the pursuit of the more important objects of his own profession.

"Natural history was a field in which he walked at every opportunity, and contemplated with infinite pleasure the wisdom, the power, and the goodness of God, in the structure of natural bodies, and in the various instincts and habits of the animal creation. But he was obliged to view these wonderful works of God, in the labors and records of others; his various and continual employments of a higher nature, not permitting him to make experiments and observations for himself.*

"As a writer, Mr. Wesley certainly possessed talents, sufficient to procure him considerable reputation. But he did not write for fame: his object was chiefly to instruct and benefit that numerous class of people who have little learning, little money, and but little time to spare for reading. In all his writings he constantly kept these circumstances in view. Content with doing good, he used no trappings merely to please, or to gain applause. The distinguishing character of his style is brevity and perspicuity. He never lost sight of the rule which Horace gives:

> '*Est brevitate opus, ut currat sententia, neu se*
> *Impediat verbis lassas onerantibus aures.*'
>
> 'Concise your diction, let your sense be clear,
> Nor with a weight of words fatigue the ear.

"In all his writings his words are well chosen, *pure, proper* to his subject, and *precise* in their meaning. His sentences commonly have the attributes of clearness, unity, and strength: and whenever he took time, and gave the necessary attention to his subject, both his manner of treating it, and his style, show the hand of a master.†

"The following is a just character of Mr. Wesley as a preacher: 'His attitude in the pulpit was graceful and easy; his action calm and natural, yet pleasing and expressive; his voice not loud, but clear and manly; his style neat, simple, and perspicuous, and admirably adapted to the capacity of his hearers. His discourses, in point of composition, were extremely different on different occa-

* He, however, employed much leisure time while at college in the study of anatomy and medicine.

† His Treatise on Original Sin, his Appeals, and some of his Sermons, are instances of finished and careful composition; and are equally to be admired for clearness of method, and the force of many passages which are truly eloquent.

sions. When he gave himself sufficient time for preparation, he succeeded; but when he did not, he frequently failed.' It was indeed manifest to his friends, for many years before he died, that his employments were too many, and that he preached too often to appear with the same advantage at all times in the pulpit. His sermons were always short: he was seldom more than half an hour in delivering a discourse, sometimes not so long. His subjects were judiciously chosen, instructive and interesting to the audience, and well adapted to gain attention and warm the heart.

"The labors of Mr. Wesley in the work of the ministry, for fifty years together, were without precedent. During this period, he traveled about four thousand, five hundred miles every year, one year with another, chiefly on horseback. It had been impossible for him to accomplish this almost incredible degree of exertion, without great punctuality and care in the management of his time. He had stated hours for every purpose: and his only relaxation was a change of employment. His rules were like the laws of the Medes and Persians, absolute and irrevocable. He had a peculiar pleasure in reading and study, and every literary man knows how apt this passion is to make him encroach on the time which ought to be employed in other duties: he had a high relish for conversation, especially with pious, learned, and sensible men: but whenever the hour came when he was to set out on a journey, he instantly quitted the company with which he might be engaged, without any apparent reluctance. For fifty-two years, or upward, he generally delivered two, frequently three or four, sermons in a day. But calculating only two sermons a day, and allowing, as a writer of his life has done, fifty annually for extraordinary occasions, the whole number of sermons he preached during this period will be forty thousand, five hundred and sixty. To these must be added an infinite number of exhortations to the societies after preaching, and in other occasional meetings at which he assisted.

"In social life, Mr. Wesley was lively and conversational. He had the talent of making himself exceedingly agreeable in company: and having been much accustomed to society, the rules of good breeding were habitual to him. The abstraction of a scholar did not appear in his behavior; but he was attentive and polite. He spoke a good deal where he saw it was expected, which was almost always the case wherever he visited. Having seen much of the world in his travels, and read more, his mind was stored with an infinite number of anecdotes and observations; and the manner in which he related them was no inconsiderable addition to the entertainment and instruction they afforded. It was impossible to be long in his company, either in public or private, without partaking of his placid cheerfulness; which was not abated by the infirmities of age, or the approach of death; but was as conspicuous at fourscore and seven, as at one and twenty.

"A remarkable feature in Mr. Wesley's character was his placability. Having an active, penetrating mind, his temper was naturally quick, and even tending to sharpness. The influence of religion, and the constant habit of patient thinking, had in a great measure corrected this disposition. In general he preserved an air of sedateness and tranquillity, which formed a striking contrast to the liveliness conspicuous in all his actions. Persecutions, abuse, and injury, he bore from strangers, not only without anger, but without any apparent emotion; and what he said of himself is strictly true, that he had a great facility in forgiving injuries. Submission, on the part of the offender, presently disarmed his resentment, and he would treat him with great kindness and cordiality. No man was ever more free from jealousy or suspicion than

Mr. Wesley, or laid himself more open to the impositions of others. Though his confidence was often abused, and circumstances sometimes took place which would have made almost any other man suspicious, yet he suspected no one; nor was it easy to convince him that any one had intentionally deceived him; and when facts had demonstrated that this was actually the case, he would allow no more than that it was so in that single instance. If the person acknowledged his fault, he believed him sincere, and would trust him again. If we view this temper of his mind in connection with the circumstance that his most private papers lay open to the inspection of those constantly about him, it will afford as strong proof as can well be given, of the integrity of his own mind, and that he was at the farthest distance from any intention to deceive, or impose upon others.

"The temperance of Mr. Wesley was extraordinary. When at college he carried this so far that his friends thought him blamable. But he never imposed upon others the same degree of rigor he exercised upon himself. He only said, I must be the best judge of what is hurtful or beneficial to me. Among other things, he was remarkable for moderation in sleep; and his notion of it can not be better explained than in his own words. Healthy men, says he, 'require about six hours' sleep; healthy women, a little above seven, in four and twenty. If any one desires to know exactly what quantity of sleep his own constitution requires, he may very easily make the experiment, which I made about sixty years ago. I then waked every night about twelve or one, and lay awake for some time. I readily concluded, that this arose from my being in bed longer than nature required. To be satisfied, I procured an alarum, which waked me the next morning at seven—nearly an hour earlier than I rose the day before—yet I lay awake again at night. The second morning I rose at six; but, notwithstanding this, I lay awake the second night. The third morning I rose at five; but, nevertheless, I lay awake the third night. The fourth morning I rose at four, as, by the grace of God, I have done ever since: and I lay awake no more. And I do not now lie awake, taking the year round, a quarter of an hour together in a month. By the same experiment, rising ealier and earlier every morning, may any one find how much sleep he wants.'

"It must, however, be observed, that, for many years before his death, Mr. Wesley slept more or less during the day; and his great readiness to fall asleep at any time when fatigued, was a considerable means of keeping up his strength, and enabling him to go through so much labor. He never could endure to sleep on a soft bed. Even in the latter part of life, when the infirmities of age pressed upon him, his whole conduct was at the greatest distance from softness or effeminacy.

"A writer of Mr. Wesley's Life, from whom some observations respecting his general character have already been taken, has farther observed, Perhaps the most charitable man in England was Mr. Wesley. His liberality to the poor knew no bounds but an empty pocket. He gave away, not merely a certain part of his income, but all that he had: his own wants provided for, he devoted all the rest to the necessities of others. He entered upon this good work at a very early period. We are told, that, 'when he had thirty pounds a year, he lived on twenty-eight, and gave away forty shillings. The next year, receiving sixty pounds, he still lived on twenty-eight, and gave away two and thirty. The third year he received ninety pounds, and gave away sixty-two. The fourth year he received one hundred and twenty pounds. Still he lived on twenty-eight, and gave to the poor ninety-two.' In this ratio he proceeded during the rest of his life; and, in the course of fifty years, it has been supposed, he gave away between twenty and thirty thousand pounds;* a great part of which most other men would have put out at interest, upon good security.

"In the distribution of his money, Mr. Wesley was as disinterested as he was charitable. He had no regard to family connections, nor even to the wants of the preachers who labored with him, in preference to strangers. He knew that these had some friends; and he thought that the poor destitute stranger might have none, and, therefore, had the first claim on his liberality. When a trifling legacy has been paid him, he has been known to dispose of it in some charitable way before he slept, that it might not remain his own property for one night. He often declared that his own hands should be his executors; and though he gained all he could by his publications, and saved all he could, not wasting so much as a sheet of paper, yet, by giving all he could, he was preserved from *laying up treasures upon earth.* He had said in print, that, if he died worth more than ten pounds, independent of his books, and the arrears of his fellowship, which he then held, he would give the world leave to call him 'a thief and a robber.' This declaration, made in the integrity of his heart, and the hight of his zeal, laid him under some inconveniences afterward, from circumstances which he could not at that time foresee. Yet in this, as all his friends expected, he literally kept his word, as far as human foresight could reach. His chaise and horses, his clothes, and a few trifles of that kind, were all, his books excepted, that he left at his death. Whatever might be the value of his books, this altered not the case, as they were placed in the hands of trustees, and the profits arising from the sale of them were to be applied to the

* Money chiefly arising from the constant and large sale of his writings, and the works he abridged.

use and benefit of the conference for public purposes; reserving only a few legacies and a rent charge of eighty-five pounds a year to be paid to his brother's widow, which was in fact a debt, in consideration for the copyright of his brother's hymns.

"Among the other excellences of Mr. Wesley, his moderation in controversy deserves to be noticed. Writers of controversy too often forget, that their own character is intimately connected with the manner in which they treat others: and if they have no regard for their opponents, they ought to have some respect for themselves. When a writer becomes personal and abusive, it affords a fair presumption against his arguments, and tends to put his readers on their guard. Most of Mr. Wesley's opponents were of this description; their *railing* was much more violent than their *reasons* were cogent. Mr. Wesley kept his temper, and wrote like a Christian, a gentleman, and a scholar. He might have taken the words of the excellent Hooker as a motto to his polemical tracts, 'To your *railing*, I say *nothing;* for your *reasons* take what follows.' He admired the temper in which Mr. Law wrote a controversy: only in some instances Mr. Law shows a contempt for his opponents, which Mr. Wesley thought highly improper."

To these remarks of Dr. Whitehead may be added two or three sketches of Mr. Wesley's character, drawn up by different persons, and printed soon after his death. The first is anonymous:

"Now that Mr. John Wesley has finished his course upon earth, I may be allowed to estimate his character, and the loss the world has sustained by his death. Upon a fair account, it appears to be such, as not only annihilates all the reproaches that have been cast upon him, but such as does honor to mankind, at the same time that it reproaches them. His natural and acquired abilities were both of the highest rank. His apprehension was lively and distinct; his learning extensive. His judgment, though not infallible, was, in most cases, excellent. His mind was steadfast and resolved. His elocution was ready and clear, graceful and easy, accurate and unaffected. As a writer, his style, though unstudied, and flowing with natural ease, yet for accuracy and perspicuity was such as may vie with the best writers in the English language. Though his temper was naturally warm, his manners were gentle, simple, and uniform. Never were such happy talents better seconded by an unrelenting perseverance in those courses which his singular endowments, and his zealous love to the interests of mankind, marked out for him. His constitution was excellent: and never was a constitution less abused, less spared, or more excellently applied, in an exact subservience to the faculties of his mind. His labors and studies were wonderful. The latter were not confined to theology only, but extended to every subject that tended either to the improvement or the rational entertainment of the mind. If we consider his reading by itself, his writings and his other labors by themselves, any one of them will appear sufficient to have kept a person of ordinary application busy during his whole life. In short, the transactions of his life could never have been performed, without the utmost exertion of two qualities, which depended, not upon his capacity, but on the uniform steadfastness of his resolution. These were inflexible temperance, and unexampled economy of time. In these he was a pattern to the age he lived in, and an example to what a surprising extent a man may render himself useful in his generation, by temperance and punctuality. His friends and followers have no reason to be ashamed of the name of Methodist, which he has entailed upon them, as, for an uninterrupted course of years, he has given the world an instance of the possibility of living without wasting a single hour, and of the advantage of a regular distribution of time, in discharging the important duties and purposes of life. Few ages have more needed such a public testimony to the value of time, and perhaps none have had a more conspicuous example of the perfection to which the improvement of it may be carried.

"As a minister, his labors were unparalleled, and such as nothing could have supported him under but the warmest zeal for the doctrine he taught, and for the eternal interests of mankind. He studied to be gentle, yet vigilant and faithful toward all. He possessed himself in patience, and preserved himself unprovoked, nay, even unruffled, in the midst of persecution, reproach, and all manner of abuse, both of his person and name. But let his own works praise him. He now enjoys the fruits of his labors, and that praise which he sought, not of men, but of God.

"To finish the portrait. Examine the general tenor of his life, and it will be found self-evidently inconsistent with his being a slave to any one passion or pursuit, that can fix a blemish on his character. Of what use were the accumulation of wealth to him, who, through his whole course, never allowed himself to taste the repose of indolence, or even of the common indulgence in the use of the necessaries of life? Free from the partiality of any party, the sketcher of this excellent character, with a friendly tear, pays it as a just tribute to the memory of so great and good a man, who, when alive, was his friend."

Of Mr. Wesley Mr. Alexander Knox says:

"Very lately I had an opportunity, for some days together, of observing Mr. Wesley with attention. I endeavored to consider him, not so much with the eye of a friend, as with the impartiality of a philosopher; and I must declare, every hour I spent in his company afforded me fresh reasons for esteem and veneration. So fine an old man I never saw. The happiness of his mind beamed forth in his countenance. Every look showed how fully he enjoyed 'the gay remembrance of a life well spent;' and wherever he went, he diffused a portion of his own felicity. Easy and affable in his demeanor, he accommodated himself to every sort of company, and showed how happily the most finished courtesy may be blended with the most perfect piety. In his conversation, we might be at a loss whether to admire most his fine classical taste, his extensive knowledge of men and things, or his overflowing goodness of heart. While the grave and serious were charmed with his wisdom, his sportive sallies of innocent mirth delighted even the young and thoughtless; and both saw, in his uninterrupted cheerfulness, the excellency of true religion. No cynical remarks on the levity of youth imbittered his discourse; no applausive retrospect to past times marked his present discontent. In him even old age appeared delightful, like an evening without a cloud; and it was impossible to observe him without wishing, fervently, 'May my latter end be like his!'

"But I find myself unequal to the task of delineating such a character. What I have said may to some appear as panegyric; but there are numbers, and those of taste and discernment too, who can bear witness to the truth, though by no means to the perfectness, of the sketch I have attempted. With such I have been frequently in his company; and every one of them, I am persuaded, would subscribe to all I have said. For my own part, I never was so happy as while with him, and scarcely ever felt more poignant regret than at parting from him; for well I knew 'I ne'er should look upon his like again.' "

The following account of Mr. Wesley appeared soon after his death in a very respectable publication, and was afterward inserted in Woodfall's Diary, London, June 17, 1791:

"His indefatigable zeal in the discharge of his duty has long been witnessed by the world; but, as mankind are not always inclined to put a generous construction on the exertions of singular talents, his motives were imputed to the love of popularity, ambition, and lucre. It now appears that he was actuated by a disinterested regard to the immortal interests of mankind. He labored, and studied, and preached, and wrote, to propagate what he believed to be the Gospel of Christ. The intervals of these engagements were employed in governing and regulating the concerns of his numerous societies; assisting the necessities, solving the difficulties, and soothing the afflictions of his hearers. He observed so rigid a temperance, and allowed himself so little repose, that he seemed to be above the infirmities of nature, and to act independent of the earthly tenement he occupied. The recital of the occurrences of every day of his life would be the greatest encomium.

"Had he loved wealth, he might have accumulated it without bounds. Had he been fond of power, his influence would have been worth courting by any party. I do not say he was without ambition; he had that which Christianity need not blush at, and which virtue is proud to confess. I do not mean that which is gratified by splendor and large possessions, but that which commands the hearts and affections, the homage and gratitude, of thousands. For him they felt sentiments of veneration, only inferior to those which they paid to Heaven: to him they looked as their father, their benefactor, their guide to glory and immortality: for him they fell prostrate before God, with prayers and tears, to spare his doom, and prolong his stay. Such a recompense as this is sufficient to repay the toils of the longest life. Short of this, greatness is contemptible impotence. Before this, lofty prelates bow, and princes hide their diminished heads.

"His zeal was not a transient blaze, but a steady and constant flame. The ardor of his spirit was neither damped by difficulty, nor subdued by age. This was ascribed by himself to the power of divine grace; by the world, to *enthusiasm*. Be it what it will, it is what philosophers must envy, and infidels respect; it is that which gives energy to the soul, and without which there can be no greatness or heroism.

"Why should we condemn that in religion which we applaud in every other profession and pursuit? He had a vigor and elevation of mind, which nothing but the belief of the Divine favor and presence could inspire. This threw a luster round his infirmities, changed his bed of sickness into a triumphal car, and made his exit resemble an apotheosis rather than a dissolution.

"He was qualified to excel in every branch of literature: he was well versed in the learned tongues, in metaphysics, in oratory, in logic, in criticism, and every requisite of a Christian minister. His style was nervous, clear, and manly; his preaching was pathetic and persuasive; his journals are artless and interesting; and his compositions and compilations to promote knowledge and piety were almost innumerable.

"I do not say he was without faults, or above mistakes; but they were lost in the multitude of his excellences and virtues.

"To gain the admiration of an ignorant and superstitious age, requires only a little artifice and address; to stand the test of these times, when all pretensions to sanctity are stigmatized as hypocrisy, is a proof of genuine piety and real usefulness. His great object was, to revive the obsolete doctrines and extinguished spirit of the Church of England; and they who are its friends can not be his enemies. Yet for this he was treated as a fanatic and impostor, and exposed to every species of slander and persecution. Even bishops and dignitaries entered the lists against him; but he never declined the combat, and generally proved victorious. He appealed to the Homilies, the

Articles, and the Scriptures, as vouchers for his doctrine; and they who could not decide upon the merits of the controversy, were witnesses of the effects of his labors; and they judged of the tree by its fruit. It is true, he did not succeed much in the higher walks of life; but that impeached his cause no more than it did that of the first planters of the Gospel. However, if he had been capable of assuming vanity on that score, he might have ranked among his friends some persons of the first distinction, who would have done honor to any party. After surviving almost all his adversaries, and acquiring respect among those who were the most distant from his principles, he lived to see the plant he had reared spreading its branches far and wide, and inviting not only these kingdoms, but the western world, to repose under its shade. No sect, since the first ages of Christianity, could boast a founder of such extensive talents and endowments. If he had been a candidate for literary fame, he might have succeeded to his utmost wishes; but he sought not the praise of man; he regarded learning only as the instrument of usefulness. The great purpose of his life was doing good. For this he relinquished all honor and preferment; to this he dedicated all his powers of body and mind; at all times and in all places, in season and out of season, by gentleness, by terror, by argument, by persuasion, by reason, by interest, by every motive and every inducement, he strove, with unwearied assiduity, to turn men from the error of their ways, and awaken them to virtue and religion. To the bed of sickness, or the couch of prosperity; to the prison, the hospital, the house of mourning, or the house of feasting, wherever there was a friend to serve, or a soul to save, he readily repaired; to administer assistance or advice, reproof or consolation. He thought no office too humiliating, no condescension too low, no undertaking too arduous, to reclaim the meanest of God's offspring. The souls of all men were equally precious in his sight, and the value of an immortal creature beyond all estimation. He penetrated the abodes of wretchedness and ignorance, to rescue the profligate from perdition; and he communicated the light of life to those who sat in darkness and the shadow of death. He changed the outcasts of society into useful members; civilized even savages, and filled those lips with prayer and praise that had been accustomed only to oaths and imprecations. But as the strongest religious impressions are apt to become languid without discipline and practice, he divided his people into classes and bands, according to their attainments. He appointed frequent meetings for prayer and conversation, where they gave an account of their experience, their hopes and fears, their joys and troubles; by which means they were united to each other, and to their common profession. They became sentinels upon each other's conduct, and securities for each other's character. Thus the seeds he sowed sprang up and flourished, bearing the rich fruits of every grace and virtue. Thus he governed and preserved his numerous societies, watching their improvement with a paternal care, and encouraging them to be faithful to the end.

"But I will not attempt to draw his full character, nor to estimate the extent of his labors and services. They will be best known when he shall deliver up his commission into the hands of his great Master."

The following is a description of Mr. Wesley's person:

"The figure of Wesley was remarkable. His stature was low; his habit of body, in every period of life, the reverse of corpulent, and expressive of strict temperance and continual exercise; and, notwithstanding his small size, his step was firm, and his appearance, till within a few years of his death, vigorous and muscular. His face, for an old man, was one of the finest we have seen. A clear, smooth forehead; an aquiline nose; an eye, the brightest and most piercing that can be conceived; and a freshness of complexion, scarcely ever to be found at his years, and expressive of the most perfect health, conspired to render him a venerable and interesting figure. Few have seen him without being struck with his appearance; and many, who had been greatly prejudiced against him, have been known to change their opinion the moment they were introduced into his presence. In his countenance and demeanor, there was a cheerfulness mingled with gravity; a sprightliness, which was the natural result of an unusual flow of spirits, and yet was accompanied with every mark of the most serene tranquillity. His aspect, particularly in profile, had a strong character of acuteness and penetration.

"In dress, he was a pattern of neatness and simplicity: a narrow, plaited stock; a coat, with a small upright collar; no buckles at his knees; no silk or velvet in any part of his apparel; and a head as white as snow, gave an idea of something primitive and apostolic; while an air of neatness and cleanliness was diffused over his whole person."

CHAPTER XV.

A few miscellaneous topics remain to be noticed. One of the chief reasons why full and willing justice has not been always done to the labors of Mr. Wesley, has doubtless arisen from the facts, that, whatever his views might be, he raised up a people who, in his lifetime, formed a religious body independent of the Church, while yet not nominally separated from it; and that since his death, although that separation does not affect all the members, yet the great mass of the societies, with all the preachers, are as completely separated from the Establishment as any body of professed Dissenters. That a strict Churchman should consider this as a great counterbalance to the good effected by Methodism is very natural; and he has a right to his opinions, provided he holds them in charity. Still, however, this subject is so frequently dwelt upon under mistaken and imperfect views, that it demands a few additional remarks.

As far as Mr. Wesley's character is concerned, enough has been said to show the sincerity with which he disavowed all intention of separating from the Church, and of making his people separatists. This, certainly, notwithstanding the freedom of his opinions on Church government, can not be charged upon him in the early period of his career; and although, in what we may call the second period, he saw so strong a tendency to separation that his fears were often excited, yet he may surely be allowed still to have proceeded straight forward, with perfect honesty of mind, in the same course, with more of hope on this subject than of fear. Several eminent writers of the Church party have thought that even modern Methodism, though existing now in a form apparently less friendly to union, might still with advantage be attached to the Church, and have seen but little difficulty in the project. Why, then, might not Mr. Wesley, even after his societies had acquired considerable maturity, still hope that those simple institutions for promoting piety, which he had commenced, might have been recognized by the Church, and hoped that the spirit of religion, revived already to so great an extent, might still farther so influence the members of the Church and its clergy, as to dispose them to view his societies with more cordiality? He took care, therefore, and all his principles and feelings favored the caution, that no obstacles should be placed in the way of the closest connection of his societies with the Establishment. Their services were very seldom held in the hours of her public service; the Meth odists formed in many parishes the great body of her communicants; thousands of them died in her communion; and the preachers were not ordinarily permitted to administer either of the sacraments to the people among whom they labored. There can be no charge, therefore, against his sincerity at this period, any more than in the first. We may think his hopes to have been without any foundation; and so they proved; and the idea of uniting the modern Methodists to the Church is a very visionary one, but has doubtless been maintained by several Churchmen with great sincerity. Separation from the Church, at a later period of Mr. Wesley's life, was certainly anticipated. That must be allowed; but an enlightened Churchman ought to think that Mr. Wesley's conduct was still worthy of praise, not of censure; for when a partial separation was in reality foreseen as probable, it had no sanction from him, and he appeared determined so to employ his influence to his last breath, that if separation did ensue it should assume the mildest form possible, and be deprived of all feelings of hostility. His example, the spirit of his writings, and his advices all tended to this; and the fact is, that, though Methodism now stands in a different relation to the Establishment than in the days of Mr. Wesley, dissent has never been formally professed by the body, and for obvious reasons. The first is, that the separation of the greater part of the society from the Church did not, in any great degree, result from the principles assumed by the professed Dissenters, and which are usually made prominent in their discussions on the subject of establishments; the second, that a considerable number of the Methodists actually continue in the communion of the Church of England to this day; and the third, that to leave that communion is not, in any sense, a condition of membership with us. All the services of the Church and her sacraments may be observed by any person in the Wesleyan societies who chooses it, and they are actually observed by many.

It was owing to these circumstances that Methodism did not rush down, but gently glided, into a state of partial division from the Church; and this, by neither arousing party passions, nor exciting discussions on abstract points of Church polity, has left the general feeling of affection to all that is excellent in the Establishment unimpaired. No intemperate attacks upon it have been ever sanctioned; the attendance of Methodists upon its services was never discouraged; and it is surely of some account that a vast mass of people throughout the country have been held in a state of friendly feeling toward a clergy who have nevertheless generally treated them with disdain and contumely, and many of whom have zealously employed themselves in nursing feelings of bigoted dislike to them among their friends and neighbors. Yet, after all, the prevalent sentiment of the Methodists, as a body, toward the Establishment has been that of friendship. It was so when the Church was in a lower religious state than it is at present; and its more recent religious improvement has not diminished the feeling. I may venture to say, that there is a warmer regard toward the Church among the body of the Methodists now, than there was in the days of Mr. Wesley; although there were then more Methodists than at present who professed to be of her communion. We have no respect at all to her exclusive claims of divine right, or her three orders of ministers; and yet have no objection to her episcopacy, when Scripturally understood, or her services. We smile at the claim she sometimes assumes to be the exclusive instructress of the people, in a country where the statute law has given them the right to be taught by whom they please, and as explicitly protects dissent as conformity; but we rejoice that she has great influence with the mass of the population, whenever that influence is used for the promotion of true religion and good morals. We wish her prosperity and perpetuity, as we wish all other Christian Churches; and the more so, as we recognize in her "the mother of us all," and can never contemplate, without the deepest admiration, her noble army of confessors and martyrs, and the illustrious train of her divines, whose writings have been, and continue to be, the light of Christendom. If Churchmen think this feeling of any importance, let them reciprocate it; and though the formal union of which some of them have spoken is visionary, a still stronger bond of friendship might be established; and each might thus become more formidable against the errors and evils of the times; for a people who have nearly half as many places of worship in the kingdom as there are parish churches, can not be without influence.

Nor have the true causes which led to the separation of the Methodists from the Church been, in general, rightly stated. Some of the violent adherents of "the old plan," as it was called, among ourselves, have, ignorantly or in a party spirit, attributed this to the ambition and intrigues of the preachers; but the true causes were, that the clergy, *generally*, did not preach the doctrines of their own Church and of the reformation, and that *many* of them did not adorn their profession by their lives. It may be added, that, in no small number of cases, the clergy were the persecutors and calumniators of the Wesleyan societies; that the sermons in the churches were often intemperate attacks upon their characters and opinions; and that the Methodists were frequently regarded as intruders at the table of the Lord, rather than as welcome communicants. These were the reasons why, long before Mr. Wesley's death, a great number of his societies were anxious to have the sacraments from the hands of their own preachers, under whose ministry they were instructed and edified, in whose characters they had confidence, and with respect to whom they knew, that if any one disgraced his profession, he would not be suffered long to exercise it.

Such were the true causes which led to the partial separation of the Methodist societies from the communion of the Church, after the death of Mr. Wesley; and this is an answer to the objection, repeated a thousand times, that we have departed from Mr. Wesley's principles. The fact is, that though full relief to the consciences of the societies in general was refused by Mr. Wesley's authority, yet he himself was obliged to allow a relaxation from his own rule in London, and some other principal towns, by giving the Lord's supper himself, or obtaining pious clergymen to administer it in his chapels. After his death it was out of the power of the conference, had they not felt the force of the reasons urged upon them, to prevent the administration of the sacraments to the people by their own preachers. Yet in the controversy which this subject excited, speculative principles had little part. The question stood on plain practical grounds: Shall the societies be obliged, from their conscientious scruples, to neglect an ordinance of God? Or shall we drive them to the Dissenters, whose peculiar doctrines they do not believe? Or shall we under certain regulations accede to their wishes? So far from Mr. Wesley's principles and views having lost their influence with the conference, the sacraments were forced upon none, and recommended to none. The old principles were held as fast as higher duties would allow. Many, indeed, of the people, and some of the preachers, opposed even these concessions; but the plan which was adopted to meet cases of conscientious scruple, and yet to avoid encouraging a departure from the primitive system, leaving every individual to act in this respect as he was persuaded in his own mind, and receive the Lord's supper at church or at chapel, was at length by both parties in England cordially acquiesced in, as warranted equally by principle and by prudence. Assuredly the Church would have gained nothing by a different measure, for the dissidents would have been compelled to join other communions. Had the Church been provided early with an evangelical and a holy ministry, that separation would not have taken place; for the controversy between the Church and the Dissenter was little known, and still less regarded by the majority of the Methodist societies at that time; and the case is not greatly altered at the present day. The clergy had lost their hold upon the people generally, through neglect; and that revival of the spirit of truth and holiness, which we are now so happy to witness among them, came too late to prevent the results just stated.

And what should we do now, if we were disposed to revert to the state of things in Mr. Wesley's time? It is true we should more rarely meet with immoral clergymen; and so that part of the case would be relieved as a matter of conscience. But would the Methodist societies meet with friendly clergymen; with men who would bear with so many communicants, in addition to those who now attend their churches? And if they were brought to attend the services of their parish churches, would they be disposed long to hear those of the clergy who never preach the doctrines of the articles of their own Church? or those who follow some great names of the present day, and *neologize* as far as decency permits? or those of the evangelical party, whose discourses are strongly impregnated with Calvinism? or those who place their speculations on the prophecies among the means of grace and salvation? Our people would neither hear such clergymen themselves, nor could they conscientiously train up their families to listen to what they believe great error; and so if we were to go back, as we have been exhorted, to Mr. Wesley's first plan, the majority of our people would, as then, neither attend Church nor sacrament, and the same process would have to be repeated again, with probably less peaceful results.

"But 'great evil' has resulted to the Church from Methodism." This has been often said, certainly never substantiated; and this defense of the hostile feeling of many Churchmen toward Mr. Wesley and his societies stands upon no solid ground. On the contrary, it seems not at all difficult to make it plainly appear that great good has resulted to the Church, as well as to the nation. When this question is under consideration by Churchmen, they look at the mere fact that a great body of people have been raised up, as they say, out of the Church, within a century past, excelling in number almost, if not entirely, the whole of the old bodies of Dissenters; and they assume that if the Wesleys and Mr. Whitefield had never appeared, the Church would have been in as improved a state as now, with none but the old Dissenters to contend with. There is great fallacy in both these views, which merits to be pointed out.

When the Messrs. Wesley, Mr. Whitefield, and their early coadjutors entered upon their itinerant career, it is a matter of fact and history, that no general plans for the illumination of the nation were either in operation or in the contemplation of any one. Nothing had this bearing. There were no persons associated in such institutions of any kind, making this a common object. The pious labors of a few zealous clergymen—and few they were—and of the ministers of other denominations, were confined to their own parishes and congregations. There were no means of general application in existence, to remove the ignorance and correct the vices which were almost universal. The measures taken by the founders of Methodism to correct existing evils were on a large scale. They acted in concert; they conceived noble designs. They visited the large towns; they labored in the populous mining, manufacturing, and commercial districts; they preached in places of public resort; they formed religious societies, and inspired them with zeal for the instruction and salvation of their neighbors; they employed men of zeal, character, and competent acquaintance with practical and experimental religion, to assist them in this work as it widened before them; and they gave it their vigilant superintendence. The benefits they were the means of producing were not confined to individuals; they influenced whole neighborhoods. Religious knowledge was spread, and religious influence exerted. The manners of the rude were civilized; barbarous sports and pastimes fell greatly into disuse; and a higher standard of morals was erected, of itself of no small importance to the reformation of manners.

It is a matter of history, that, beside those means which were afforded by their personal labors, and by the auxiliaries they brought forward to their assistance, in order to revive and extend the spirit of religion in the nation, for a great number of years no other means of extensive application were employed to promote this end. The effects which were thus produced began, however, after a considerable time had elapsed, to operate collaterally as well as directly. Many of the clergy were aroused, and the doctrines of the Articles and the Homilies began to be heard more distinctly and more frequently in their pulpits. Holy and zealous men in different denominations began to labor for the public instruction and reformation. The institution of Sunday schools, though devised by a Churchman, was, at first, but slowly encouraged. The Methodists and Dissenters were carrying those schools to a great extent when the members of the Church followed: some from a fear, laudable enough, lest the body of the poor should be alienated from the Establishment; others, as perceiving in the institution the means of conveying instruction and religious influence to those who most needed them. The circulation of the Scriptures by Bible societies followed; but still that was an effect of the new order of principles and feelings which had been introduced into the nation. These principles of zeal for the moral improvement of society farther led, at a later period, to general measures for the education of the poor by the two great national education societies, which promise so much benefit to the country. All these efforts for enlightening and moralizing the people may be traced to several intermediate causes; but it is only justice to the memory of such men as the Wesleys and Whitefield, men so often flippantly branded as enthusiasts, to state, that they all primarily sprung from that spirit, which, under God, they were the means of exciting in a slumbering Church, and in a dark and neglected land. This is a point not to be denied; for long before any of those efforts for public instruction and reformation which could be considered national were called forth, those aspersed men were pursuing their gigantic labors among the profligate population of London, and of the principal towns of the kingdom; among the miners of Cornwall, the colliers of Kingswood and Newcastle, and the manufacturers of Yorkshire and Lancashire; while the preachers they employed were every year spreading themselves into dark, semi-barbarous villages in the most secluded parts of the kingdom; enduring bitter privations, and encountering, almost daily, the insults of rude mobs, that they might convey to them the knowledge of religion.

Now, in order to judge of these efforts, and to ascertain what "evil" has resulted to the Church of England from Mr. Wesley's measures, it is but fair to consider what the state of the country and of the Church must in all human probability have been, had he and his associates never appeared, or confined themselves to the obscurity of Epworth and similar parishes. It is not denied that other means and agents might have been raised up by God to effect the purposes of his mercy; but it is denied that any such were raised up—for this is matter of fact. No agency has appeared in the Church, or out of it, tending to the general instruction and evangelizing of the nation, and operating on a large scale, which is not much subsequent in its origin to the exertions of the Messrs. Wesley and Whitefield, and which may not be traced to the spirit which they excited, and often into the very bosoms of those who derived their first light and influence, either directly or indirectly, from them. What *was* and not what *might have been,* can only be made the ground of argument.

But for their labors, therefore, and the labors of those persons in the Church, among the Dissenters, and their own people, whom they imbued with the same spirit, that state of things in the Church of England, and in the country at large, which has been already described, must have continued, at least, for many years, for any thing which appears to the contrary; for no substitute for their exertions was supplied by any party. They took the place of none who were exerting themselves: they opposed no obstacle to the operation of any plan of usefulness, had it been in preparation. If they, therefore, had not appeared, and kindled that flame of religious feeling which ultimately spread into many denominations of Christians, and thus gave birth to that variety of effort which now diffuses itself through the land, it is a very erroneous conclusion to suppose, that a later period would have found the nation and the Church at all improved. The probability, almost amounting to certainty, is, that both would have been found still more deteriorated, and in a state which would have presented obstacles much more formidable to their recovery. For all who have given attention to such subjects must know, that a number of those demoralizing causes were then coming into operation, which, with all the counteractions since supplied by the Church, and the different religious sects, by schools, and by Bibles, have produced very injurious effects upon the morals and principles of the nation; that the tide of an unprecedented commercial prosperity began then to flow into the country, and continued, for a long succession of years, to render the means of sensual indulgence more ample, and to corrupt more deeply all ranks of society; that, in consequence of the independence thus given to the lower orders in many of the most populous districts, the moral control and influence of the higher became gradually weaker; that the agitation of political subjects, during the American quarrel and the French revolution, with the part which even the operative classes were able to take in such discussions by means of an extended education, produced, as will always be the case among the half-informed, a strong tendency to republicanism, a restless desire of political change on every pinching of the times, and its constant concomitant, an aversion to the National Establishment, partly as the result of ill-digested theories, and partly because this feeling was encouraged by the negligent habits of many of the clergy, and the absence of that influence which they might have acquired in their parishes by careful pastoral attentions. To all this is to be added the diffusion of infidel principles, both of foreign and home growth, which, from the studies of the learned, descended into the shop of the mechanic, and, embodied in cheap and popular works, found their way into every part of the empire. To counteract agencies and principles so active and so pernicious, it is granted that no means have yet been applied of complete adequacy. This is the reason why their effects are so rife in the present day, and that we are now in the midst of a state of things which no considerate man can contemplate without some anxiety. These circumstances, so devastating to morals and good principles, could only have been fully neutralized by the ardent exertions of every clergyman in his parish, of every dissenting minister in his congregation, of every Methodist preacher in his circuit, of every private Christian in his own circle, or in the place which useful and pious institutions of various kinds would have assigned him; and even then the special blessing of God would have been necessary to give effect to the whole. But had no correctives been applied, what had been the present state of the nation and of the Church? The labors of the founders of Methodism were, from the beginning, directly counteractive of the evils just mentioned; and those have little reason to stigmatize them who deplore such evils most, and yet have done least for their correction and restraint. Wherever these men went, they planted the principles of religion in the minds of the multitudes who heard them; they acted on the *offensive* against immorality, infidelity, and error; the societies they raised were employed in doing good to all; the persons they associated with them in the work of national reformation were always engaged in diffusing piety; and though great multitudes were beyond their reach, they spread themselves into every part of the land, turning the attention of men to religious concerns, calming their passions, guarding them against the strifes of the world, enjoining the Scriptural principles of "obedience to magistrates," and a sober, temperate, peaceable, and benevolent conduct. The direct effect of their exertions was great; and it increased in energy and extent as the demoralizing causes before mentioned acquired also greater activity; and when their indirect influence began to appear more fully in the National Church, and in other religious bodies, remedies more commensurate with the evils existing in the country began to be applied. I shall not affect to say what would have been the state of the Church of England under the uncontrolled operation of all the causes of moral deterioration, and civil strife, to which I have adverted; or what hold that Church would have had upon the people at this day, if the spirit of religion had not been revived in the country, and if, when ancient prejudices were destroyed or weakened by the general spread of information among men, no new bond between it and the nation at large had been created. But if, as I am happy to believe, the National Church has much more influence and much more respect now than formerly, and if its influence and the respect due to it are increasing with the increase of its evangelical clergy, all this is owing to the existence of a stronger spirit of piety; and in producing that, the first great instruments were the men whose labors have been mentioned in the preceding pages. Not only has the spirit which they excited improved the religious state of the Church, but it has disposed the great body of religious people, not of the Church, to admire and respect those numerous members of the Establishment, both clergymen and laics, whose eminent piety, talents, and usefulness, have done more to abate the prejudices arising from different views of Church government, than a thousand treatises could have effected, however eloquently written, or ably argued.

It may also be asked, Who are the persons whom the Methodists have alienated from the Church? In this, too, the Church writers have labored under great mistakes. They have "alienated" those, for the most part, who never were, in any substantial sense, and never would have been, of the Church. Very few of her pious members have at any time been separated from her communion by a connection with us; and many who became serious through the Methodist ministry, continued attendants on her services, and observers of her sacraments. This was the case during the life of Mr. Wesley, and in many instances is so still; and when an actual separation of a few persons has occurred, it has been much more than compensated by a return of others from us to the Church, especially of opulent persons, or their children, in consequence of that superior influence which an established Church must always exert upon people of that class. For the rest, they have been brought chiefly from the ranks of the ignorant and the careless; persons who had little knowledge, and no experience of the power of religion; negligent of religious worship of every kind, and many of whom, but for the agency of Methodism, would have swelled the ranks of those who are equally disaffected to Church and state. If such persons are not now Churchmen, they are influenced by no feelings hostile to the institutions of their country.

Such considerations may tend to convey more sober views on a subject often taken up in heat: that they will quite disarm the feeling against which they are leveled is more than can be hoped for, considering the effects of party spirit, and the many forms of virtue which it simulates. However, it is nothing new for the Methodists to endure reproach, and to be subject to misrepresentations. Perhaps something of an exclusive spirit may have grown up among us in consequence; but, if so, it has this palliation, that we are quite as expansive as the circumstances in which we have ever been placed could lead any reasonable man to anticipate. It might almost be said of us, "Lo, the people shall dwell alone." The high Churchman has persecuted us because we are separatists; the high Dissenter has often looked upon us with hostility, because we would not see that an establishment necessarily, and *in se*—in itself—involved a sin against the supremacy of Christ; the rigid Calvinist has disliked us because we hold the redemption of all men; the Pelagianized Arminian, because we contend for salvation by grace; the Antinomian, because we insist upon the perpetual obligation of the moral law; the moralist, because we exalt faith; the disaffected, because we hold that loyalty and religion are inseparable; the political tory, because he can not think that separatists from the Church can be loyal to the throne; the philosopher, because he deems us fanatics; while semi-infidel liberals generally exclude us from all share in their liberality, except it be in their liberality of abuse. In the mean time we have occasionally been favored with a smile, though somewhat of a *condescending* one, from the lofty Churchman; and often with a fraternal embrace from pious and liberal Dissenters: and if we act upon the principles left us by our great founder, we shall make a meek and lowly temper an essential part of our religion; and, after his example, move onward in the path of doing good, through "honor and dishonor, through evil report and good report," remembering that one fundamental principle of Wesleyan Methodism is ANTI-SECTARIANISM AND A CATHOLIC SPIRIT.

To return, however, to Mr. Wesley: Among the censures which have been frequently directed against him, are his alleged love of power, and his credulity. The first is a vice; the second but a weakness; and they stand therefore upon different grounds.

As to the love of power, it may be granted that, like many minds who seem born to direct, he desired to acquire influence; and, when he attained it, he employed his one talent so as to make it gain more talents. If he had loved power for its own sake, or to minister to selfish purposes, or to injure others, this would have been a great blemish; but he sacrificed no principle of his own, and no interest or right of others, for its gratification. He gained power, as all great and good men gain it, by the very greatness and goodness with which they are endowed, and of which others are always more sensible than themselves. It devolved upon him without any contrivance; and when he knew he possessed it, no instance is on record of his having abused it. This is surely virtue, not vice, and virtue of the highest order. The only proof attempted to be given that he loved power, is, that he never devolved his authority over the societies upon others; but this is capable of an easy explanation. He could not have shared his power among *many*, without drawing up a formal constitution of Church government for his societies, which would have amounted to a formal separation from the Church; and it would have been an insane action had he devolved it upon *one*, and placed himself, and the work he had effected under the management of any individual to whom his societies could not stand in the same filial relation as to himself. He, however, exercised his influence by aid of the counsel of others; and allowed the free discussion of all prudential matters in the conference. Had he been armed with legal power to inflict pains and penalties, he ought to have distrusted himself, as every wise and good man would do, and to have voluntarily put himself beyond the reach of temptation to abuse what mere man, without check, can seldom use aright. This I grant; but the control to which he was subject was, that the union of his societies with him was perfectly voluntary, so that over them he could have no influence at all but what was founded upon character, and public spirit, and fatherly affection. The power which he exercised has descended to the conference of preachers; and, as in his case, this has been often very absurdly complained of, as though it were parallel to the power of civil government, or to that of an established Church, supported by statutes and the civil arm. But this power, like his, is moral influence only, founded upon the pastoral character, and can exist only upon the basis of the confidence inspired by the fact of its generally just and salutary exercise among a people who neither are nor can be under any compulsion.*

On the charge of credulity, it may be observed, that Mr. Wesley lived in an age in which he thought men in danger of believing too little, rather than too much, and his belief in apparitions is at least no proof of a credulousness peculiar to himself. With respect to the "strange accounts" which he inserted in his Magazine, and strange indeed some of them were, it has been falsely assumed that he himself believed them entirely. This is not true. He frequently remarks, that he gives no opinion, or that "he knows not what to make of the account," or that "he leaves every one to form his own judgment concerning it." He met with those relations in reading; or received them from persons deemed by him credible, and he put them on record as facts reported to have happened. Now, as to an unbeliever, one sees not what sound objection he can make to that being recorded which has commanded the faith of others; for, as a part of the history of human opinions, such accounts are curious, and have their use. It neither followed, that the editor of the work believed every account, nor that his readers should consider it true because it was printed. It was for them to judge of the evidence on which the relation stood. Many of these accounts, however, Mr. Wesley did credit, because he thought that they stood on credible testimony; and he published them

[* This topic is one on which the calumniators of Methodism in America also have often harped. The just and obvious view of it so forcibly exhibited above by Mr. Watson, has been repeatedly presented, too, in answer to the croakers in this country. It is one which can neither be misapprehended nor resisted, except by sheer ignorance, or by an invincible determination to persist in calumny for its own sake.—AMERICAN EDIT.]

for that very purpose, for which he believed they were permitted to occur—to confirm the faith of men in an invisible state, and in the immortality of the soul. These were his motives for inserting such articles in his Magazine; and to the censure which has been passed upon him on this account, may be opposed the words of the learned Dr. Henry More, in his Letter to Glanville, the author of "*Sadducismus Triumphatus:*" [Sadducism triumphed over:] "Wherefore let the small philosophic Sir Toplings of this present age deride as much as they will, those that lay out their pains in committing to writing certain well-attested stories of apparitions, do real service to true religion and sound philosophy; and they most effectually contribute to the confounding of infidelity and Atheism, even in the judgment of the Atheists themselves, who are as much afraid of the truth of these stories as an ape is of a whip, and, therefore, force themselves with might and main to disbelieve them, by reason of the dreadful consequence of them, as to themselves." It is sensibly observed by Jortin, in his remarks on the diabolical possessions in the age of our Lord, that "one reason for which divine Providence should suffer evil spirits to exert their malignant powers at that time, might be to give a check to Sadducism among the Jews, and Atheism among the Gentiles, and to remove in some measure these two great impediments to the reception of the Gospel." For moral uses, supernatural visitations may have been allowed in subsequent ages; and he who believes in them, only spreads their moral the farther by giving them publicity. Before such a person can be fairly censured, the ground of his faith ought to be disproved, for he only acts consistently with that faith. This task would, however, prove somewhat difficult.

Mr. Wesley was a voluminous writer; and as he was one of the great instruments in reviving the spirit of religion in these lands, so he led the way in those praiseworthy attempts which have been made to diffuse useful information of every kind, and to smooth the path of knowledge to the middle and lower ranks of society. Beside books on religious subjects, he published many small and cheap treatises on various branches of science; plain and excellent grammars of the dead languages; expurgated editions of the classic authors; histories, civil and ecclesiastical; and numerous abridgments of important works.*

It is his especial praise, that he took an early part in denouncing the iniquities of the African slave-trade, and in arousing the conscience of the nation on the subject. In Bristol, at that time a dark den of slave-traders, he courageously preached openly against it, defying the rage of the slave merchants and the mob; and his spirited and ably-reasoned tract on slavery continues to be admired and quoted to the present time. It may be added, that one of the last letters he ever wrote was to Mr. Wilberforce, exhorting him to perseverance in a work, of which he was one of the leading instruments—the effecting the abolition of the traffic in the nerves and blood of man.

* Mr. Wesley's principal writings are, his Translation of the New Testament, with Explanatory Notes, quarto; his Journals, 6 vols., duodecimo; his Sermons, 9 volumes, duodecimo; his Appeal to Men of Reason and Religion; his defense of the Doctrine of Original Sin, in Answer to Dr. Taylor; his answers to Mr. Church, and Bishops Lavington and Warburton; and his Predestination Calmly Considered, beside many smaller tracts on various important subjects. His works were published by himself in thirty-two volumes, duodecimo, in the year 1771. An edition of them in fourteen large octavo volumes has just been completed; with his work on the New Testament in two volumes of the same size. In addition to his original compositions, Mr. Wesley published upward of a hundred and twenty different works, mostly abridged from other authors; among which are grammars in five different languages; the Christian Library, in fifty duodecimo volumes; thirteen volumes of the Arminian Magazine; a History of England, and a general Ecclesiastical History, in four volumes each; a Compendium of Natural Philosophy in five volumes; and an Exposition of the Old Testament, in three quarto volumes.

At the time of Mr. Wesley's death, the number of members in connection with him in Europe, America, and the West India Islands, was 80,000. At the last conference, 1830, the numbers returned were, in Great Britain 249,278; in Ireland 22,897; in the foreign missions 41,186; total 313,360, exclusive of near half a million of persons in the societies in the states of America. As to the field of labor at home, the number of circuits in the United Kingdom was, at the time of his death, 115. At present they are 399. The number of mission stations was 8 in the West Indies, and 8 in British America: at present there are 150. The number of preachers left by him was 312. It is now 993, in the United Kingdom; and 193 in the foreign missions. In the United States of America the number of preachers is about 2,000.

Such have been the results of the labors of this great and good man. Whether they are still to diffuse a hallowing influence through the country, and convey the blessings of Christianity to heathen lands with the same rapidity and with the same vigor, will, under the Divine blessing, depend upon those who have received from him *the trust* of a system of religious agency, to be employed with the same singleness of heart, the same benevolent zeal for the spiritual benefit of mankind, and the same dependence upon the Holy Spirit. I know not that it bears upon it any marks of decay, although it may require to be accommodated, in a few particulars, to the new circumstances with which it is surrounded. The doctrinal views which Mr. Wesley held, were probably never better understood, or more accurately stated in the discourses of the preachers; and the moral discipline of the body, in all its essential parts, was never more cordially approved by the people generally, or enforced with greater faithfulness by their pastors. Very numerous are the converts who are every year won from the world, brought under religious influence, and placed in the enjoyment of means and ordinances favorable to their growth in religious knowledge and holy habits; and many are constantly passing into eternity, of whose "good hope through grace," the testimony is in the highest degree satisfactory. If Methodism continue in vigor and purity to future ages, it will still be associated with the name of its founder, and encircle his memory with increasing luster; and if it should fall into the formality and decays which have proved the lot of many other religious bodies, he will not lose his reward. Still a glorious harvest of saved souls is laid up in the heavenly garner, which will be his "rejoicing in the day of the Lord;" while the indirect influence of his labors upon the other religious bodies and institutions of the country will justly entitle him to be considered as one of the most honored instruments of reviving and extending the influence of religion that, since the time of the apostles, have been raised up by the providence of God.

THE END.

www.ingramcontent.com/pod-product-compliance
Lightning Source LLC
LaVergne TN
LVHW020125110826
845151LV00001B/273

9781425541682